OUR ISLAND STORY

OUR ISLAND STORY

H. E. MARSHALL

WLC

OUR ISLAND STORY

Originally published in 1905. This edition
published by WLC Books in 2009.

CONTENTS

CHAPTER I

THE STORIES OF ALBION AND BRUTUS

ONCE upon a time there was a giant called Neptune. When he was quite a tiny boy, Neptune loved the sea. All day long he played in it, swimming, diving, and laughing gleefully as the waves dashed over him.

As he grew older he came to know and love the sea so well that the sea and the waves loved him too, and acknowledged him to be their king. At last people said he was not only king of the waves, but god of the sea.

Neptune had a very beautiful wife who was called Amphitrite. He had also many sons. As each son became old enough to reign, Neptune made him king over an island.

Neptune's fourth son was called Albion. When it came to his turn to receive a kingdom, a great council was called to decide upon an island for him.

Now Neptune and Amphitrite loved Albion more than any of their other children. This made it very difficult to chose which island should be his.

The mermaids and mermen, as the wonderful people who live in the sea are called, came from all parts of the world with news of beautiful islands. But after hearing about them, Neptune and Amphitrite would shake their heads and say, "No, that is not good enough for Albion."

At last a little mermaid swam into the pink and white coral cave in which the council was held. She was more beautiful than any mermaid who had yet come to the council. Her eyes were merry and honest, and they were blue as the sky and the sea. Her hair was as yellow as fine gold, and in her cheeks a lovely pink came and went. When she spoke, her voice sounded as clear as a bell and as soft as the whisper of the waves, as they ripple upon the shore.

"O Father Neptune," she said, "let Albion come to my island. It is a beautiful little island. It lies like a gem in the bluest of waters. There the trees and the grass are green, the cliffs are white and the sands are golden. There the sun shines and the birds sing. It is a land of beauty. Mountains and valleys, broad lakes and swift-flowing rivers, all are there. Let Albion come to my island."

"Where is this island?" said Neptune and Amphitrite both at once. They thought it must indeed be a beautiful land if it were only half as lovely as the little mermaid said.

"Oh, come, and I will show it to you," replied she. Then she swam away in a great hurry to show her beautiful island, and Neptune, Amphitrite, and all the mermaids and mermen followed.

It was a wonderful sight to see them as they swam along. Their white arms gleamed in the sunshine, and their golden hair floated out over the water like fine seaweed. Never before had so many of the sea-folk been gathered together at one place, and the noise of their tails flapping through the water brought all the little fishes and great sea monsters out, eager to know what was happening. They swam and swam until they came to the little green island with the white cliffs and yellow sands.

As soon as it came in sight, Neptune raised himself on a big wave, and when he saw the little island lying before him, like a beautiful gem in the blue water, just as the mermaid had said, he cried out in joy, "This is the island of my love. Albion shall rule it and Albion it shall be called."

So Albion took possession of the little island, which until then had been called Samothea, and he changed its name to Albion, as Neptune had said should be done.

For seven years Albion reigned over his little island. At the end of that time he was killed in a fight with the hero Hercules. This was a great grief to Neptune and Amphitrite. But because of the love they bore to their son Albion, they continued to love and watch over the little green island which was called by his name.

For many years after the death of Albion the little island had no ruler. At last, one day there came sailing from the far-off city of Troy a prince called Brutus. He, seeing the fair island, with white cliffs and golden sands, landed with all his mighty men of war. There were many giants in the land in those days, but Brutus fought and conquered them. He made himself king, not only over Albion, but over all the islands which lay around. He called them the kingdom of Britain or Britannia after his own name, Brutus, and Albion he called Great Britain because it was the largest of the islands.

Although after this the little island was no longer called Albion, Neptune still loved it. When he grew old and had no more strength to rule, he gave his sceptre to the islands called Britannia, for we know—

"Britannia rules the waves."

This is a story of many thousand years ago. Some people think it is only a fairy tale. But however that may be, the little island is still sometimes called Albion, although it is nearly always called Britain.

In this book you will find the story of the people of Britain. The story tells how they grew to be a great people, till the little green island set in the lonely sea was no longer large enough to contain them all. Then they sailed away over the blue waves to far-distant countries. Now the people of the little island possess lands all over the world. These lands form the empire of Greater Britain.

Many of these lands are far, far larger than the little island itself. Yet the people who live in them still look back lovingly to the little island, from which they or their fathers came, and call it "Home."

CHAPTER II

THE COMING OF THE ROMANS

HUNDREDS of years passed after Brutus conquered Albion and changed its name to Britain, during which time many kings and queens reigned over the island. Our great poet Shakespeare has written about one of these kings who was called King Lear. Some day you must read his story.

There were many good and wise rulers among these ancient British kings. But it would take too long to tell of them, so we must pass on to the time when another great warrior heard of the little lonely island and came to conquer it.

The name of this great warrior was Julius Cæsar. He was a Roman. At that time the Romans were a very powerful people. They called themselves the masters of the world.

It is true they were very clever. They had taught themselves how to fight, how to make swords and armour, and how to build fortresses, better than any of the peoples who lived then. So it happened that the Romans generally won the victory over all who fought against them.

But they were a very greedy people and, as soon as they heard of a new country, they wanted to conquer it and call it part of the Roman Empire.

Julius Cæsar had been fighting in Gaul, or France as we now call it. While there, he heard of the little island with white cliffs over the sea. He was told that the people were very big and brave and fierce. He also heard that it was a rich land full of tin, lead, and other useful metals, and that the shores were strewn with precious pearls. So he resolved to conquer this land and add it to the Roman Empire.

Cæsar gathered together about eighty ships, twelve thousand men, and a great many horses. These he thought would be enough with which to conquer the wild men of Britain. One fine day he set sail from France and soon came in sight of the island. The Britons in some way or other had heard of his coming and had gathered to meet him. As he drew near, Cæsar saw with surprise that the whole shore was covered with men ready for battle. He also saw that the place which he had chosen for landing was not good, for there were high, steep cliffs upon which the Britons could stand and shower darts upon his soldiers. So he turned his ships and sailed along the coast until he came to a place where the shore was flat.

The Roman ships were called galleys. They had sails, but were also moved by oars. The rowers sat in long lines down each side of the galley. Sometimes there were two or three tiers of them sitting one above the other. These rowers were generally slaves and worked in chains. They were often soldiers who had been taken prisoner in war, or wicked men who were punished for their misdeeds by being made to row in these galleys.

It was a dreadful life. The work was very hard, and in a storm if the vessel was wrecked, as often happened, the poor galley slaves were almost sure to be drowned, because their heavy chains prevented them from swimming.

As the Roman galleys sailed along the coast, the British warriors with their horses and war chariots followed on land.

The war chariots of the British were very terrible. They were like light carts and held several men; one to drive the horses and the others to fight. On either side, from the centre of the wheels, swords stuck out. As the wheels went round these swords cut down, killed, or wounded every one who came within reach. The Britons trained their horses so well, that they would rush madly into battle or stand stock still in a moment. It was a fearful sight to see these war chariots charge an enemy.

After sailing along the coast a little way, Cæsar found a good place at which to land, and turned his vessels inshore. But the great galleys required so much water in which to sail that they could not come quite close to land.

Seeing this, Cæsar told his soldiers to jump into the water. But the soldiers hesitated, for the Britons had rushed into the water to meet them and the Romans did not like the idea of fighting in the sea.

Although the Romans were very good soldiers, they were not such good sailors as might have been expected. They did not love the water as the Britons did.

These fierce "barbarians," as the Romans called the Britons, urging their horses into the waves, greeted the enemy with loud shouts. Every inch of the shore was known to them. They knew exactly where it was shallow and where it was deep, so they galloped through the water without fear.

Suddenly a brave Roman, when he saw how the soldiers hesitated, seized a standard and leaped overboard crying, "Leap forth now, soldiers, if you will not betray your ensign to the enemy, for I surely will bear myself as is my duty."

The Romans did not have flags such as we have in our army. Their standard was an eagle which was carried upon a pole. The eagle was of gold, or gilded to look like gold. Wherever the eagle led, there the soldiers followed, for it was the emblem of their honour, and they fought for and guarded it as their most precious possession.

So now, when the Roman soldiers saw their standard in the midst of the enemy, they followed with all haste. Their fear was great lest it should be taken. It was counted as a terrible disgrace to the Romans if they returned from battle without their standard. Death was better than disgrace, so they leaped into the water to meet the fierce Britons.

A fearful fight followed. The Romans could not keep their proper order, neither could they find firm footing. Weighed down with their heavy armour, they sank in the sand or slipped upon the rocks. All the while the Britons showered darts upon them and struck at them fiercely with their battle-axes and swords.

The Britons were very brave, but they had not learned the best ways of fighting as the Romans had. So after a terrible struggle the Romans reached the land. On shore they formed in close ranks and charged the Britons.

The Britons in their turn charged the Romans with their war chariots. The horses tore wildly along, neighing and champing their bits, and trampling underfoot those who were not cut down with the swords on the wheels. As they galloped, the fighting men in the cars threw darts and arrows everywhere among the enemy. When they were in the thickest of the fray the horses would suddenly stand still. Then the soldiers, springing out of the chariot, would fight fiercely for a few minutes with their battle-axes, killing every one within reach. Again they would leap into the cart, the horses would start forward and once more gallop wildly through the ranks of the enemy, leaving a track of dead behind them wherever they passed. But in spite of all their wild bravery the Britons were beaten at last and fled before the Romans.

Thus Cæsar first landed upon the shores of Britain. But so many of his soldiers were killed and wounded that he was glad to make peace with these brave islanders.

He sailed away again in such of his ships as had not been destroyed. For fierce storms had arisen a few days after his landing and wrecked many of his vessels.

Cæsar did not gain much glory from this fight. Indeed, when he went away, it seemed rather as if he were fleeing from a foe than leaving a conquered land.

CHAPTER III

THE ROMANS COME AGAIN

CAESAR must have felt that he had not really conquered the Britons for, as soon as he arrived safely in France, he began to gather together another army. In the spring of the following year, he again sailed over to Britain. He came now not with eighty, but with eight hundred ships and many thousands of men. But this time there was no one to meet him when he landed. The Britons indeed had heard of his coming, and had gathered in great force to resist him. But, when they saw such a huge number of ships, their hearts were filled with fear, and they fled into the forests and hills to hide.

It must have been a wonderful sight, in the eyes of the ancient Britons, to see so many ships sailing on the sea all at once. They knew scarcely anything of the great lands which lay beyond the blue sea surrounding their little island. They had not even dreamed that the whole world contained as many ships as they now saw. So it was not surprising that at first they were afraid and fled. But they did not lose courage for long. They soon returned and many battles were fought.

The Romans seemed to think that they won all these battles, but the Britons were not at all sure of it. Certainly a great many people on both sides were killed. If the Britons had been less brave than they were, they would have been very badly beaten, for the Romans wore strong armour and carried shields made of steel, while the Britons had little armour, if any at all, and their shields were made of wood covered with skins of animals. The Roman swords too were strong and sharp, while those of the Britons were made of copper. Copper is a very soft metal, and swords made of it are easily bent and so made useless.

The Britons at this time were divided into many tribes, each following their own chief. They often used to quarrel among themselves. Now, however, they joined together against their great enemy and chose a brave man, called Cassivellaunus, to be their leader.

Cassivellaunus led the Britons so well, and Cæsar found it such a difficult task to conquer them, that at last he was glad to make peace again and sail back to his own country.

He did not like to go away as if he had been defeated, so he sent messengers to the British chief, saying, "If you let me take some of your warriors back to Rome as a sign that you are now Roman subjects and will not rebel against me, I will go away."

The Britons were only too glad to be rid of Cæsar and his soldiers at any price. They gave him some British soldiers to take back to Rome, and even promised to pay him a certain sum of money every year.

But it almost seemed as if Neptune had been doing battle for his beloved Albion with his winds and waves. For while Cæsar had been fighting the Britons, such fierce storms arose that his ships were thrown upon the rocky shore and many of them dashed to pieces. Indeed so few of his ships remained fit to put to sea again that Cæsar could not take all his soldiers away at one time. As many went as could, and the ships came back again for the others.

Cæsar did not leave any soldiers in Britain at all, so it does not seem as if he had really conquered the land. These things happened in the year 54 B.C., that is, fifty-four years before Christ was born. All Christian lands count time from the year in which Christ was born, because His coming is the most wonderful thing which has ever happened. Anything that took place before Christ was born is said to be in such and such a year B.C. Everything which has taken place since then is said to be A.D. or Anno Domini, which means, "in the year of our Lord." For instance, this book is written in the year 1905 A.D. or 1905 years after the birth of Christ.

CHAPTER IV

HOW CALIGULA CONQUERED BRITAIN, AND HOW CARACTACUS REFUSED TO BE CONQUERED

AFTER the second coming of Cæsar, years passed during which the Romans left the Britons in peace. But they had by no means forgotten about the little green island in the blue sea.

Julius Cæsar had been dead many years when a Roman emperor called Caligula said he would go to Britain and thoroughly conquer the island. He did not mean to land and fight in one small part of it as Julius Cæsar had done. He meant to march over the island, north, south, east, and west, and bring it all under the power of Rome. That is what he said he was going to do. What he really did was something quite different.

He gathered a great army and marched from Italy right through France till he reached the coast. There news came to him that Guilderius, the king of Britain, had heard of his coming and had also gathered his soldiers together.

Caligula must have been afraid when he heard that the brave Britons were ready to fight him, for this is how he conquered Britain.

He drew his soldiers up in battle array upon the shore. Then he himself went into his galley and told his sailors to row him out to sea. After they had rowed him a short way he told them to return. When he had landed again he climbed into a high seat like a pulpit, which he had built on the sands. Then he sounded a trumpet and ordered his soldiers to advance as if to battle.

But there was no enemy there. In front of the soldiers there was nothing but the blue sea and the sandy shore covered with shells. They could not fight against the waves and the sand, and the brave Britons, whom they had come to fight, were far away on the other side of the water and quite out of reach.

So the soldiers stood and wondered what to do. Then Caligula ordered them to kneel down upon the sand and gather as many shells as they could.

The first thing a Roman was taught, was to obey. So now the soldiers did as their general commanded and gathered the cockle shells which lay around in hundreds.

It must have been a curious sight to see all these strong soldiers, armed with sword, shield, and helmet, picking up shells upon the sea-shore.

When they had gathered a great quantity, Caligula made a speech. He thanked the soldiers as if they had done him some great service. He told them that now he had conquered the ocean and the islands in it, and that these shells were the spoils of war. He praised the soldiers for their bravery, and said that the shells should be placed in the temples of Rome in remembrance of it. Then he rewarded them richly and they marched home again.

That was how Caligula conquered Britain.

After the death of Caligula, another Roman called Claudius tried to conquer Britain. He sent generals and came himself, but he could not thoroughly subdue the Britons. A few chiefs indeed owned themselves beaten, but others would not. They would rather die than be slaves of Rome, they said.

Among those who would not yield was a brave man called Caractacus. A great many of the Britons joined him and fought under his orders. Caractacus and his men fought well and bravely, but in the end the Romans defeated them.

After many battles Caractacus chose for his camp a place on the top of a hill on the borders of Shropshire, Cheshire, and Lancashire. There he made a very strong fortress surrounded by three walls and a deep ditch. The walls were so well built that after all these long years they can still be seen quite plainly to-day.

When the Roman soldiers came to the foot of the hill, Caractacus prepared for battle. He called his soldiers together and made a speech to them. "Show yourselves to be men," he said. "To-day is either the beginning of Liberty or of eternal bondage. Remember how your forefathers fought against Julius Cæsar, and fight now for your homes, as they did for theirs."

Then all the Britons called out, "We will die for our country." The noise of their shouts was carried by the wind to the camp of the Romans. It sounded to them as if the Britons were rejoicing. The Romans feared Caractacus. They knew how brave he and his men were. They knew that it would be very difficult to take his strong fortress. Yet they felt quite sure of taking it in the end, and they wondered what cause the Britons had for rejoicing.

And it happened as the Romans expected. After fierce fighting and great slaughter on both sides the camp was taken. Caractacus, his wife and daughter, and all his brothers were made prisoner and led in chains to Rome, and there was great sorrow in Britain.

Whenever a Roman emperor returned from battle and victory, he used to have what was called a Triumph. Every one in Rome had a holiday; the streets were gay with flowers and green wreaths. The conqueror, dressed in beautiful robes and wearing a crown of bay leaves, rode through the streets. He was followed by his soldiers, servants, and friends. Then came a long train of the captives he had made during the war, with the armour, weapons, jewels, and other riches he had taken from the conquered people.

After the war with Britain was over Claudius had a Triumph. The fame of Caractacus had already reached Rome, and when it became known that he had been taken prisoner and would walk in the Triumph there was great excitement. The people crowded into the streets eager to see this brave warrior. And although in chains he looked so proud and noble that many even of the Romans were sorry for him.

When he was brought before the Emperor and Empress, Claudius and Agrippina, he did not behave like a slave or a captive, but like the freeborn king and Briton he was.

"I am as nobly born as you," he said proudly to Claudius. "I had men and horses, lands and great riches. Was it wonderful that I wished to keep them? You fight to gain possession of the whole world and make all men your slaves, but I fought for my own land and for freedom. Kill me now and people will think little of you: but if you grant me my life, all men will know that you are not only powerful but merciful."

Instead of being angry, Claudius was pleased with the proud words of Caractacus. He was so pleased that he set him at liberty with his wife and all his family. But whether Caractacus ever returned to his dear country, or whether he died in that far-off land, we do not know. We do not hear anything more about him.

CHAPTER V

THE STORY OF A WARRIOR QUEEN

ALTHOUGH the Britons had lost their great general Caractacus, still they would not yield to the Roman tyrants.

Soon another brave leader arose. This leader was a woman. Her name was Boadicea, and she was a queen. She ruled over that part of the country which is now called Norfolk and Suffolk.

As I said before, the Romans were a very greedy people. They wanted to take away the freedom of Britain and make the island into a Roman province. They also wanted to get all the money and possessions which belonged to the Britons for themselves.

The husband of Boadicea knew how greedy the Romans were, and when he was about to die he became very sad. He was afraid that the Roman Emperor would rob his wife and daughters of all their money, when he was no longer there to take care of them. So, to prevent this, he made the Emperor a present of half of his money and lands, and gave the other half to his wife and children. Then he died happy, thinking that his dear ones would be left in peace.

But the greedy Romans were not pleased with only half of the dead king's wealth. They wanted the whole. So they came and took it by force. Boadicea was a very brave woman. She was not afraid of the Romans, and she tried to make them give back what they had stolen from her.

Then these cruel, wicked men laughed at her. And because she was a woman and had, they thought, no one to protect her, they beat her with rods and were rude to her daughters.

But although the Romans were clever, they sometimes did stupid things. They thought very little of their own women, and they did not understand that many of the women of Britain were as brave and as wise as the men, and quite as difficult to conquer.

After Boadicea had been so cruelly and unjustly treated, she burned with anger against the Romans. Her heart was full only of thoughts of revenge. She called her people together, and, standing on a mound of earth so that they could see and hear her, she made a speech to them. She told them first how shamefully the Romans had behaved to her, their Queen. Then, like Caractacus, she reminded them how their forefathers had fought against Julius Cæsar, and had driven the Romans away for a time at least. "Is it not better to be poor and free than to have great wealth and be slaves?" she asked. "And the Romans take not only our freedom but our wealth. They want to make us both slaves and beggars. Let us rise. O brothers and sisters, let us rise, and drive these robbers out of our land! Let us kill them every one! Let us teach them that they are no better than hares and foxes, and no match for greyhounds! We will fight, and if we cannot conquer, then let us die—yes, every one of us—die rather than submit."

Queen Boadicea looked so beautiful and fierce as she stood there, with her blue eyes flashing, and her golden hair blowing round her in the wind, that the hearts of her people were filled with love for her, and anger against the Romans. As she spoke, fierce desires for revenge grew in them. They had hated their Roman conquerors before, now the hatred became a madness.

So, when Boadicea had finished speaking, a cry of rage rose from the Britons. They beat upon their shields with their swords, and swore to avenge their Queen, to fight and die for her and for their country.

Then Boadicea, leaning with one hand upon her spear, and lifting the other to heaven—prayed. She prayed to the goddess of war, and her prayer was as fierce as her speech, for she had never heard of a God who taught men to forgive their enemies.

As she stood there praying, Boadicea looked more beautiful than ever. Her proud head was thrown back and the sun shone upon her lovely hair and upon the golden band which bound her forehead. Her dark cloak, slipping from her shoulders, showed the splendid robe she wore beneath, and the thick and heavy chain of gold round her neck. At her feet knelt her daughters, sobbing with hope and fear.

It was a grand and awful moment, and deep silence fell upon the warriors as they listened to the solemn words. Then, with wild cries, they marched forward to battle, forgetful of everything but revenge.

The battles which followed were terrible indeed. The words of Queen Boadicea had stirred the Britons until they were mad with thoughts of revenge, and hopes of freedom. They gave no mercy, and they asked none. They utterly destroyed the towns of London and of St. Albans, or Verulamium as it was then called, killing every one, man, woman and child.

Again and again the Romans were defeated, till it almost seemed as if the Britons really would succeed in driving them out of the country. Boadicea herself led the soldiers, encouraging them with her brave words. "It is better to die with honour than to live in slavery," she said. "I am a woman, but I would rather die than yield. Will you follow me, men?" and of course the men followed her gladly.

At last the Roman leader was so downcast with his many defeats that he went himself to the British camp, bearing in his hand a green branch as a sign of peace. When Boadicea was told that an ambassador from the Romans wished to speak to her, she replied proudly, "My sword alone shall speak to the Romans." And when the Roman leader asked for peace, she answered, "You shall have peace, peace, but no submission. A British heart will choose death rather than lose liberty. There can be peace only if you promise to leave the country."

Of course the Romans would not promise to go away from Britain, so the war continued, and for a time the Britons triumphed.

But their triumph did not last long. The Roman soldiers were better armed and better drilled than the British. There came a dark day when the Britons were utterly defeated and many thousands were slain.

When Boadicea saw that all hope was gone, she called her daughters to her. "My children," she said sadly, as she took them by the hand and drew them towards her, "my children, it has not pleased the gods of battle to deliver us from the power of the Romans. But there is yet one way of escape." Tears were in her blue eyes as she kissed her daughters. She was no longer a queen of fury but a loving mother.

Then taking a golden cup in her hands, "Drink," she said gently.

The eldest daughter obeyed proudly and gladly, but the younger one was afraid. "Must I, mother?" she asked timidly.

"Yes, dear one," said Boadicea gently. "I too will drink, and we shall meet again."

When the Roman soldiers burst in upon them, they found the great queen dead, with her daughters in her arms.

She had poisoned both herself and them, rather than that they should fall again into the hands of the Romans.

CHAPTER VI

THE LAST OF THE ROMANS

CARACTACUS was dead, Boadicea was dead, many other brave British leaders were dead, but the Britons still continued to give the Romans a great deal of trouble.

At last Vespasian, who was then Emperor of the Romans, sent a general called Julius Agricola to see if he could subdue the people and govern the island of Britain.

Julius Agricola was a very clever soldier and a wise man. When he had gained one or two victories over the Britons, he tried what kindness would do. This was something the Romans had never done before.

Julius Agricola tried to understand the people. He was just and fair. He not only took away many of the heavy taxes which the Romans had made the British pay, but he built schools and had the people taught to read and write. For up to this time the Britons had had no teachers and no schools. None of them could read or write, and perhaps there was not a single book in the whole island.

Of course, books in those days were quite different from what they are now. There was no paper, and printing was unknown, so when people wanted to make a book they wrote upon strips of parchment, which was made from the skins of animals. These strips were then rolled up, and looked very much like the maps we hang upon the wall, only they were smaller.

Besides building schools, Agricola built public halls and courts where the people might come and ask for justice, whenever they had been wronged. He taught the Britons what obedience, law and order meant, and in every way tried to make them live good lives.

Soon the Britons began to understand that the Romans could give them some things which were worth having. So there was much more peace in the land.

Julius Agricola also built a line of forts across the island from the Forth to the Clyde. He did this to keep back the wild Picts and Scots, or people of the north. For as they could not be brought under Roman rule nor tamed in any way, he thought it was better to try to shut them into their own country. Later on an emperor, called Antonine, built a great wall along the line of Agricola's forts for the same purpose.

But while Julius Agricola was doing all this good work in Britain, the emperor who had sent him died, and another ruled instead.

This emperor was jealous of Agricola because he managed the people of Britain so well. He was so jealous that he told Agricola to come back to Rome, and sent another man to govern Britain instead of him.

It was very foolish of a great emperor to be angry with his general because he did his work well. He ought rather to have been glad.

The people of Britain soon showed him how foolish he had been, for they once more rebelled against Roman rule.

Later on another great emperor who was called Hadrian reigned, and he himself came to Britain. He found the wild people of the north very troublesome, so he built a wall across Britain from the Tyne to the Solway. He did not try to drive these wild people so far north as Agricola had done. The wall which Hadrian built is still called by his name, and is still to be seen to this day; so you can imagine what a very strong wall it was and what a fierce people they were who lived beyond it.

Hadrian was wise as Agricola had been. He taught the Britons many things which were good and useful to know. But very soon after he left the island, the people rebelled again.

And so it went on until, at last, nearly five hundred years after the first coming of Julius Cæsar, the Romans gave up and left Britain altogether. That was about the year 410 A.D. The wonder is that they had stayed so long, for the Britons had certainly given them a great deal of trouble.

But after all, although the Britons always fought against the Romans, they had learned many things from them.

Before the Romans came, the Britons had been very ignorant and wild. In many parts of the country they wore no clothes at all. Instead, they stained their bodies blue with a dye called woad. Their houses were only little round huts, with a hole in the middle of the roof which let some light in and the smoke of the fire out. There were no schools, and little boys and girls were taught nothing except how to fish and hunt, and how to fight and kill people in battle.

There were hardly any roads and there were no churches.

The ancient Britons were heathen. They worshipped the oak-tree and the mistletoe.

The British priests were called Druids. It is said that they received their name from Druis, who was a very wise king of Albion in far-off times.

The Druids were the wisest people in the land. When any one was in doubt or difficulty he would go to them for advice. They were very solemn and grand old men with long white beards and beautiful robes. There were no churches, as I said, but the people worshipped in dark hollows in the woods and in open spaces surrounded by great oak-trees. Some of the teaching of the Druids was very beautiful, but some of it was very dreadful, and they even killed human beings in their sacrifices.

But the Romans taught the Britons many things. They taught them how to build better houses and how to make good roads, how to read and write, and much more that was good and useful. And presently priests came from Rome, bringing tidings of a new and beautiful religion.

They came to tell the people of Britain how the Son of God came to earth to teach men not to hate and kill each other, but to love each other, and above all to love their enemies.

It is difficult to understand what a wonderful story this must have seemed to the wild island people. For they were a people who were born and who lived and died among wars and hatred. Yet many of them believed and followed this new religion. Gradually the Druids disappeared, and the priests of Christ took their place.

Although the religion of Christ came from Rome, the Romans themselves were nearly all pagans. And one of the last Roman emperors who tried to rule Britain hated the Christians very much. He forbade the worship of God and Christ, and killed and tortured those who disobeyed his orders.

But the people who had once become Christian would not again become heathen. They chose rather to die. A person who dies for his religion is called a martyr.

In the next chapter is the story of the first Christian martyr in Britain.

CHAPTER VI

THE STORY OF ST. ALBAN

THE first Christian martyr in Britain was called Alban. He lived in the town called Verulamium. He was a Briton, but he was one of those who had learned many things from the Romans. When he was a boy he had even travelled to Rome, and had seen the beautiful city from which these conquerors took their name. And all that he had seen and learned had helped him to grow up a noble, generous man.

Alban had a great deal of money, and with it he used to help the poor people who lived around him. Every one loved and trusted him. Even the Christians loved and trusted him although he was a heathen. If any one was in trouble he would go for help to Alban the great, rich, kind man.

When the wicked Roman Emperor sent men to kill the Christians in Britain, a holy man called Amphibalus, who also lived in Verulamium, fled to the house of Alban for shelter.

"My lord," said this old man, "the soldiers of the emperor seek me to take my life. Hide me, and God will reward you."

"What evil have you done?" asked Alban.

"I have done no evil," replied Amphibalus. "I am a Christian, that is all."

"Then fear nothing," said Alban kindly. "I have heard much of the Christians, but nothing that is bad."

Then Alban took Amphibalus into his house and hid him. He seemed quite safe there, as the soldiers did not think of looking for him in the house of a man who was a heathen.

Alban talked every day with Amphibalus, who told him all the story of Christ. It seemed to Alban very beautiful and wonderful that any one should die to save others. He felt that this religion of love and gentleness was much better than the fierce teaching of the Druids.

For some days Amphibalus lived in peace. But one day while he sat talking with Alban, a frightened servant came to say that soldiers were at the gate. They had found out where Amphibalus was hiding.

"My son," said the old man trembling, "I must say farewell, for I am about to die."

"No," replied Alban, "I will save you yet. Give me your robe."

Then hastily taking off his own beautiful robe he threw it over the old man's shoulders, and thrust a purse of gold into his hand. "God," he said, "go quickly; my servant will take you by secret ways. I will keep the soldiers from pursuing you. But bless me, father, before you go."

Alban knelt, and Amphibalus gently laid his hand upon the bowed head.

"May God the Father reward you, and may the Holy Spirit lead you in the true way of Christ. Farewell, my son." Then he made the sign of the cross over him, and was gone.

Alban wrapped himself in the robe which Amphibalus had taken off and, drawing the hood over his head, waited.

The soldiers, having at last forced a way into the house, rushed in upon him. Seeing a man in the robe of a priest, they seized and bound him, never doubting that it was Amphibalus the Christian.

Alban was then led before the Roman Governor. There his hands were unbound, and he threw off his long robe. Great was the astonishment of the soldiers when they discovered that their prisoner was not the Christian priest for whom they had been seeking, but the heathen lord, Alban.

The Governor happened to be offering up sacrificed to idols, when Alban was led before him. He was very angry with the soldiers for allowing Amphibalus to escape, and still more angry with Alban for helping him to do so.

"Who are you, and how dare you hide wicked and rebellious people in your house?" he asked. "You must tell me where this Christian is hiding, and offer sacrifices to the gods to show that you are sorry for what you have done."

"I can do neither of these things," replied Alban.

"Who are you, that you dare to defy me?" demanded the Governor.

"What does it matter to you who I am?" replied Alban.

"I asked for your name," repeated the Governor in furious anger. "Tell it to me at once."

"My parents called me Alban," he then replied.

"Then, Alban, if you would have the gods forgive you, you must offer sacrifices to them, and repent of your wicked words and deeds."

"I cannot," replied Alban. "I no longer believe in these old gods. They teach men to be cruel and wicked. I shall never sacrifice to them again. Amphibalus is a good and gentle old man. He has never hurt nor wronged any one, yet these gods tell you to torture and kill him. I will not believe in them any more. I would rather believe in the God of Amphibalus, who teaches people to love one another."

Then the Governor cried out, "This man is too wicked to live. Take him and put him to death."

The soldiers led Alban away, and it soon became known all over the town that Alban, who was good and kind and loved by every one, was to be put to death. So a great crowd followed him as he was led across the river and up the grassy slope to the top of a hill. Indeed so many people followed that no one was left in the town, except the wicked Governor. Perhaps when he was alone in the terrible silence of the empty streets, he felt sorry for what he had done. But it was too late. Alban had gone to death, and there was not one person remaining in the town whom the Governor could send after him to bring him back.

With tears and sobs the people followed and pressed round Alban. Every one was eager to show his love for him, and to say a last good-by.

When they came to the little bridge over the river, the crowd was so great that it was impossible for Alban to pass. So the soldiers, impatient and angry, said he must walk through the water. Then, we are told, a wonderful thing happened. The water of the river dried up, and Alban passed over on dry land.

On they went up the hillside. It was a beautiful green, grassy slope where the children used to play in the summer sunshine. Sweet-scented wild-flowers made it gay with their bright colors. Pretty butterflies fluttered about, and the air was full of the hum of bees and the song of birds.

On the top of the hill Alban knelt down, feeling tired and thirsty. Just at that moment there seemed to spring from the ground a clear stream of water which no one had noticed before. Alban bent down, drank from it and felt refreshed.

A tall soldier had been walking beside Alban, carrying a great sword with which to cut off his head. But when he saw how gentle and good Alban was and how the people loved him, he began to feel sorry for what he had to do.

As Alban knelt upon the grass the soldier threw down his sword, crying out, "This is a holy man. I cannot kill him."

The captain of the soldiers was very angry at this. "Take up your sword," he said, "and do your duty."

"I cannot," replied the man, "I would rather die."

"Then you shall die," replied the captain. And drawing his own sword, with one blow he cut off Alban's head and with a second the head of the soldier. At the same moment, we are told, the captain lost his sight and remained blind for the rest of his life.

This is the story of how the first martyr in Britain died. He was brave, and wise, and kind and, like Christ, he gave his life for others.

After his death Alban was called St. Alban, and the name of the town in which he had lived was changed from Verulamium to St. Albans. The sorrowing people built a church on the spot where he died and, when it became so old that it fell into ruins, a still more beautiful one was built. That church remains to this day, and people still worship God on the very spot where the first Christian martyr in Britain died.

Although we need not believe the wonderful stories of what happened at St. Alban's death, it is interesting to know that there is still a spring called Holywell at St. Albans, and that the hill up which the people followed the saint is still called Holywell Hill.

CHAPTER VIII

VORTIGERN AND KING CONSTANS

DURING nearly all the time that the Romans remained in Britain, the Britons fought with them and rebelled against them. But, strange to say, hardly had the Romans gone away than the Britons wanted them to come back.

While they remained in Britain the Romans took all the strongest and bravest of the Britons for soldiers. They made them go into the Roman army and taught them how to fight like the Romans. When they left Britain they took away all these British soldiers as well as their own. So the poor country was left with very few men who were able to fight. There were no great generals either like Cassivelaunus, Caractacus or Boadicea to lead them. And in those days, when people were almost always fighting and quarrelling, it was very necessary not only to have brave soldiers, but wise generals.

You will remember that the Romans built two walls across Britain, in order to keep back the wild people who lived in the north—that is, in the part of the island which we now call Scotland.

As long as the Romans remained in Britain they rebuilt and repaired these walls whenever it was necessary. Soldiers, too, lived in the forts, which were placed at short distances along the walls. These soldiers kept watch so that the Picts and Scots had not much chance of getting into the south part of the island.

But when the Romans went away, there was no one to guard and repair these walls. The Picts and Scots soon found this out. They broke down the walls and overran the whole south country, reaching even as far as London. Fierce and brave as the Britons were, they were no match for the Picts and Scots. Besides, they had very few soldiers left, and no great leader. So in despair they sent a letter to the Roman Emperor, asking for help. This letter was so sad, that it was called "The groans of the Britons."

"Come and help us," it said, "for the barbarians drive us into the sea, and the sea drives us back again to the barbarians. So those of us who are not killed in battle are drowned, and soon there will be none of us left at all."

The Romans, you remember, called the Britons barbarians, and now the Britons in their turn called the Picts and Scots barbarians.

But by this time the Romans had as much as they could do to fight their own battles. They could spare no soldiers to send to Britain, so the Britons had to help themselves as best they could.

It was a very sad and miserable time for Britain, till at last a wise king called Constantine began to reign, and he succeeded in driving the Picts and Scots back into their own country.

But one day a wicked Pict killed this wise king, and things became as bad as ever, if not worse. For the people, besides fighting with their enemies, began to quarrel among themselves as to who should be king next.

King Constantine had three sons. The eldest, Constans, was a monk. A monk is a man who takes a vow that he will not marry and have a home of his own. He lives in a big house with other monks, and spends his time in praying, in reading good books, and in helping people who are poor or ill.

Constantine's eldest son was a man like this; his two younger sons, who were called Aurelius Ambrosius and Uther Pendragon, were little boys.

Now some people said, "We cannot have a monk for our king." Others said, "We cannot have little boys." So they quarrelled.

Among the nobles of Britain was a prince called Vortigern. He was very wise, but not very good. He now went to Constans and said to him, "Your father is dead. Your brothers are only little boys. You ought to be king. Be a monk no longer, but trust yourself to me and I will make you king. Only you must promise to take me for your chief adviser."

It is considered a very wicked thing for a man to break his vows and cease to be a monk, after he has promised to be one for all his life. But perhaps Constans was rather tired of that way of living, for he promised to do everything that Vortigern asked.

Vortigern took Constans away from the monastery, as the house in which monks live is called. They went to London together and Vortigern marched into the king's palace, took the crown, and put it on Constans's head. Then he told the people that Constans was their new king.

The people were not very pleased at having a king chosen for them in this way, but, as Vortigern was such a powerful prince, they were afraid to fight with him. So they let Constans be king.

Now Vortigern really wanted to get the whole of the power for himself. He knew that Constans, having lived all his life in a monastery, could not know much about ruling people. So, although Constans was called king, it was really Vortigern who ruled. First, Vortigern took charge of the king's money. Next, he got all the strong castles into his hands, and filled them with his own soldiers. Then he said to the King, "I hear that the Picts and Scots are coming to fight against us again. We ought to have more soldiers."

King Constans replied, "I leave everything to you. Get more soldiers if you think we need them."

Then Vortigern said, "I think the Picts would be the very best soldiers to get. They will come and fight for us, if we pay them well." In those days people did not always fight for their own country. There were many soldiers who would fight for any country and any cause, if only they were paid well.

So Vortigern sent to Scotland for a hundred Picts. When they came he treated them very kindly. He gave them more money and better food and clothes than any of the other soldiers. The Picts thought Vortigern was a very kind master. They soon saw that he really had all the power, and that Constans was only a pretence king.

Now Vortigern wanted these Picts to murder Constans. But he was too cunning to tell them this plainly, so one day he appeared with a sad face and told the Picts that Constans gave him so little money that he could not afford to live in Britain any more, and must go somewhere else.

This made the Picts very angry with Constans. They were so afraid of losing their kind master, that they resolved to kill Constans and make Vortigern king.

That night, while Constans was asleep, they rushed into his room, cut off his head, and carried it to Vortigern.

Vortigern was really delighted that his plan had succeeded so well. But he pretended to be very sad at the death of Constans, and very angry with those who had killed him. He ordered all the Picts to be put into prison, and then had their heads cut off. He did this because he was afraid they might say afterwards that he had told them to murder Constans.

When the two little boys, Aurelius Ambrosius and Uther Pendragon, heard what had happened to their brother, King Constans, they were afraid that Vortigern might kill them too. For although Vortigern tried hard to make believe that he had had nothing to do with the murder of Constans, the people felt quite sure that he was really to blame for it. So Aurelius Ambrosius and Uther Pendragon fled away to that part of France called Brittany, where they remained in safety for many years.

CHAPTER IX

THE STORY OF THE COMING OF HENGIST AND HORSA

VORTIGERN now became king, for he was so powerful that none of the other princes dared to oppose him. But the Picts and Scots were very angry when they heard how their friends had been treated. They resolved to avenge them and at once made war on the Britons. They defeated Vortigern in many battles, and killed more than half of his soldiers.

The Britons were in despair. Then Vortigern called all the nobles and princes together in council, to discuss what was best to do.

At this time there were really no very clever men among the nobles of Britain. They were all in great fear of the Picts and Scots, and they had no good counsel to offer. Vortigern therefore was able to do very much as he liked.

"We must have help," he said, "if we are not to be thoroughly conquered by these wild barbarians from the north. The Romans will not help us. We must ask some one else. Across the sea, called the North Sea, there is a great country called Germany. The people who live in this country are Saxons. They are very brave and valiant fighters. Let us send over to Germany and ask the Saxons to come and help us."

Then all the nobles and princes said, "That is good advice; let it be done."

So Vortigern sent messengers to Germany with promises of money and land to the Saxons, if they would come to fight against the Picts and Scots. The Saxons were very glad to come, and soon there appeared sailing over the sea three ships, filled with some of their strongest and bravest men. Their captains were two brothers, called Hengist and Horsa. Both these names, in the old Saxon language, mean horse. They were so called because they were strong and brave.

The Saxons landed in Britain in 449 A.D. And little did the Britons think that they had come, not only to help, but to conquer them.

As soon as the strangers landed, Vortigern led them northward to fight the Picts and Scots. There was a terrible battle. Both sides fought with the fiercest bravery, and on both sides many soldiers were killed. But in the end the Saxons had the best of it, and the Picts and Scots were driven back to their own country.

The Britons were greatly delighted, and rewarded the Saxons with money and lands. Then Hengist and Horsa, seeing what a fine country Britain was, resolved never to go away again. They resolved rather to stay and conquer it for themselves.

So they first told Vortigern that Aurelius Ambrosius and Uther Pendragon, the brothers of the dead King Constans, were coming to fight against him, and then they advised him to send over to Germany for more soldiers.

Vortigern was very much afraid of the dead king's brothers, so he said, "Send messengers to Germany and ask whom you like to come. I can refuse you nothing, since you have freed us from the Picts and Scots."

Then Hengist said, "You have indeed given us lands and houses, but as we have helped you so much I think you should give me a castle and make me a prince."

"I cannot do that," replied Vortigern. "Only Britons are allowed to be princes in this land. You are strangers and you are heathen. My people would be very angry if I made any one but a Christian a prince."

At that Hengist made a low bow, pretending to be very humble. "Give your servant then just so much land as can be surrounded by a leather thong," he said.

Vortigern thought there could be no harm in doing that, so he said, "Yes, you may have so much." But he did not know what a cunning fellow Hengist was.

As soon as Vortigern had given his consent, Hengist and Horsa killed the largest bullock they could find. Then they took its skin and cut it round and round into one long narrow strip of leather. This they stretched out and laid upon the ground in a large circle, enclosing a piece of land big enough upon which to build a fortress.

If you do not quite understand how Hengist and Horsa managed to cut the skin of a bullock into one long strip, get a piece of paper and a pair of scissors. Begin at the edge and cut the paper round and round in circles till you come to the middle. you will then find that you have a string of paper quite long enough to surround a brick castle. If you are not allowed to use scissors, ask some kind person to do it for you.

Vortigern was very angry when he learned how he had been cheated by Hengist and Horsa. But he was beginning to be rather afraid of them, so he said nothing, but allowed them to build their fortress. It was called Thong Castle, and stood not far from Lincoln, at a place now called Caistor.

While this fortress was being built, messengers were sent to Germany for more men. They returned with eighteen ships full of the bravest soldiers they could find. In one of the ships, too, was a very beautiful lady. This was Rowena, Hengist's daughter.

Soon after these soldiers and this beautiful lady arrived, the castle was finished. Then Hengist gave a great feast and asked Vortigern to it.

Vortigern came and admired the castle very much, although he was still rather angry with Hengist for having cheated him about the land.

Towards the end of the feast, Rowena came into the room, carrying a beautiful golden cup in her hands. Vortigern stared at her in surprise. He had never seen any one so pretty before. He thought that she must be a fairy, she was so lovely.

Rowena went up to Vortigern, and kneeling before him held out the cup, speaking in the Saxon language.

Vortigern did not understand. "What does she say?" he asked Hengist.

"She calls you 'Lord, King,' and offers to drink your health. You must say, 'Drinc heil,' " he answered.

Vortigern said "Drinc heil," although he did not know what it meant.

Rowena then drank some of the wine and handed the cup to Vortigern, who drank the rest.

Then Vortigern made Rowena sit beside him. They could not talk to each other because he could only speak British and she could only speak Saxon. But they looked at each other all the more. Vortigern loved Rowena. He loved her so much that he wanted to marry her.

This was just what Hengist had hoped would happen. He knew he would have a great deal of power in Britain when his daughter was queen. But at first he pretended to object, and only consented at last as if it were a great favour. He made Vortigern give him the whole of Kent, too, in return for allowing him to marry Rowena.

When the people heard that the King had married a Saxon lady, they were very angry. Vortigern had been married before, and his sons, who were now men, were very angry too. But the Prince of Kent was most angry of all, when he heard that his land had been given to the Saxons.

Hengist, seeing how angry the Britons were, though it would be safer to have more of his own people round him. So he sent over to Germany for men, and almost every day more and more Saxons landed in Britain. And Vortigern loved Rowena so much that he allowed her father Hengist to do anything he liked.

But the Britons did not mean to let their country be conquered a second time, so they rebelled against Vortigern and chose his son Vortimer to be king.

Vortimer was young and brave, and loved his country. Under his leadership the Britons fought so well that they soon drove the Saxons away. Horsa was killed in one of the battles, and soon afterwards Hengist and most of his soldiers took their ships and fled back to Germany. They left their wives and children behind them, however, which looked very much as if they expected to come back again some day.

CHAPTER X

HENGIST'S TREACHERY

THE Britons were very glad to see the last of these heathen Saxons, and Vortimer began to restore order, and rebuild the towns and churches, which Hengist and Horsa and their men had destroyed.

Vortimer was a very good king and his people loved him and obeyed him. But there was one person in the land who hated him. That person was his stepmother, Rowena. She hated him because he had driven her father, Hengist, and all her countrymen away.

Rowena tried in many ways to kill Vortimer, but she could not succeed. His people loved him so much that they guarded him well. At last, however, she found a wicked man who, because she promised him a great sum of money, agreed to poison Vortimer. So one day the people were told the sad news that their good king was dead. After this we do not hear very much more of Rowena, nor do we know if she was ever punished for her wickedness.

As soon as Vortigern heard that his son was dead, he came from the castle in Wales where he had been hiding, and made himself king again.

Then Rowena sent messengers to her father, and he gathered all his ships and men together, and came sailing over the sea to Britain once more.

When the Britons heard that Hengist was coming, they were very angry, and prepared to fight. Vortigern was frightened too. He sent a message to Hengist telling him that he must go away again. "The Britons are ready for battle," he said, "and you and your men will all be killed if you try to land."

But Hengist was as cunning as ever. He sent back a message to Vortigern saying that he did not know that Vortimer was dead. "I came to fight for you, to help you to regain your throne," he said. "But now that you are King again there is no need to fight. Let us be friends. Let us all, Britons and Saxons, meet together at a great feast. Let us forget our quarrels and make peace. Then I will go home again with my soldiers."

Vortigern told the British nobles that Hengist wanted to make friends. The Britons really did not wish to fight any more, so they readily agreed to meet Hengist in a friendly way on the Plain of Salisbury, and feast together.

A day was fixed. It was in May. The grass was green and the sky blue, and the birds sang on this bright spring day. From all sides came the British nobles in their gayest holiday clothes, wearing no armour and carrying no weapons.

The Saxons, too, came gaudily clad and seemingly unarmed.

There was laughter, and talk and friendly greeting, and the feast began. Suddenly, over the noise of the feasting, the voice of Hengist sounded loud, "Draw your daggers."

Then every Saxon drew his dagger, which he had hidden in his stocking, and stabbed the Briton next to him. The Britons fought and struggled bravely, but they had no chance. They had only their bare hands with which to defend themselves, for they had not dreamed of such treachery.

Only two of all the Britons were saved. One was Vortigern, the king, because Hengist had ordered his soldiers not to kill him; the other was Edol, Earl of Gloucester. He found a wooden stake lying on the ground, and defended himself so bravely with it that, it is said, he killed seventy of the Saxons, and then escaped with his life.

After this wicked and cowardly slaughter of unarmed men, Hengist took possession of Britain. His wild, heathen soldiers swarmed all over the land, killing people, burning towns and making terrible havoc everywhere. The Britons fled in terror to the mountains and forests. Vortigern himself fled into a lonely part of Wales. There he built a strong castle in which to hide, for he was very much afraid. He was afraid of Hengist and the Saxons, and he was afraid of the Britons. He was also afraid of Aurelius Ambrosius and Uther Pendragon, the two brothers of King Constans. For by this time they were no longer little boys, but had grown up into brave men.

Vortigern had need to be afraid of Aurelius and Uther, for, hearing how Hengist had taken possession of Britain, they thought it was now time to fight for their country. So they gathered ships and soldiers together, and came sailing over from France to Britain.

When the Britons heard that Aurelius Ambrosius and his brother had landed, they took heart again. They came out from the places in which they had been hiding from the Saxons. Joyfully they offered themselves to fight under the banner of the brothers.

As soon as Aurelius and Uther had collected their army, they marched straight to Wales to besiege Vortigern in his castle. They had not forgotten that he had murdered their brother, Constans, and they meant to punish him.

But the castle was very, very strong. Try how they might, the Britons could not take it. Vortigern sat behind the thick walls, and laughed at all their efforts.

At last the Britons fell upon a plan. They cut down trees and gathered dry sticks and leaves from the forests round about. These they piled high round the castle. Day by day Vortigern watched the pile of wood rising, and wondered what was going to happen.

When the Britons had gathered enough wood, they set fire to it in several places at once. So one morning Vortigern awoke to hear the crackle, crackle of newly-lit fires. He looked out and saw smoke and flames all around him.

Wherever he looked he saw little tongues of fire. Soon the little tongues grew longer and longer. Higher and higher leapt the flames. Fiercer and fiercer grew the heat. Vortigern's laughter was turned to wild shrieks. In vain he prayed the Britons to have mercy on him and let him escape. "Had you any mercy on our brother, Constans?" said Ambrosius and Uther. "Had you any mercy on our fathers and brothers when you let Hengist slay them on Salisbury Plain?" asked the Britons. "You had no mercy. You shall find none."

The roar of the fire drowned all else. The flames leaped higher. With a crash the roof of the strong castle fell in. Vortigern, the betrayer of his people, was dead.

CHAPTER XI

THE STORY OF HOW THE GIANT'S DANCE WAS BROUGHT TO BRITAIN

VORTIGERN was dead, but the Saxons whom he had brought to Britain were still rulers of the land. So after burningf the castle of Vortigern, Aurelius Ambrosius and Uther Pendragon marched against the Saxons. They defeated them in a great battle, and Hengist was taken prisoner.

Then Aurelius Ambrosius called all the British nobles together in council to decide what should be done with Hengist. Aurelius was a very brave man, but he was not cruel. He was noble, and above all things he hated a lie. Hengist was brave too, but he was cruel, revengeful, and deceitful.

Aurelius would have spared Hengist's life, because he was such a brave man. But Edol, Earl of Gloucester, that noble who fought so well when the Britons were destroyed on Salisbury Plain, stood up. "It is not right," he said, "that Hengist should live. He has brought much sorrow on our land. Through his fault nearly all our nobles were killed on Salisbury Plain. Let him die."

Then all the people shouted, "Let him die."

So Aurelius bowed his head and said, "It is just. Let him die."

Edol then led Hengist away and cut off his head.

But although their leader was gone, many Saxons still remained in Britain, and afterwards you will hear how powerful they became.

Aurelius was now chosen to be King of Britain and, like Vortimer, he began to restore order and rebuild the churches and towns which the heathen Saxons had a second time destroyed. The land which the Saxons had stolen he gave back to those of the Britons to whom it really belonged. He revised the laws, and once more peace and justice reigned in the kingdom.

When Aurelius had put everything in good order, he went to Salisbury Plain to see the place where so many of his people had been put to death by Hengist and his wicked Saxons.

As he stood upon the great plain, he felt very sad. Turning to his nobles who surrounded him, he said, "My people died trying to make peace for their country. Yet there is no stone to mark the spot. I will have a noble monument raised, so that the wickedness of Hengist and the bravery of my people may be remembered for ever."

Then Aurelius sent for all the best builders and masons in the country, and told them to make a splendid monument. But, one after another, they refused. "We are not clever enough to do such a great thing," they said.

This made Aurelius sorry, for he wished very much that people should not forget these British heroes.

Then a wise man came to him and said, "Send for Merlin. If any one can build a great monument he can."

"Who is Merlin?" asked Aurelius.

"Merlin is a great magician," replied the wise man. "He used to live with Vortigern and do wonderful things for him. Since Vortigern's death he has been hiding somewhere in Wales. If you can find him he will build the monument for you."

A magician is a person who can do difficult things quite easily. His real home is in fairyland, and he understands fairy language. The fairies come and whisper their wonderful secrets to him, although no one else can see or hear them.

Aurelius was very glad to hear about Merlin. He sent messengers into all the land to look for him. They searched about for a long time, until at last they found Merlin and brought him to the king.

As soon as Merlin knew what Aurelius wanted, he said, "If you really wish to honour the burying-place of these men with a monument which will last for ever, send to Ireland for the Giant's Dance."

"What is the Giant's Dance?" asked Aurelius.

"The Giant's Dance is a great ring of stones," replied Merlin. "They are so wonderful and so old that no one is sure how they came there. But it is said that long, long ago giants brought these stones from a far-off country called Africa."

When Aurelius heard that, he burst out laughing. "How is it possible," he asked, "to remove such big stones from a far-off country? Have we not enough stones in Britain with which to build a monument?" and he laughed again.

"Do not laugh," said Merlin gravely. "They are wonderful stones. Every one of them will cure some kind of illness. They are fairy stones."

When the Britons heard that, they made up their minds to have these stones, and Uther Pendragon was chosen to go with Merlin to bring them. So, taking a great army of men and many ships, they set sail for Ireland.

When they arrived in Ireland they sent a message to the king, asking him to let them take the Giant's Dance away.

It was now the King of Ireland's turn to laugh. "What mad people these Britons are!" he said. "Was ever such folly heard of? Have they not enough stones in their own country, that they must come to take mine? I shall certainly not give them one single stone of the Giant's Dance. Tell them to go home again and not to be so foolish."

But the Britons had quite made up their minds to have the Giant's Dance. As the King of Ireland would not give it to them, they resolved to fight for it. This they did, and soon put the Irish to flight.

Then Merlin led the Britons to the place where the Giant's Dance stood. When they saw it, they were filled with joy and wonder, and set to work at once to move the stones. But try how they might, they could not move even the smallest of them one single inch. They pulled and pushed, struggled and strained, till they were hot and tired, but the stones stood as firm as rocks.

Merlin sat by, watching them and smiling. Then when they were all worn out, and cross and tired, he rose. "Now let me try," he said, "it is really quite easy." And in a very short time, with the help of his wonderful magic, he had moved all the stones and put them on board the ships. The people looked on in amazement and, as soon as he had finished, they set sail for Britain with great rejoicing.

When they landed, messengers were sent to tell King Aurelius Ambrosius. He gathered all the nobles and clergy, and wearing his crown and royal robes, rode to Salisbury Plain. There, with great feasting and ceremony, the stones were set up as a memorial to the dead British heroes. They were placed in exactly the same order as they were found in Ireland. Aurelius changed the name from Giant's Dance to Stonehenge, and the great monument may be seen on Salisbury Plain to this day.

Most people say this is a fairy tale, and ought not to be put in a history book. They say that the stones on Stonehenge were there long before Merlin lived, long before Hengist and his Saxons, or Cæsar and his Romans, even long before Brutus of Troy, came. They say that probably no one will ever find out how these stones came to be there, or why they were placed as they are. I dare say they are right, but fairy tales are very interesting, and this fairy tale (if it is one) is to be found in some of the first histories of Britain that were ever written. So certainly at one time people must have believed it to be true.

Unfortunately, soon after this, a wicked Saxon poisoned the good king, Aurelius Ambrosius. The Britons were very sad at his loss, and they buried him within the Giant's Dance, where so many other noble Britons lay. Then, because Aurelius had no children, the people chose his brother Uther Pendragon to be king.

He, too, was good and wise, but he had to spend most of his time fighting against the Saxons. After the death of Hengist very many Saxons had remained in Britain, and now many more came again in ships from Germany. Fierce and terrible battles were fought, and although the Saxons were often defeated, the Britons could not succeed in driving them away altogether.

But the name of Uther Pendragon became a terror to these heathen. It is said that when he was so old and feeble that he could not stand, he was carried to battle in a litter. And so great was the power and fame of his courage, that the Saxons were utterly defeated. "Ah," he said, laughing, "these heathen call me the half-dead king. And so indeed I am. Yet victory to me half dead is better than to be safe and sound and vanquished. For to die with honour is better than to live with disgrace."

But alas! Uther Pendragon, like so many of the good kings before him, was also poisoned by the wicked Saxons. So he died, and the people buried him close to his brother, Aurelius Ambrosius, within the Giant's Dance on Salisbury Plain.

CHAPTER XII

THE COMING OF ARTHUR

AS soon as Uther Pendragon was dead, the mighty nobles of Britain began to quarrel among themselves as to who should be king next. Each noble thought he had the best right, so the quarrelling was dreadful.

While they were all gathered together, fighting and shouting at each other, Merlin came among them, leading a tall, fair-haired boy by the hand. When the nobles saw Merlin, they stopped fighting and were silent. They knew how clever he was, and what wonderful things he could do, and they were rather afraid of him.

Merlin stood quietly looking at them all from under his bushy eyebrows. He was a very old man. But he was tall and strong and splendid, with a long white beard and fierce, glittering eyes. It was no wonder that the Britons felt afraid of him.

"Lords of Britain," said Merlin at last, "why fight ye thus? It were more meet that ye prepare to do honour to your king. Uther Pendragon is indeed dead, but Arthur, his son, reigns in his stead."

"Who is this Arthur? Where is he?" asked the nobles angrily. "Uther Pendragon had no son."

"Hear me," said Merlin, "Uther Pendragon had a son. It was told to me that he should be the greatest king who should ever reign in Britain. So when he was born, lest any harm should befall him, he was given into my care till the time should come for him to reign. He has dwelt in the land of Avilon, where the wise fairies have kept him from evil and whispered wisdom in his ear. Here is your king, honour him."

Then Merlin lifted Arthur up and placed him upon his shoulders, so that all the people could see him. There was something so noble and splendid about Arthur, even although he was only a boy, that the great lords felt awed. Yet they would not believe that he was the son of Uther Pendragon. "Who is this Arthur?" they said again. "We do not believe what you say. Uther Pendragon had no son."

Then Merlin's bright eyes seemed to flash fire. "You dare to doubt the word of Merlin?" he shouted. "O vain and foolish Britons, follow me."

Taking Arthur with him, Merlin turned and strode out of the hall, and all the nobles followed him. As they passed through the streets, the people of the town and the women and children followed too. On they went, the crowd growing bigger and bigger, till they reached the great door of the cathedral. There Merlin stopped, and the knights and nobles gathered around him; those behind pushing and pressing forward, eager to see what was happening.

There was indeed something wonderful to be seen. In front of the doorway was a large stone which had not been there before. Standing upright in the stone was a sword, the hilt of which glittered with gems. Beneath it was written, "Whoso can draw me from this stone is the rightful king of Britain."

One after another the nobles tried to remove the sword. They pulled and tugged till their muscles cracked. They strained and struggled till they were hot and breathless, for each one was anxious to be king. But it was all in vain. The sword remained firm and fast in the rock.

Then last of all Arthur tried. He took the sword by the hilt and drew it from the stone quite easily.

A cry of wonder went through the crowd, and the nobles fell back in astonishment leaving a clear space round the king. Then as he stood there, holding the magic sword in his hand, the British nobles one after another knelt to Arthur, acknowledging him to be their lord.

" 'Be thou the king and we will work thy will,
Who love thee.' Then the king in low deep tones
And simple words of great authority
Bound them by so strait vows to his own self
That when they rose, knighted from kneeling, some
Were pale as at the passing of a ghost,
Some flushed, and others dazed, as one who wakes
Half-blinded at the coming of a light."

Arthur was only fifteen when he was made king, but he was the bravest, wisest and best king that had ever ruled in Britain. As soon as he was crowned, he determined to free his kingdom from the Saxons. He swore a solemn oath that he would drive the heathen out of the land. His knights he bound by the same solemn oath.

Then, taking the sword which he had won, and which was called Excalibur, and his mighty spear called Ron, he rode forth at the head of his army.

Twelve great battles did Arthur fight and win against the Saxons. Always in the foremost of the battle he was to be seen, in his armour of gold and blue, the figure of the Virgin upon his shield, a golden dragon and crown upon his helmet. He was so brave that no one could stand against him, yet so careless of danger that many times he would have been killed, had it not been for the magic might of his sword Excalibur, and of his spear Ron.

And at last the Saxons were driven from the land.

CHAPTER XIII

THE FOUNDING OF THE ROUND TABLE

IT is said that Arthur not only drove the Saxons out of Britain, but that he conquered many parts of Europe, until at last he ruled over thirty kingdoms. Then for some years there was peace.

During these years, Arthur did much for his people. He taught them to love truth and goodness, and to be Christian and gentle. No king had ever been loved as Arthur was loved.

"Liberal to each man, I ween,
Knight with the best, wondrous keen,
To the young he was as father,
To the old as comforter.
Wondrous stern to the unwise,
Wrong could he suffer nowise,
Right, dear exceeding was to him.
Now was Arthur right good king,
His folk and all peoples lovéd him."

In those fierce and far-off days, when men spent most of their time fighting, it was very necessary for them to be brave and strong, in order to protect their dear ones, but they were very often cruel as well and nearly always fierce. Arthur taught people that it was possible to be brave yet kind, strong yet gentle. Afterwards people forgot this again, but in the days of Arthur the fame of his court and of his gentle knights spread far and wide.

No noble thought himself perfect unless his armour, and clothes even, were made like those of Arthur's knights. No man thought himself worthy of love until, fighting for the right against the wrong, he had three times conquered an enemy.

Many pretty stories are told of Arthur and his gentle, courteous knights, although they did not learn all their gentleness and their courtesy at once, as you shall hear.

Upon an Easter Day, Arthur called together all his knights and nobles, from his many kingdoms, to a great feast. They came from far and near, kings, earls, barons and knights, gay in splendid clothes, glittering with jewels and gold.

As they waited for the King they laughed and talked together. But secretly each heart was full of proud thoughts. Each man thought himself nobler and grander than any of the others.

The tables were spread for the feast. They were covered with white silk cloths. Silver baskets piled with loaves, golden bowls and cups full of wine stood ready, and, as the knights and nobles talked and waited, they began to choose where they would sit.

In those days master and servants all sat together at the same table for meals. The master and his family sat at the top, and the servants and poor people at the bottom of the table. So it came to be considered that the seats near the top were the best. The further down the table any one sat, the less honour was paid him.

At his feast no servants nor poor people were going to sit at table, yet all the nobles wanted places at the top. "We will not sit in the seats of scullions and beggars," they said.

So they began to push each other aside, and to say, "Make way, this is my seat."

"Nay, I am more honourable than you. You must sit below me."

"How dare you? My name is more noble than yours. That is my seat."

"Give place, I say."

At first it was only words. Soon it came to blows. They had come to the feast unarmed, so they had only their hands with which to fight, but as they grew angrier and angrier, they seized the bowls of wine and threw them at each other. Next the loaves of bread and the gold and silver cups were thrown about, the tables and benches were overturned, howls and yells filled the hall, and everything was in dreadful confusion.

When the noise was at its worst, the door opened and the King appeared. His face was stern and grand as he looked down on the struggling, yelling crowd.

"Sit ye, sit ye down quickly, every man in the place where he is," he cried. "Whoso will not, he shall be put to death."

At the sound of their King's stern voice, the foolish nobles were filled with shame. Silently they sat down; the tables and benches were put back in their places and the feast began.

But Arthur was sad at heart. "How can I teach my people to be gentle and kind, if my knights will not even sit at meat in peace," he said to himself. Then as he sat sorrowfully wondering what he could do, Merlin came to him.

"Be not sad, O King," he said, "but listen to my advice. Tell your carpenters to make a great round table at which there shall be a place for every knight. Then there can be no more quarrelling. For at a round table there is neither top nor bottom, so no knight can say that he sits above or below another. All shall be equal."

Then Arthur was sad no longer. He did as Merlin advised, and had a great round table made, at which there was a seat for each one of his knights. After that there was no more quarrelling as to who should have the best place, for all were equal, and Arthur's knights became known as The Knights of the Round Table.

But, alas! the time of peace did not last. Again came days of war and strife. In a great and terrible battle, Arthur and nearly all his knights were killed. Once more the fierce heathen swept over the land, filling it with sorrow and bloodshed, and the glory and beauty of knighthood were forgotten in Britain.

But some people think that Arthur did not die. They say that when he was wounded so that he could fight no more, the wise fairies came to take him back to fairyland. They say that he is still there, and that some day he will come again.

Other people say the stories about Arthur and his knights are not true, but at least we may believe that in those far-off, fierce, fighting days there was a king who taught his people that to be gentle was not cowardly and that to be cruel was not brave;—

> *"Who reverenced his conscience as his king;*
> *Whose glory was redressing human wrong;*
> *Who spake no slander, no, nor listened to it,*
> *Who loved one only and who clave to her."*

CHAPTER XIV

THE STORY OF GREGORY AND THE PRETTY CHILDREN

YOU remember that the Romans came to Britain and, in a manner, conquered it. But after staying several hundred years, they again went away. When the Romans came to the island, the people who lived there were Britons. When the Romans left the island, the people who lived there were still Britons. The Romans could not make the Britons Romans, however hard they tried. They could not even make them speak Latin, which was the language of the Romans. The Britons learned many things from the Romans, but in spite of all they learned, they never forgot that they were Britons.

When the Saxons came to Britain, things happened very differently. You remember that first of all Vortigern asked the Saxons to come, and that afterwards every British king fought against them and tried to drive them away.

It seemed sometimes as if the Britons might succeed, but it never seemed so for long. In fact, from the day Hengist and Horsa landed, Britain had never really been free from these fierce heathen people. As time went on, they came in greater and greater numbers from over the sea. They were all Saxons, but there were many different tribes of them, some called Jutes, some Angles, and some by other names.

The Britons fought nobly for their country, but all in vain. However many of the Saxons were killed did not seem to matter, for their ships always brought more and more of them from over the sea. At last the Saxons had killed nearly all the Britons, and the few who remained took refuge in the mountains, in that part of the country which we now call Wales, and in Cornwall. So to this day the men of Cornwall and the Welsh are the descendants of the ancient Britons, and the language they speak is very like the language spoken by the ancient Britons.

I want you to understand that the kings and people of whom you are now going to read are not British but Saxon, the new people from over the sea who had gradually taken possession of the whole of the south of Britain. There were other British kings after Arthur, but as nearly all their time was taken up with fighting against the Saxons, the story of their lives is not very interesting.

These wild Saxons did not at once settle down quietly into one kingdom. No, they had many leaders, and each leader seized a part of Britain for himself and his followers, so there arose seven different kingdoms. And although they were really all one race of people, and spoke almost the same language, they were always fighting with each other. This lasted until Egbert, one of the kings of one of the seven kingdoms, succeeded in making the others own him as a kind of over-lord. He was an Angle, and he changed the name of the country from Britain to Angleland or England. So we may say that he was the first king of England.

The Saxons were heathen as you know, and they pulled down the churches and killed the Christian priests. So all the land became heathen again. Only in the wild mountains of Wales, the teaching of Arthur and his Christian knights was remembered.

But once again the story of Christ was brought to Britain, and you shall now hear how it happened.

In those days slavery was allowed, that is, people used to buy and sell men and women, and little boys and girls, just as if they were cattle.

The merchants who came to trade with Britain used to take away slaves to sell in far-off countries. One day a good man called Gregory was walking through the market-place in Rome. It was market day and the square was crowded with people buying and selling. It was very noisy and gay. Fine gentlemen strolled about, careful housewives went from stall to stall trying to find what was cheapest and best, friends met and chatted, and through all the noise and bustle Gregory walked with his head bent, deep in thought.

Suddenly he stood still. He had been awakened from his dream by the sound of children's voices, and now he stopped to watch them, as they laughed and played together. These children had fair faces and rosy cheeks, their eyes were merry and blue, and their hair shone like gold in the sunshine. Gregory thought they were the prettiest children that he had ever seen.

A very tender look came into Gregory's eyes as he stood and watched them playing. Then he sighed, for he saw by the chains round their necks that they were to be sold as slaves. "Poor children," he said, "so far from home!" He knew they must come from some far-off country because all the people in his own land had dark faces and black hair.

"Where do these children come from?" he asked, turning to the man who had charge of them.

"From the island called Britain," replied the man, "but the people are called Angles."

"Angles," said Gregory, as he gently put his hand on their curly heads, "nay, not Angles but angels they should be called."

The children could not understand what Gregory said, but they knew from his voice that it was something kind. They ceased their play, and stood round him, looking up trustingly into his face, with their big blue eyes.

Gregory stroked their curly heads, and as he bent over them he felt love for the pretty fair-haired children grow in his heart. He asked many question about them, and when he heard that they were heathen, he made up his mind to buy them and teach them to be Christians.

Gregory took the pretty children home with him. He was very kind to them, and taught them how to grow up into good men and women. They loved him, you may be sure, and he loved them so much, that he made up his mind to go to Britain to teach all their brothers and sisters there to be Christians too.

But the people of his own land were so fond of Gregory that they would not let him go. So, although it was a great sorrow to him, he was obliged to give up his plan.

But Gregory did not forget about it. Some years after this he was made Bishop of Rome, and so became a very powerful and important person. And one of the first things he did after he became powerful was to send a good man called Augustine to preach about Christ to the Angles.

Augustine took about forty other good men with him, and set out for Britain. We are not told if the pretty children, whom Gregory had bought in the Roman market-place so many years before, were among these men, but I think very likely they were. They would be so glad to go back to their own country to teach their brothers and sisters all the good things they had learned from Gregory.

It is a long way from Italy to England, and in those days when there were no trains and travelling was both difficult and dangerous, it seemed very long indeed. But after many adventures Augustine and his men arrived safely on the seashore of France. There they had to wait for a ship to take them across to Britain, or England as we must now call it.

While they waited, Augustine and his men heard such stories about the fierceness of the Angles and the Saxons that they were frightened. They were so frightened that they turned back to Rome.

When Gregory heard that they had returned he was very angry. "I am ashamed that you should be so cowardly," he said to Augustine. "Go back again. If the people of England kill you, you die for others, even as Christ did."

So Augustine set out again. This time he reached England.

Although the Saxons were fierce and lawless, they treated Augustine and his followers very kindly. Ethelbert, who was King of Kent, one of the seven kingdoms into which England was divided, was the first to listen to them. He was a heathen, but he had married a Christian lady, and so had already heard something of the story of Christ. Soon he and all his people were baptized.

Augustine does not seem to have had any difficulty in persuading the Saxons to leave off worshipping idols. One would think that the heathen priests at least would have been very angry, and that they would have tried to stop the teaching of this new religion. But they did not.

A story is told of a priest whose name was Coifi. He sat one day among the people listening very attentively to the story of God and Christ. When the preacher had finished speaking there was a great silence. This new religion seemed to the people to be very beautiful, but they were so accustomed to believing that their idols had power to punish them, if they neglected them or disobeyed them, that they were afraid. Then Coifi rose. "No one," he said, "has ever served the old gods more faithfully than I have. I have tried to believe in them all my life, yet they have never done anything to make me better or happier. This new teaching seems to me to be good. Let us destroy our old gods and turn to the teaching of Christ."

Then while the astonished people looked on in fear, Coifi took a spear in his hand, mounted upon a horse, and riding at full speed knocked over the great idol which for so many years he had worshipped as God.

When the people saw their god fallen and broken, they trembled. They felt sure something dreadful would happen to Coifi for his wickedness. But nothing happened. So, taking heart and following the example of Coifi, the people set fire to their temple, which was soon burned to the ground, and the idols with it. Then all the people were baptized and became Christians.

In time Augustine or his followers went through all the seven kingdoms of England. It took a long time, but at last the whole land became Christian, although of course the people did not learn all at once to live as good Christians ought.

CHAPTER XV

HOW KING ALFRED LEARNED TO READ

WHEN the Saxons first came to England, they came only to fight and kill, but soon they began to love their new home and, when two or three hundred years had passed, they forgot that they had ever lived in any other country. So, instead of fighting against England, they began to fight for and love the land as their own.

Then English kings arose who tried to make good laws and rule the people well, as some of the British kings had done. But just as the Romans had come to conquer Britain, and as the Saxons themselves had come, so now another people came.

These new enemies were the Northmen or Danes. They came from the countries which we now call Denmark, Norway, and Sweden.

These Danes, as we shall call them all, were fierce, wild men. They loved to sail upon the sea; they loved to fight. They were heathen too, just as the Saxons had been when they first came to England.

Many and long were the battles which were fought between the English and the Danes, but year by year the Danes grew stronger, and the English weaker, till it seemed as if the land was going to be conquered once again. But at last a great English king, called Alfred, began to rule. He beat the Danes in many battles, and nearly drove them out of the country.

Alfred was the youngest son of Ethelwulf, who was King of Wessex, one of the seven kingdoms into which England was divided. He was also the grandson of Egbert, that king who changed the name of Britain to England.

Although Ethelwulf was really king only of Wessex, he was "over-lord" over all the rulers of the other seven kingdoms of England. So you must remember, when we speak of the King of England at this time, that we do not mean that he was the only king in the land. But Wessex was the chief of the seven kingdoms, and the King of Wessex was the chief of the seven kings. In the end the King of Wessex became real king of all England, while the other kingdoms disappeared and their kings were forgotten.

King Ethelwulf's wife was called Osburga. She was a good and wise woman, and a very kind mother to her little children. She was clever, too, and fond of reading, which was rather uncommon in those days when very few people could read or cared about it.

In the time of the Romans, you remember, books were written on strips of parchment, and rolled up like maps. Now they were shaped and bound just like our books, only as there was no paper and no printing, they were still written on parchment and the pictures were all painted by hand. It took a long time to make a book, and required a great deal of money to buy one.

One day when Alfred, the youngest son of King Ethelwulf, was quite a tiny boy, he was playing with his big brothers, while Osburga, his mother, sat watching them, and reading.

The book she read was one of old English songs. Osburga was very fond of these songs, and used to say them to her little boys when they were tired of play. It was a pretty book, full of pictured and bright letters in gold, and blue, and red.

As Osburga turned the pages Alfred saw the pretty pictures, so he left his play, and came to lean against his mother's knee, to look at them.

"What a pretty book it is, mother!" he said.

"Do you like it, little one?" said Osburga.

"Yes, mother, I do," replied Alfred.

Then all the other boys came crowding round their mother to see the pretty book too. They pressed against her, and leaned over her shoulder till nothing was to be seen but five curly heads close together.

"Oh, isn't it lovely!" they said, as Osburga slowly turned the pages, explaining the pictures, and letting them look at the beautiful colored letters at the beginnings of the songs.

When Osburga saw how they all liked the book, she was very much pleased. She pushed them all away from her a little, and looked round their happy eager faces. You see in those days even kings' sons had no picture-books, such as every child has now, and it was quite a treat for these princes to be allowed to look at this beautiful one.

"Do you truly like this book?" asked Osburga.

"Oh yes, mother, we do," they all answered at once.

"Then, boys," she said, "I will give it to the one who first learns to read it."

"O mother, do you mean it? May I try too?" asked Alfred.

"Yes, I do mean it, and, of course, you may try," answered Osburga, smiling at him. And perhaps she hoped that he would win the prize, for both his father and his mother loved Alfred best of all their children.

And Alfred did win the prize. He was so eager to have the book that he worked hard all day long. And one morning, while his big brothers were still trying to read the book, he came to his mother and read it without making any mistakes.

Then Osburga kissed him and gave him the prize, as she had promised. All his life afterwards Alfred was fond of books; and even when he became king, and had many, many other things to do, he still found time not only to read, but to write them.

CHAPTER XVI

KING ALFRED IN THE COWHERD'S COTTAGE

WHEN Ethelwulf, Alfred's father, died, each of his sons became king in turn. During these reigns the Danes became more and more troublesome. Nearly all the time was spent in fighting, so that the country came to be in a very sad state indeed.

When Ethelred (who was the last of Ethelwulf's sons except Alfred) came to the throne, Alfred had grown to be a man, and although he was still very young, he helped his brother a great deal. And when Ethelred died, the people chose Alfred to be their king. For although Ethelred had two sons, they were little boys, and no one thought of making either of them king. The people knew that a strong and wise man was needed to rule in England, and Alfred was both strong and wise.

No king has ever had to fight more bravely for his kingdom than Alfred had. When he came to the throne, the Danes were growing more and more bold. They did not now only come in their ships to plunder and rob, and then sail away again. They came now to live in the land, killing the people, and then taking their houses for themselves.

So all the first years of Alfred's reign were spent in fighting these fierce enemies. But Alfred did not only fight bravely, he thought too.

The Danes were brave and daring sailors, just as the English had been before they came to live in England. But somehow after the English settled down, they seem to have forgotten about how to build ships and how to sail upon the sea.

But Alfred was wise and saw how much better it would be to stop the Danes before they landed at all. So he built ships and went in them to fight the Danes on the sea.

In the year 875 A.D., King Alfred and his ships met the Danes and their ships and fought a great battle and won a great victory. That was the first of many, many sea-victories which the English have won, and ever since the days of Alfred, England has had a navy and Britannia has ruled the waves.

"Ye mariners of England
That guard our native seas,
Whose flag had braved a thousand years
The battle and the breeze;
Your glorious standard launch again
To match another foe
And sweep through the deep,
While the stormy winds do blow;
While the battle rages loud and long,

And the stormy winds do blow.
Britannia needs no bulwarks,
No towers along the steep;
Her march is on the mountain waves,
Her home is on the deep.
With thunders from her native oak
She quells the floods below,
As they roar on the shore,
When the stormy winds do blow;
When the battle rages loud and long,
And the stormy winds do blow."

But even although Alfred gained this battle at sea, the Danes were not beaten altogether. Again and again Alfred had to fight, but at last he forced the Danes to make peace. They swore by a most solemn and dreadful oath that they would go away and never make war against the English again. This vow was taken with great ceremony. Sheep and cattle were killed and offered in sacrifice to the heathen gods, for the Danes, you remember were heathen. A beautiful ring of gold, called the holy bracelet, was dipped in the blood of the animals. The bracelet was then placed upon an altar and, laying their hands upon it, the Danish chiefs swore to fight no more against the English.

This was not the first time that the Danes had promised to go away and fight no more, but they had always broken their promises. Now Alfred thought they would be sure to keep their word, because of the very solemn vow they had taken.

But the Danes did not mean to keep this promise any more than the others. Very soon they came back again as bold as before, or bolder. Once more fierce battles raged, till at last, weary of fighting, and forsaken by nearly all his followers, Alfred was forced to hide for a time in the marshes of Somerset.

This was the saddest part of Alfred's life. He was a king, yet he had neither crown nor royal robes, neither palace nor servants. He was so poor that he went to live in the cottage of a cowherd called Denewulf. His clothes were so old and worn that the cowherd's wife thought that he was a friend of her husband, and so she treated him as if he had been a common man and not a great king.

One day Denewulf's wife was very busy. She had been baking cakes, and had still many things to do. Alfred meanwhile was sitting by the fire. He had been mending his bow and arrows, but they had dropped from his hand, for, thinking deeply about his kingdom and his people, and of how he could free them from the Danes, he had forgotten all else.

It seemed to Denewulf's wife that Alfred was a lazy sort of fellow. She did not know the great matters he had to think of, and she wondered how any one could sit for hours by the fire doing nothing, while she and her husband had to work so hard.

Now, she said to herself, this lazy fellow can at least look after my cakes, while I go to do something else.

"Here, good man," she said to him, "just mind my cakes for me. And don't let them burn. When they are nice and brown on one side, turn them over on to the other side, like this—" and she showed him how to do it.

"All right, good wife, I will look after your cakes for you," replied Alfred.

But when the good woman had gone, Alfred sank once more deep in thought. As he watched the cakes, he looked into the fire. Soon, in the red glow of the burning ashes, he saw wonderful things. The cakes and the cowherd's cottage vanished. Once again he was leading his army, his banner with its golden dragons fluttered in the breeze, his spear was in his hand, his crown upon his head. He heard the shout of his soldiers as they charged the Danes. The ranks of the enemy broke, they fled—to their ships they fled. Fast behind them came the English. They set fire to the Danish ships. He smelt the smoke as it rolled upward, heard the crackle of the flames, the shrieks of the dying, the shouts of victory. England was saved.

Then suddenly he was awakened out of his dream by a blow to his shoulder, and an angry voice in his ear,

"Canst thee not mind the cakes, man?
And doesn't thee see them burn?
I's bound thee'll eat them fast enough
As soon as 'tis thy turn."

Alas! the cakes, and not the Danish ships, were burning. Alfred was a great king, but he had proved a poor cook; and the good wife was very angry.

She scolded him well, little thinking that she was scolding her King. She was still rating when Denewulf came in.

"Hush thee, woman, hush thee," he said, ashamed and frightened.

"Hush, shall I?" she cried angrily. "The lazy loon, the idle good-for-naught, to sit by the fire, and see the cakes burn, and never stir a finger."

"Hush thee, woman," said Denewulf again in despair. "It is the King."

"The King!" cried the good wife, astonished, and a little frightened too. "Well, king or no king," she added grumblingly after a minute, "he ought to have minded the cakes."

Alfred was not angry, as Denewulf feared he would be, and afterwards, when he came to his kingdom again, Alfred made the cowherd a bishop, for he had found out while hiding in his cottage that Denewulf was a good and wise man. So his wife became a great lady, and perhaps never baked any more cakes. Certainly she never again had a king to watch them for her.

CHAPTER XVII

MORE ABOUT ALFRED THE GREAT

SOON, Alfred was joined in his hiding-place in Somerset by his wife and children and a few of his nobles. They chose a hill which rose above the surrounding marshes for their camp, and there Alfred and his nobles worked like common men, building a strong fort. Because of this, the place was called Athelney, which means the Isle of Nobles.

While Alfred worked on the Isle of Nobles, he sent messengers secretly among his people, telling them where he was. Soon a small but faithful band gathered round him. Then, one day, some of Alfred's friends suddenly attacked the Danes, won a victory, and seized the great Danish banner called the Raven.

The Danes were very sad at the loss of this banner, for they believed it to be a magic one. They said that when they were going to win a battle the Raven would spread its wings as if to fly, but when they were going to lose, the Raven drooped its wings in sorrow. Now that their precious banner had been taken, they were always afraid of losing.

This victory cheered the English very much, and when the people heard of it, more and more of them gathered round their king.

Alfred now began to feel that the time for striking a blow had come. But first he wanted to find out exactly how many Danes there were and what plans they had. So he dressed himself like a minstrel or singer, and taking his harp, he went to the Danish camp. There he began to play upon his harp and to sing the songs he had learned when he was a boy.

The Danes were a fierce, wild people, yet they loved music and poetry. They were delighted with Alfred's songs, and he was allowed to wander through the camp wherever he liked.

Alfred stayed in the Danish camp for several days, singing his songs and playing sweet music, and all the time watching and listening. He found out how many Danes there were, and where the camp was strong and where it was weak. He listened to the king as he talked to his captains and, when he had found out everything he could, he slipped quietly away and went back to the Isle of Nobles.

The Danes were sorry when they found that the gentle minstrel had gone. And little did they think that it was the great and brave King Alfred who had been singing and playing to them.

Alfred now knew that his army was strong enough to fight the Danes. So he left his fort on the Isle of Nobles and boldly marched against them. A battle was fought in which the Danes were defeated, and from that time onwards Alfred was victorious. The dark days were over. The power of the

Danes was crushed. Their king, Guthorm, submitted to Alfred, and even became a Christian. When he was baptized, Alfred stood as godfather to him, and changed his name from Guthorm to the English name of Æthelstan.

Then Alfred made a peace with the Danes, called the peace of Wedmore. And although the Danes did not leave England, they did not fight any more, and they left Wessex and kept within the land which was given to them in the north. Afterwards, this part was called the Danelagh or Daneland.

And not it was, in the time of peace, that Alfred began to do great things for his people, the things by which he earned his name of Alfred the Great. He collected the laws and wrote them out so that people could understand them. He did away with the laws which he thought were bad, and made others. One law he made was, that a man who had done wrong could not be punished unless twelve men agreed that he really had been wicked, and ought to be punished. This was called trial by jury, and means trial by those who have promised to do justly. Our word jury comes from a Latin word which means to promise or swear.

It was a very good law, for sometimes if a man hated another man he would say he had done something wicked in order to have him punished. But when twelve men had to agree about it, it was not easy to have an innocent person unjustly punished.

Alfred was much loved. He made good laws, and the people kept them. They kept them so well, that it is said that golden chains and bracelets might be hung upon the hedges and no one would touch them.

King Alfred was fond of reading and learning, and he tried to make his people fond of learning too. In those days the monasteries were the chief places to which people went to learn. But the Danes had destroyed nearly all the monasteries, so Alfred began to build them again, and he also founded schools. Then, as nearly all the books which were worth reading were written in Latin, he translated into English several of the best he had read. He did this because he saw how much more difficult it was for people to learn to read when they had to do so in a foreign language.

Alfred built more great ships, and sent people into far countries to bring back news of them to England. He encouraged the English to make all kinds of things, in order to trade with these far-off countries. In fact, during all his life Alfred was thinking only of his people and of what was best for them.

You will wonder how he found time to do all these things, and indeed it is wonderful, especially in those days when there were no clocks to strike the hours and remind people how time was flying.

Yet Alfred divided the day into three parts: eight hours for work, eight hours for study, and eight hours for rest. He invented a kind of clock for himself. He had great candles made which were marked off into parts, each part burning for an hour. A man watched the candle and, when the flame burned down to the mark, he went to the King, and said, "O king, another hour has fled."

Alfred was good, and wise and kind. There never was a better king in England. He had to fight many battles, and war is terrible and cruel, but he did not fight for love of conquering, as other kings did. He fought only to save his country and his people. We never hear of him doing one unjust or unkind act. He was truthful and fearless in everything. It is no wonder, then, that we call him Alfred the Great, Alfred the Truthteller, England's Darling.

CHAPTER XVIII

ETHELRED THE UNREADY

ALFRED died in 901 A.D. and his son, Edward, became king after him. He is called Edward the Elder, because he was the first of a great many kings of that name. He was a good king and was greatly helped by his sister, Ethelfleda, who was called the Lady of Mercia. She was a brave, wise woman and, like Boadicea, often led her soldiers in battle. For the Danes began to be troublesome again, and Edward and Ethelfleda had to fight many battles with them.

When Edward the Elder and Ethelfleda both died, Edward's son, Athelstane, came to the throne. He, too, was a good king, and he, too, had to fight with the Danes. After him came six kings who have been called the "boy kings," because they were all so young when they came to the throne. Some of these boy kings were wise and good, and all of them had to fight with the Danes.

Year by year the Danes were becoming more and more powerful in England. They not only came and went in their ships, but many more of them settled in the country. They made their homes in England and forgot about their old homes in Denmark. That would not have mattered much, if they had become good English subjects, willing to obey an English king. But that is what they did not do. Instead, they rebelled always against the king, and so wars and fighting went on.

Now you shall hear about the last of the "boy kings." His name was Ethelred, and because he was foolish and slow, he was also called the Unready. He lived about a hundred years after Alfred.

In his reign everything seemed to go wrong. The Danes soon found out what a foolish man he was, and they came in greater numbers than ever. Ethelred had not spirit enough to be a good leader. He was never sure of what he wanted to do, so his soldiers lost heart and his captains quarrelled among themselves.

He built ships, but they were shattered by storms. The city of London caught fire by accident and was burnt to the ground. Everywhere there was misery and misfortune.

Then Ethelred thought of an unhappy plan for ridding the country of the Danes. He said to them, "I will give you a large sum of money if you will go away."

The Danes, of course, were delighted at the idea of getting money so easily, and they gladly promised. Ethelred gave them the gold, and they sailed away and the English people rejoiced.

But the Danes, as you know, were never careful about keeping their promises. They went home, it is true, but when they had spent all the money which Ethelred had given them, they said, "Let us go to England again and rob the people. Perhaps their foolish king will give us more money."

And so they sailed to England. Ethelred again gave them money to go back to Denmark; again they sailed away, but when the money was spent, once more they returned.

Over and over again the same thing happened, Ethelred always giving the Danes larger and larger sums, for they grew more and more greedy when they saw how easy it was to make the foolish English king give them money.

How did Ethelred get all the money which he gave to the Danes? Was it his own? No. In order to get the money, Ethelred taxed the people, that is, he made each person pay a certain sum every year, and this was called Danegelt or Danemoney.

The English were already accustomed to pay taxes for various things, and at first they did not mind paying this new one. Indeed they were glad to do it, in the hope of getting rid of their terrible enemies. But when the Danes returned time after time, when year by year the tax grew heavier and heavier, the people grew wary of it, and angry.

"We strive and toil," they said, "to earn money, that we may live in peace and comfort, but it is of no use. The King takes our money and gives it to these idle heathen. We will work and pay no more." So the people grew moody, and the country was in greater misery than before.

Then Ethelred thought of another plan by which to get rid of the Danes. This plan was both terrible and wicked.

He sent messengers into every part of England, telling the English that, on the 13th of November, they were to kill all the Danes, men, women and children.

This was a most cruel and wicked order. Besides, it was not the Danes who were living in England who gave the greatest trouble, but those who year by year came across the sea in their ships, to plunder and kill. But Ethelred was weak and cowardly. He dared not fight the fierce sea-kings as they were called, so he thought he would murder their peaceful brothers and sisters.

And the most dreadful thing is that Englishmen all over the country were found willing to carry out the cruel order. Yet we must not think too hardly of these old Englishmen, for they had suffered so much from the Danes that it was little wonder that they hated them.

Even those Danes, who were living peaceably in England, were so proud and haughty that the English hated them. They always thought they should have the best of everything, they expected to be called "Lord Dane," they treated the English like slaves, and if an Englishman and a Dane met in a narrow passage or on a bridge the Englishman had to go back until "my

Lord Dane" had passed.

So when the 13th of November came, the Englishmen rose and slaughtered the Danes, every one, man, woman and child, rich and poor, high and low. None were saved.

Among those who were killed was the Princess Gunhilda, sister of the King of Denmark. She had married an English lord and was living with him in England. She was not only very beautiful, but good. The Danes were heathen, but Gunhilda had become Christian, and in her gentle way she tried to bring about peace between the English and the Danes.

When the terrible slaughter began, and the air was filled with shrieks, Gunhilda's husband, son and servants gathered round her, to protect her. Bravely they fought for her, but all in vain. First her husband and then her son fell dead at her feet, pierced by many spears.

Then a cruel man seized the beautiful Gunhilda by the hair and buried his sword in her heart.

"Alas!" she said, as she sank dying to the ground, "my death will bring great sorrow upon England."

CHAPTER XIX

HOW EDMUND IRONSIDE FOUGHT FOR THE CROWN

GUNHILDA was right. This act of Ethelred's proved to be not only wicked, but foolish, and it brought great sorrow upon England. For as soon as Sweyn, King of Denmark, heard of the cruel murder, he determined to avenge his sister's death. Gathering a great company of soldiers and a most wonderful fleet of ships, he set sail for England.

Over the blue waves came the fierce sea-kings in their splendid ships, with purple sails and glittering, golden prows. Beasts and birds, dragons and serpents were carved upon the painted and gilded ships, and it seemed as if all the monsters of fairyland were gathered to terrify and conquer the people of England.

No storm stayed the ships. Soft winds blew gently over sunny sparkling waters, as nearer and nearer they came. Never before had the Danes come in such splendour and such force. The frightened people fled as these fierce sea-warriors landed, and where they landed, and on through all the country, wherever they passed, they left behind them a track of death and desolation. The people were killed, the towns were burned, the crops and cattle trampled and destroyed; hunger, misery and tears filled the land. Ethelred, weak and cowardly as ever, deserting his country in the hour of need, fled to France with his wife and children.

Ethelred fled to France because his wife, Emma, was the daughter of the Duke of Normandy. Normandy is part of France. Queen Emma's father received them kindly, and no doubt Ethelred enjoyed himself very much at the Norman court, riding and hunting, and quite forgetting his poor country.

So Sweyn, King of Denmark, was master of England. But though he was proclaimed king, he never wore the crown, for he died suddenly, leaving the throne to his son Canute.

But Englishmen could not forget the great Alfred and his good sons. They longed to have a king of their own people again. So when Sweyn died, they sent messengers to France, begging Ethelred to come back, and promising to be true to him and to fight for him, if only he would rule a little better than he had done.

Ethelred came back, and had he had a little courage, he might soon have won all England again. For his people were ready and willing to die for their country. They only waited for a brave man to lead them. But Ethelred was neither better nor wiser than before. Soon his soldiers lost heart again, and some of them even deserted and went to fight for Canute the Dane. This, too, in spite of all that Edmund Ironside, the brave son of Ethelred, could do.

Edmund was called Ironside because of his strength and courage. He tried to keep the army together, but he could not hide his father's cowardice and weakness from the soldiers. Soon, however, Ethelred died, and the people immediately crowned Edmund king.

But some of the wise men and nobles thought it was of no use to try to fight against the Danes any longer, so they crowned Canute king. Thus there were two kings in England, an English king and a Danish, and the wars between the two nations continued as fiercely as ever.

But now the English had a wise king and brave leader. That was all they asked. They took heart again and joyfully followed him. Five great battles were fought, and in nearly all of them the English were victorious. That seems to show that it was truly Ethelred's fault that the English were ever beaten. He did not love his people, and he did not care what happened to them. He thought only of his own pleasure and comfort.

But Edmund Ironside was different. He thought only of his country, and although he was winning battle after battle, it made him sad and sick at heart to see his people die. The horror of war had filled the land for so many years that he longed for peace.

One day as the two armies lay opposite each other ready for battle, Edmund sat in his tent sad and weary. The summer sun shone on unplowed fields and ruined homes. All around there was sorrow and desolation. As Edmund looked across the land with sad eyes, he thought to himself that he would gladly die, if he could bring peace to his dear country.

He sat some time in thought, then suddenly calling one of his captains, he said to him, "Go to Canute the Dane. Say to him that I, Edmund Ironside, King of England, send him greeting, that, weary of battle and death, I challenge him to fight in single combat with me alone. He who dies shall die and be buried as befits a king. He who lives shall be ruler over all England."

The captain bowed low before the King, and mounting upon his horse, he rode off to the Danish camp with this strange message.

When Canute heard it, he sat silently thinking for some time. Then turning to the messenger, he said, "Go, tell Edmund Ironside that I will meet him and, please God, although I am the lesser man, I shall conquer him and still be King of England."

Both kings then arrayed themselves in splendid armour with shield and sword and spear, and rode out to fight. The two armies stood around watching in hope and fear. At first the kings fought with their spears while riding upon their horses, then leaping to the ground they attacked each other fiercely with their swords.

Both were strong, but Edmund was the taller, and Canute soon began to feel that he was being beaten. So in a loud voice he cried out, "Why should we fight thus? Two kings as we should be brothers, not enemies. Let us stop fighting, and divide the kingdom and be at peace."

Then King Edmund, throwing down his sword, held out his hands to Canute. "Brother." He said, "we will be kings together."

So once more England was divided. Edmund Ironside, the Englishman, ruled over the south part, and Canute the Dane ruled over the north part, and there was peace in the land. But this did not last for long, for very soon Edmund died. Altogether he had only reigned seven months, and much of that time had been spent in fighting, yet he had done more for his people than Ethelred had done in many years.

CHAPTER XX

CANUTE AND THE WAVES

WHEN Edmund Ironside died, Canute became king over all England, as it had been agreed between them that whoever lived the longest should have the whole kingdom. Edmund had two sons, and Canute was afraid that the people might wish to make one of them king, so he sent both to a far-off country called Hungary. Perhaps it was wrong to banish these children, but at least it was better than killing them, as some people say he wanted to do.

Canute did not begin by being a good king. At first he was bad and cruel. But he ended by being very good and wise. In fact he seems to have ruled so well that the English came to love him almost as if he had been an English king.

They loved him, but they flattered him too. He was certainly a great king, for he ruled not only over England, but over Denmark, Norway, and Sweden. The nobles thought it pleased Canute to be told of his greatness, so they used often to let him hear them praise him.

One day as they were walking upon the seashore, the nobles began, as usual, to tell Canute how powerful he was.

"All England obeys you," they said.

"And not only England, but Denmark, Norway, and Sweden."

"Should you desire it, you need but command all the nations of the world and they will kneel before you as their king and lord."

"You are king on sea and land. Even the waves obey you."

Now this was foolish talk, and Canute, who was a wise man, did not like it. He thought he would teach these silly nobles a lesson. So he ordered his servants to bring a chair.

When they had brought it, he made them set it on the shore, close to the waves. The servants did as they were told, and Canute sat down, while the nobles stood around him.

Then Canute spoke to the waves. "Go back," he said, "I am your lord and master, and I command you not to flow over my land. Go back, and do not dare to wet my feet."

But the sea, of course, neither heard nor obeyed him. The tide was coming in, and the waves rolled nearer and nearer, until the king's feet and robe were wet.

Then Canute rose, and turning sternly to his nobles said, "Do you still tell me that I have power over the waves? Oh! foolish men, do you not know that to God alone belongs such power? He alone rules earth and sky and sea, and we and they alike are His subjects, and must obey Him."

The nobles felt how foolish they had been, and did not again try to flatter Canute in such a silly way. From that day, too, Canute never wore his crown, but it placed it upon the figure of Christ in the minster at Winchester, as a proof of his humility. From this story we learn that Canute was a Christian, although many of the Danes were still heathen, but no doubt they very soon followed the example of their king, and became Christians too.

Gradually the differences between the Danes and the English passed away. The Danes began to forget that they had ever lived in any other country, and lived like Englishmen, taking English ways and customs for their own. So once more England became a united kingdom. But this, of course, did not happen all at once. It was many years before the English and the Danes quite forgot their quarrels.

As Canute had other countries to govern as well as England, he felt the need of some one to help him to rule. So he divided England into four earldoms, and placed an earl over each part. These earls ruled the kingdom under the king. Over the part which was called Wessex, Canute placed a man named Godwin, who afterwards became of very great importance in English history.

In the year 1035 A.D. King Canute died, and was buried in the minster at Winchester.

After him his two sons, Harold Harefoot and Hardicanute, reigned. Neither of them was good and, at the death of Hardicanute, the English were easily persuaded by Earl Godwin not to have any more Danish rulers. Following his advice they chose Edward, the son of Ethelred the Unready, to be their king.

CHAPTER XXII

EDWARD THE CONFESSOR

YOU remember that, when the Danes invaded England in the time of Sweyn, Canute's father, Ethelred, who was then king, fled to France with his wife and children. After Ethelred's death Edmund Ironside, one of his sons, became king, shared the kingdom with Canute, and died after a reign of only seven months. Edward, whom the English now chose to be king, was Edmund Ironside's brother, another son of King Ethelred the Unready.

Edward was a boy when he was first taken to Normandy, so although he was English, he had lived all his life in Normandy, and he liked the Normans better than the English.

He brought Norman friends over from France with him. The Norman language, Norman customs and fashions were soon heard and seen everywhere in England.

It had been greatly through the advice of Godwin, Earl of Wessex, that Edward had been chosen, and now the earl was sorry when he found that the king seemed not to be English, but Norman.

However, Godwin thought that an English wife might make Edward love England better, so he persuaded the King to marry his daughter Edith. But although Edward married this beautiful and good lady, he never loved her. Indeed, although he was perhaps not really cruel to her, he was not kind, and he hardly ever even spoke to her. So she had no chance of making him love England better.

The Normans, like the Danes, were very proud and haughty. And Edward's friends behaved so haughtily towards the English, that very soon they were hated, just as the Danes had been hated. The hatred grew and grew, and at last it broke out into fighting.

It happened that one of Edward's friends, called Eustace, Count of Boulogne, was going back to France, after having visited the King. Like most of the Normans Eustace was proud, and he and his company rode into Dover, on their way to their ships, with jingling swords and clanking armour, making a great noise and stir, and behaving as if the whole town belonged to them.

They went to the best houses, rudely demanding food and lodging. They entered the houses without leave, and took what they wanted without a word of thanks.

Now the English have ever been hospitable, but an Englishman's house is his castle. He will give freely, but he does not like to be bullied and robbed. So one brave man refused to allow the Normans to enter his house. Angry at that, a Norman soldier struck him in the face. The man returned the blow. It was enough. In a few minutes a fierce fight had begun, the Normans against the men of Dover.

The Englishmen fought well. They were glad to have a chance of showing their dislike of the Normans, they beat them thoroughly, and drove them out of the town.

Back to King Edward rode Count Eustace in furious rage. "See," he cried, bursting into the room where the King was, "see how these Englishmen of yours have treated us. They set upon us as we rode peaceably through Dover. They have killed twenty of my men, and I myself have barely escaped with my life. Is this the way to treat your friend and guest, my lord king?

Count Eustace, you see, did not tell the story truly. He did not tell King Edward that he and his men had begun the quarrel and were to blame.

King Edward was very angry with the English. He sent at once for Earl Godwin, as Dover was in his earldom. Godwin came, but when he had heard the story of the fight, he felt sure that the fault was not all on the side of the English. So when the King told him to take an army and go to punish the brave men of Dover, he refused. "You have only heard one side of the story," he said. "You have no right to blame or punish the Englishmen until you have heard what they have to say. I will not go."

King Edward was so angry at this, that he banished Earl Godwin and his sons from the land, and gave their earldoms to other people. Then he shut Queen Edith up in a convent, because she was Godwin's daughter.

Now there was no one to hinder the King from doing just as he wanted. He brought more people than ever from France, and among them came his cousin, the Duke of Normandy.

William of Normandy only came for a visit, but many of the other nobles remained in England, and Edward gave them all the best places at court.

William thought England was a very beautiful country, and before he went away he made Edward promise that he should be king next. And Edward was so fond of his cousin that he promised.

Of course Edward had no right to do this. He could not give away the crown of England to any one without the consent of the people. And certainly the people did not wish a Norman king. The kings of England had really no power to act in great matters without calling together a council of the nobles and wise men. The English had always been a free people, who had a share in governing themselves. Their kings had been kings, not tyrants.

Nearly all the chief men at court were now Normans, and the people longed for Godwin and his sons to return and free them from these hated strangers. At last they did return.

Edward was angry when he heard that these banished men had come back without leave. But the people rejoiced and flocked to join the great earl, and it seemed as if there might be war. But there was none. Earl Godwin was very clever, and somehow he forced the king to send away his Norman favourites, and put Englishmen in their places, without any fighting at all. Then Frenchmen fled back to their own country, and the things went better in England.

Soon after this, Earl Godwin died and his son Harold took his place. During what remained of Edward's reign it was really Harold who ruled, for the king was growing old and feeble. And Harold governed well, for love of England filled his heart. He even banished his own brother, Tostig, who was Earl of Northumbria, because he governed his earldom badly. This was a difficult thing for Harold to do. But although he loved his brother, he loved his country more, and when he had to choose between them, he chose his country.

Now a very sad thing happened which, together with Edward's foolish promise, made a great difference in the lives of the English people, and perhaps changed all our island story.

One day Harold was sailing upon the sea when a terrible storm arose. The sailors worked hard and tried to get into a safe port, but it was of no use. The masts were broken, the sails torn away. The ship drifted helplessly, and at last was dashed to pieces on the rocky coast of Normandy. Harold and some of the sailors escaped drowning, but they fell into the hands of Duke William.

Now Duke William had never forgotten what a beautiful country England was, and he still hoped to be its king. He knew that Harold was a very great man in England, and he was glad to have him in his power.

Duke William pretended to treat Harold very kindly, but he really kept him prisoner. He would not let him go home until he promised to help him to become king when Edward died.

At last Harold promised. Now of course Harold had no more right to do this than Edward had. But there was more excuse for Harold than for Edward, because the King was a free man in his own country, while Harold was a prisoner in a foreign country, and to make this promise was his only hope of freedom. We must blame Harold for making a promise which he did not mean to keep, but we must blame William more for forcing him to make it, as he took a mean advantage of a helpless prisoner.

Harold went back home, glad to be free, but sad at heart at the remembrance of what William had forced him to do, and hating the Normans more than ever.

Very soon after this, on 5th January 1066 A.D., King Edward died. He was buried with great pomp and ceremony in the grand new church at Westminster, which he had built and which had been finished only a few days before.

King Edward on the whole was a good king, but he had not those things in him which make a great king. He was gentle and pious, and after his death people began to think that he was really a holy man and called him

Edward the Confessor, by which name we remember him in history.

If his reign was a happy one for England, it was partly because the great Earl Godwin and his noble son Harold were so powerful that they forced the King to act justly.

Edward did not feel as all great kings must feel, that they are put in their high position, not to please themselves but to do what is best for their people. Edward did not love his people, and he pleased himself by bringing his proud Norman friends from France, and by giving them all the chief posts in England. He thought more about building churches and buying relics or bones of holy men, long since dead, than of strengthening his castles and trying to make the lives of his people peaceful and happy. This and his foolish promise to his cousin, Duke William of Normandy, brought great sorrow upon the country.

CHAPTER XXII

HAROLD

WHEN Edward the Confessor died, the people chose Harold Godwin to be their king, although he was not the real heir to the throne. The real heir was Edgar Ætheling, Edward's grand-nephew and grandson of Edmund Ironside, that king who had such a short and troubled reign and who fought so bravely against Canute the Dane.

But Edgar Ætheling was only a little boy. It seemed to the people as if he was not even an English boy, because he had lived all his life in a far-off country called Hungary, to which Canute had banished his father, and had come to England only a few months before Edward, his grand-uncle, had died. He did not understand the English language nor English ways, so nearly all the people looked upon him as a stranger. They were very tired of the strangers and foreigners with whom Edward had filled his court, and so they said, "Let us have a real Englishman to rule over us, and one who is brave and wise."

They knew Harold was brave, for he had already led them many times in battle. They knew that he was wise, because Edward, during the last years of his life, had been very ill and week, and had allowed Harold to rule for him. And above all they knew Harold bitterly hated Edward's friends, the Norman nobles, and they were sure he would drive them out of the country. But they did not know what was perhaps Harold's chief reason for hating the Normans. They did not know that he had promised the crown of England to the most powerful of them all, William, Duke of Normandy.

So it came about that the day after Edward the Confessor was buried, the people crowded again to the grand new church at Westminster. This time they came to see the new king crowned. The church was filled with the nobles and the great people of the land. Outside the common folk and those who could not get inside waited, impatient to know what was happening.

It was in the beginning of January, and the weather was bitterly cold, but the people did not seem to mind that, so eager were they to see their new king as he passed. Although the wind blew keenly from the north, the sky was blue, and the winter sun shone brightly on the gay colours of their holiday clothes, making the gold ornaments of the women, and the helmets and shields of the soldiers, glitter and sparkle.

The day before, the streets had been full of grave and mourning crowds, sorrowing for the death of their king. This day there was no mourning, everything seemed joyful and glad, and hope shone in the faces of all. Only here and there in the crowd could be seen a few scowling Normans, but they soon slunk away, afraid of the fierce looks and angry words with which the

Saxons greeted them.

Within the church all was solemn and quiet. After earnest prayer to God, the Archbishop of York, holding the crown in his hand, turned to the people. Harold knelt humbly at the steps of the high altar, while a breathless hush filled the great church from end to end. Then in the silence the voice of the old archbishop rang out clear and sharp, "Do you choose Harold, Earl of Wessex, son of Godwin, to be your king?

Like the thunder of the waves as they break upon the beach came the answer, "We do, we do."

The words sounded again and again through the aisles of the great church, echoing and re-echoing from the vaulted roof, till it seemed as if all England had answered. Outside the church the people took up the cry, "Harold, son of Godwin, Harold, son of Godwin, Harold the Englishman for our king."

In the silence which followed, Harold placed his hands between those of the archbishop, and promised to fear God, to rule wisely, and to keep the laws of the land.

Then the archbishop, speaking solemn words, anointed him with holy oil, placed the crown of England upon his head, and the sceptre in his hand.

Harold rose from his knees, no longer Earl of Wessex, but King of England. As he turned to the people he looked so brave, handsome, and kingly, that a cry of love and gratitude rose from them, and once again the arches of the great church rang with shouts. One after another the lords and mighty men of England passed before their king. They knelt to him, promising to be true to him, to fight for and obey him, just as he had promised them that he would try to rule well and be a good king.

At last the solemn ceremony was over. Harold passed down the long aisles, followed by the archbishop and bishops in their splendid robes, and the lords and knights in their shining armour. Out of the dim church into the open air they went; out into the sunshine where the people were waiting for their king. When Harold appeared, wearing the crown and royal robes and carrying the sceptre in his hand, they shouted and cheered again and again for joy. "Harold for ever; Harold the King!" they cried.

So Harold was crowned, and all England was glad and at peace.

But the peace and the gladness did not last long. As soon as Harold was crowned, the few Normans who still remained in England fled to Normandy. They went to Rouen, the town in Normandy where Duke William lived.

Nowadays, if one wants to speak to a king, or great prince, it is not always easy, for soldiers and servants guard the doors. But in those days it was much more easy, so one of these Normans who fled from England went to find Duke William, for he knew he had great news to tell. William was out hunting when this messenger from England arrived. He was so eager to tell the news that he could not wait until the duke returned, but followed him into the park. He searched about for some time, and at last saw William riding towards him surrounded by all his lords and ladies, his falcon on his wrist, and his bow in his hand. The duke looked so splendid and powerful that the messenger was almost afraid to tell the news he brought. "My lord," he said, dropping on his knees, "Edward, King of England, is dead."

Duke William's bright eyes shone with joy.

"Ah!" he exclaimed.

"And Harold, son of Godwin, is crowned king in his stead," went on the man.

Then Duke William's eyes flashed fire, his bow dropped from his hand, his face grew red and dark with anger.

"The Saxon dog, the oath-breaker," he thundered, in a voice which made those who heard him tremble. Then he was silent, and those around him were silent too, trembling in fear before the awful wrath of their lord.

For many minutes William sat in dumb rage, clasping and unclasping the rich cloak which fell from his shoulders. Then, still without uttering a word, he turned and rode back to his palace. He seemed neither to see nor hear anything, but throwing himself on a couch, he buried his face in his cloak, and gave himself up to angry thoughts.

His courtiers stood round whispering and frightened. At last one, more bold than the others, went up to him, and laying his hand upon the duke's shoulder, "Rouse yourself, my lord," he said, "you have a message to send to Harold Godwinson, before the common folk hear how he has insulted you."

"Ay, that have I," said William fiercely. Then he called for the man who had brought the news.

He came in fear and trembling, but William only looked darkly at him. "Go," he said after a pause, "go back to England. Tell Harold Godwinson (he would not call him King Harold) that I, William of Normandy, demand the crown and throne of England. Tell him if he will not give it peaceably, that I will come and take it by force."

So the messenger returned to England, and came to Harold as he was sitting in state surrounded by his lords and nobles. Harold listened quietly to the message. Then in a clear and calm voice he replied, "Go tell your master that the crown and throne of England are not mine to give and take at will. Tell him that the people of England have given them to me in trust, and that while I live, I will keep and guard them as best I can. Let William of Normandy beware!"

When the messenger returned to Rouen with this message, William's anger was terrible. At first he could neither speak nor think for rage, but soon he recovered himself and called all his lords together. He asked them to go with him over the sea, to help him to fight Harold and make himself King of England.

But his lords and nobles refused. "It is a very dangerous thing to do," they said. "These English are a great and brave people. They will kill us all. We will not go."

Although William was lord over these men, he could not force them to go across the sea with him. He could only ask them to go. He was very angry with them for refusing, so he broke up the council and sent all the nobles away. Then he made each one come to him alone, and tried to persuade them, one by one, to go with him over the sea to England.

But it was of no use, one after another they refused. "It is all very well for you," they said, "if you win you will have the crown of England; but as for us, those of us who are not killed will return poorer than before. We will not go."

Then Duke William said, "If you will only come with me I will give you fair lands, strong castles, and great stores of money. England is a rich country, and when I have conquered the people, I will take their lands and money away from them and give them to you."

Then all the nobles answered, "We will go."

After that they went to their own homes to gather their soldiers together, and to prepare armour and weapons for battle. But William was not content with the soldiers which his own Norman nobles had promised. He sent messengers into all parts of France, with the promise of land and money as reward, to every one who would come to fight for him.

Very many came. From far and near they flocked to the court of William, glad at the thought of possessing the green fields and broad forest lands of England.

But William had not ships enough to carry so large a company over the sea, so he bought ships, and made people build them for him, paying sometimes with money, sometimes with promises of English land.

Never was such a wonderful army and so great a fleet gathered together in so short a time.

But William was a great leader. He was fierce, strong, and determined. He had set his heart on being King of England, and King of England he meant to be. So night and day he planned and worked, persuading and forcing people in one way or another to help him.

CHAPTER XXIII

THE BATTLE OF STAMFORD BRIDGE

MEANWHILE Harold was ruling England quietly and well. The people loved him, and were glad they had chosen such a brave and generous man to rule over them. Harold was kind to every one, but he was specially kind to Edgar Ætheling. He knew that it would have been a very bad thing for England had the people chosen an ignorant little boy as king. Yet he felt sorry for Edgar, and tried to make him grow into a brave and honest English boy.

Harold kept the good laws which had been made before the time of Edward, and altered the unjust ones. He was always thinking of the happiness of his people and the good of his country. Often and often he looked anxiously across the blue sea to the shores of France, watching for the white sails of Duke William's ships.

Months passed, and still they did not appear. But Harold knew that one day they would come although William sent no more messages. Harold's friends crossed the sea to find out what the great duke was doing. They brought back news of the mighty army which was gathering on the shores of the river Dive. So Harold watched and waited, and he too gathered together men and horses, swords and armour.

Often King Harold sighed to see that there were no strong castles and fortresses to guard the shores of his dear land. For Edward, instead of building ships and castles to keep the country safe from enemies, had spent his people's money in building great churches, and in buying the bones of holy men who had lived and died long, long ago. These bones, he foolishly thought, would keep wicked men away from his shores.

One day while Harold watched and waited for the coming of William, a messenger all breathless arrived from the north. He was covered with dust and worn and tired with long travelling. He burst into the room, where the King sat, and threw himself on his knees. "My lord and King," he cried, "Tostig, thy brother, and Harold Hardrada, King of Norway, have landed in the north with a mighty army of heathen folk. They have defeated Earl Morcar. They have taken York. They slay and burn without mercy. Through fear, many of thy subjects have joined the banner of Tostig. Now they are making ready to march south to take London, and Harold Hardrada of Norway will be master of all England."

Then the messenger was silent, fainting for weariness and lack of food.

This news made Harold very sorry. Tostig was his brother, and he did not wish to fight against his own brother, but for the sake of England he knew he must. For Harold loved England better than all the world. It is said that, after he was dead, people found the word "England" printed on his breast just over his heart, but whether that is true or not, this is true, that Harold held England in his heart and in his thoughts, and always tried to do what was best for his country.

So now Harold gathered all his own soldiers or huscarles as they were called, and set out for Yorkshire to meet the enemy.

At this time England had not a great army, as it has now, ready at all times for battle. The king only kept a few soldiers always near him. They were called his "huscarles" or his "body guard," as their duty was to guard his house when he was at home and his person wherever he went.

The rest of the soldiers were the servants of the great nobles and rich merchants. Whenever the king had need of them, he used to call them together, and when the fighting was over they went back again to their own homes, and to their own masters.

Harold had called these men together to be ready for William, but as months passed and the dreadful duke did not come, they grew tired of waiting and went home. For by this time it was autumn, the fields were yellow with the ripe grain, and the orchards were laden with fruit, so the men who had come to fight went home again to gather the fruit and cut the corn before the winter set in.

But hardly had they gone, when the messenger came with the terrible news from Yorkshire.

Harold did not stop to gather his army together again, but set out as quickly as he could with the few soldiers he had.

As he rode northward, he looked back with many a sigh. He looked across the blue waters which separated him from Duke William, straining his eyes anxiously, but there was no sign of a sail. "Please God," he murmured, "I may yet return in time to meet the Norman wolf."

In those days, the roads were very bad. Some of them were only tracks worn by the feet of horses. There was no means, either, of going from place to place, except by walking or riding. But there was one great road, which the Romans had made long, long before. This stretched all the way from York to London. Harold was so clever that in a few days he brought his little army along this road from the very south to the middle of England. By 24th September he had arrived at York. On the 25th a great battle was fought at a place near there, called Stamford Bridge. In memory of that great fight it was afterwards called Battle Bridge.

Before the fighting began, the two armies stood facing each other.

Up and down the lines of the Norwegian army rode a very tall man on a lovely black horse. He was dressed in splendid steel armour, and a beautiful blue cloak hung from his shoulders. As he rode, his horse stumbled and fell, and the tall man was thrown to the ground. He sprang up again with a laugh. "Oh!" he said, "a fall means good luck to a traveller."

But Harold, who had been watching, turned to some one beside him. "Who is that tall man with the blue cloak and beautiful helmet?" he asked.

"That is Harold Hardrada, King of Norway," was the reply.

"He has had a fall," said Harold of England. "That means bad luck to him."

One side, you see, thought it was good luck, and the other thought it was bad, although really, of course, it made no difference one way or another. But, in those days, people were very superstitious, that is, they found a meaning in things that had no meaning at all.

Harold of England looked sadly along the lines of the army opposite. He was looking for the banner of his brother Tostig. When he saw it he rode, almost alone, right up to the Norwegian army. His men looked on in surprise and fear as he rode so near the enemy, attended only by a few knights. When he was quite close to them, he stopped his horse, and called out, "Is Earl Tostig, son of Godwin, in this army?"

Tostig himself answered, "Yes, what want you with him?" and he rode out to meet the king.

Although Tostig's face was hidden by his helmet, King Harold knew his brother's voice. So his tone was kind and gentle, as he answered: "Your brother, King Harold, sends you greeting. He does not wish to fight against you. If you will send away these soldiers, he will forgive you all the wrong you have done, and he will give you the earldom of Northumbria once more."

"And if I accept his offer," said Tostig, "what will he give to my friend Harold Hardrada?"

King Harold's voice grew stern as he answered, "He shall have seven feet of English ground for a grave, or a little more perhaps, as he is so much taller than other men."

"Then," said the earl, "go and tell King Harold to get ready for battle, for it shall never be said that Tostig brought his friend to England to betray him."

Then the brothers parted, sad and angry, each riding back to his own side.

"Who was that fine man with whom you have been speaking?" asked Harold Hardrada, as Tostig came back.

"That was King Harold of England," replied the earl.

"Why did you not tell me?" said the king. "He was so near! So near death, for had I known who he was, he would never have gone back to his own people."

But although Tostig was a wild, wicked man, he was not altogether bad. He looked sadly at King Harold Hardrada and said, "He came to offer me peace and forgiveness. He is my brother, though my enemy. Had I betrayed him to you, I should have been not only his foe, but his murderer."

Then it seemed as if Harold Hardrada was ashamed.

Soon the battle began. Harold Hardrada rode in front singing a loud battle song.

"Advance! Advance!
No helmets glance,
But blue swords play
In our array.
Advance! Advance!
No mail coats glance
But hearts are here
That ne'er knew fear."

He sang that because these Northmen, as they were called, often fought in their shirts and wore no armour or protection of any kind. So they got the name of "Berserkers," and in Scotland to this day the work "sark" is used to mean shirt.

The fight was fierce and long. Sometimes it seemed as if the English would win, sometimes the Northmen. In the very thickest of the fight rode the two kings, each cheering on his men.

"When battle storm was ringing,
Where arrow cloud was singing,
Harold stood there,
Of armour bare,
His deadly sword still swinging.
The foemen felt its bite;
His horsemen rush to fight,
Danger to share
With Harold there,
Where steel on steel was ringing."

But at last both Earl Tostig and King Harold Hardrada were killed, and their soldiers fled in all directions.

King Harold of England was very kind to those who were not killed. He did not take them prisoners, but allowed them to go away with their ships to their own country, having first made them promise never to fight against England again.

CHAPTER XXIV

THE BATTLE OF HASTINGS

WHILE these things were happening in York, the great duke had finished his preparations. He had gathered together his huge army and his mighty fleet of ships. The wind blew fair from the coast of France, and he set sail for England.

Over the blue sea they came, the white-sailed vessels crowded with knights in armour, champing war-horses, bowmen, and spearmen. Such an army had seldom before been seen. Duke William's vessel was the gayest and proudest of them all. The sails were crimson, the deck and masts were gaily painted. A golden boy was on the prow, leaning forward as if to catch the first glimpse of England. By day the proud banner, embroidered with the three golden lions of Normandy, fluttered in the breeze. By night a crescent of light shone from the masthead, so that all could see their lord's ship and follow where he led. On they came, day and night till, with a shout, they greeted the shores of England.

No army was awaiting them. King Harold who had, for so many months, watched anxiously for their coming, was far away fighting another foe. And when at last the white sails glimmered in the distance, only the frightened fisherfolk stood upon the shore watching, and the peasants fled in fear to hide.

On came the duke's fleet, till the vessels touched the shore. Duke William was the first to spring to land, but as he did so he stumbled and fell.

"Alas! what bad luck," cried the soldiers around him; but William sprang up with a laugh, and turning to them showed his hands full of earth.

"See," he cried, "I have already taken hold of my kingdom."

Then a soldier, who had sprung ashore after the duke, ran to a cottage, and tearing from it some thatch, said, "Take hold not only of England, but of what England holds."

"I accept it," said the duke. "May God be with us."

Soon the whole army landed. The duke then caused all the ships to be sunk or pulled far up the shore, so that they could not be put out to sea again. "For," said he, "we will either conquer or die. We will never return to Normandy disgraced."

Now, after the battle of Stamford Bridge, while Harold and his men were resting in York before going southward again, the clatter of horses' hoofs was heard at the castle gate, and in a few minutes a breathless messenger flung himself at the king's feet.

"My lord," he cried, "my lord, William of Normandy has landed in England. I myself have seen him. He has come with a great and fierce host, and is laying waste all the land. I have not rested night nor day, but have hasted with the tidings."

This was very terrible news. Harold's men were wounded and weary with fighting, but before an hour had passed he and they were again on the great Roman road marching southward.

As he went, King Harold sent messages into all the country, calling the soldiers together. From every side they came to him, for they loved their king and country.

Harold had done a very wonderful thing when he marched his men north in so short a time. Now he did an even more wonderful thing when he brought them back again, for it is said that he arrived in London on 6th October, and they had to ride and walk all the way from York, which they only left on 27th September.

Here in London they rested a few days until more soldiers were gathered together. And here Gurth, his brother, tried to make Harold remain behind and let him go forward with the army to meet William. "It will not matter so much if I am killed," he said, "and besides, I have made no promises to William, so I can fight him better. Then you must burn all the houses, cut down the trees, and lay waste the cornfields between here and the seacoast, so that if I cannot keep William back, he will find no food nor shelter for his army when he arrives."

But Harold looked proudly at his brother. "I am the King," he said. "I will never harm an English village nor an English house. I will never harm the goods nor lands of any Englishman. How can I hurt the people who are given me to rule?"

So once more the King set out at the head of his army and on 12th October they arrived in sight of the Normans, who had camped near Hastings, on the south coast.

Harold camped on the hill called Senlac, and there it was that the battle took place. And from the names of the two camps, the battle is sometimes called Hastings, sometimes Senlac.

The English army was not nearly so large as the Norman, but Harold chose a very good place on the top of a hill. He also built a strong fence all round his camp.

When the battle began, the first person who advanced from the Norman side was not a soldier, but a minstrel or singer called Taillefer.

He rode out from the ranks, gaily dressed. He was tall and handsome, and had a laughing, merry face. On he came, riding not as if in battle, but as if in play.

His horse capered and pranced while he whirled his sword, throwing it high into the air, and catching it again and again.

And as he so rode and played, he sang. The song he sang was an old song of France, telling of the wonderful deeds of the great hero, Roland. It stirred the hearts of the Frenchmen, making them eager to fight and conquer. So, led by their minstrel, the whole army took up the song, and as they marched, the air was full of the music of men's voices.

" 'O Roland, sound your ivory horn,
To the ear of Karl shall the blast be borne.
He will bid his legions backward bend,
And all his barons their aid will lend.'
'Now God forbid it, for very shame,
That for me my kindred were stained with blame,
Or that gentle France to such vileness fell.
This good sword that hath served me well
My Durindana such strokes shall deal
That with blood encrimsoned shall be the steel.
By their evil star are the felons led;
They shall all be numbered among the dead.' "

Taillefer whirled his sword, struck a mighty blow, and the first Englishman fell dead.

" 'I will not sound on mine ivory horn;
It shall never be spoken of me in scorn,
That for heathen felons one blast I blew.
I may not dishonour my lineage true,
But I will strike ere this fight be o'er
A thousand strokes and seven hundred more.
And my Durindana shall drip with gore.
Our Franks will bear them like vassals brave,
The Saracens flock but to find a grave.' "

Again the sword of Taillefer flashed in the sunlight, and again an Englishmen lay dead. It seemed as if he rode alone to defy the whole English army, but behind him marched a mighty host singing:—

"God and His angels of heaven defend,
That France through me from her glory bend,
Death were better than fame laid low,
Our emperor loveth a downright blow."

"Then from the Franks resounded high—
'Mountjoie!' Whoever had heard that cry
Would hold remembrance of chivalry.
Then ride they—how proudly, O God, they ride!
With rowels dashed in their coursers' side.
Fearless too are their paynim foes,
Franks and Saracens thus they close."

So the fight began, and all through the long day it raged. Sometimes it seemed as if one side would win, sometimes as if the other.

Once a cry went through the Norman ranks that Duke William was killed. Hearing that they would have fled, but Duke William rode among them bareheaded, calling to them and cheering them on. And when the Normans saw their great duke's face, they took heart and turned once more to the fight.

As the day drew to an end it was seen, alas, that the English were beaten. They gathered close around their king and his standard, fighting fiercely and bravely to the last. And when Harold fell, pierced with an arrow, his brave knights fought still over his dead body. But when night came, all the bravest and the best men of England lay with their king, dead upon the field.

The splendid standard of Harold was torn, bloodstained, and trampled in the dust, and the three lions of Normandy, fluttering in the cold autumn wind, kept watch over the dead.

"William came o'er the sea,
With bloody sword came he,
Cold heart and bloody hand
Now rule the English land."

King Harold was buried on the seashore, not far from where he fell. Even William, fierce and cruel though he was, must have felt some pity for the man who had fought so bravely for his country. "Let him lie by the seashore," he said. "He guarded it well while he lived. Let him still guard it in death."

So, wrapped in a purple robe, as befits a king, they buried him by the sounding sea, beneath the great arch of heaven. Over his grave William caused a stone to be placed. Upon it in Latin were engraved the words:—
"Here lies Harold the unhappy."

But after many years the body was removed to Waltham Abbey, which Harold himself had founded. On the spot where Harold fell, William of Normandy, perhaps in sorrow and remorse, built another great abbey, which he called Battle Abbey, and the remains of both may be seen to this day.

So died Harold, the last of the English kings. He had reigned only nine months, and died, fighting for the freedom of his people and his country, on Saturday, October 15, 1066.

CHAPTER XXV

WILLIAM THE CONQUEROR— THE STORY OF HEREWARD THE WAKE

WILLIAM of Normandy had won the battle of Hastings, but he had not won England. Harold was dead, but the people would not call William king. For five days after the battle he waited, expecting the English lords to come to do homage to him, as their new master. But not one came. The people were full of grief and anger at the death of Harold, and of sullen hate for the conqueror. They would not own him as king.

After five days, William waited no longer. More soldiers had come from Normandy to replace those who had been killed at the battle of Hastings. With these new soldiers William marched through the land, and so fierce and terrible was he, that he forced the people to own him as king. By December all the south of England was in William's power, and on Christmas Day he was crowned at Westminster.

Scarcely a year before, the people had crowded to the same place to see Harold, and to cheer and welcome him as their king. Now all was changed. The people were sullen and silent, the way was lined with Norman soldiers, and Norman faces and Norman costumes were everywhere to be seen.

Stigand, the archbishop who had crowned Harold, refused to crown William, and William in wrath retorted that he was no true bishop, and that he did not wish to be crowned by him. Yet William forced Stigand to be present at the coronation.

Once again, as so short a time before, the voice of the bishop rang through the great church, "Do you take William of Normandy to be your king?" Once again the answer came, "We do." But this time the question was asked and answered in French, and the English voices were silent. So the question was asked again in English, and the answer came from unwilling English lips, but not from English hearts, "We do." Then an echoing cry was heard without—not the shout of a glad people, but a cry of agony and despair. The Norman soldiers, instead of keeping order, had begun to fight and kill. They had set fire to the houses near the church, and were slaying and robbing. Those within the church rushed out, some in fear, others eager to join the robbers. William was left alone with only the bishops and the priests.

Then for the first time in his life the great William was afraid. Through the windows of the church he could see the flicker of flames, and could hear the savage yells of soldiers and the shrieks of frightened women and children. Yet he did not know whether the English had risen in revolt, or whether it was only his own wild soldiers who were attacking the people.

But whatever it might be William meant to be King of England—a king crowned and anointed. So although his cheek was pale and his voice shook, he forced the archbishop to go on with the ceremony.

With trembling hands the archbishop placed the crown upon William's head—not Harold's crown, but a new one glittering with splendid gems—and in a hurried and mumbling voice he finished the service. Then William, kneeling at the altar, promised to fear God, to rule the people well, and to keep the laws of Alfred and Edward, "so that the people be true to me," he added.

As he stood up no shout greeted him, the church was silent and empty. He passed down the aisle in lonely splendour, followed only by the trembling priests, while without was heard the sound of the crackling flames mingled with fierce yells and curses.

William was crowned, but the English rejected him as king. They wanted an English king. But alas! there was no strong man whom they could choose. Harold's brave brothers had all died with him as Hastings. There, too, had fallen the noblest and the best of the English lords. There was no one left who seemed to have any right to the throne, except the little boy Edgar the Ætheling, Edmund Ironside's grandson. Even he did not seem to be English, for he had lived nearly all his life in Hungary, and could hardly speak his own language. But at least he was not Norman, so the English chose him to be king.

The people of Northumberland rose in fierce rebellion against William, and he in as fierce anger marched against them with his soldiers. From north to south he laid waste to the country, burning towns, destroying farms, killing cattle, murdering the people, till the whole of Northumberland was one dreary desert. So fierce and terrible was his wrath that even the ploughs and farming tools were destroyed, and the land lay untilled and desolate. Those of the people who were not killed in battle died miserably of cold and hunger. When William marched south again, he left only blackened ruins and dismal waste, where happy homes and smiling fields had been. From very need, most of English lords now bowed to William and owned him master. Even Edgar came to him to do homage and strange to say William treated him kindly. Perhaps he felt that he was so strong and Edgar so weak, that he had no need to fear him.

Still the English were not all conquered. In the Isle of Ely, in what is called the Fen country, the people made one last stand. There, under the leadership of a brave Englishman called Hereward, they held out against William.

In the time of Edward the Confessor, Hereward had been banished for some reason, perhaps because he had quarrelled with one of Edward's Norman friends. He had lived for many years across the sea in a country called Flanders. But when he heard that Edward was dead, that Harold was also dead, and that William the Norman had seized the crown of England,

Hereward came back determined to fight for his own land.

All the noblest and bravest of the English who still resisted William gathered to Hereward and they made their camp in the Isle of Ely. The monks who already lived there shared their monastery with the soldiers. So in the great hall peaceful monks and warlike men sat side by side at meals, and the walls which had been hung with holy relics and pictures of saints were now covered with weapons and armour.

Hereward built a castle at Ely, but it was a wooden one, while all through England the Normans were building strong fortresses of stone, such as the English had never seen before.

Hereward hoped that, from his castle at Ely, he would gradually win all England again. But the hope was vain, for William was too strong. Yet it took him a long time to conquer Hereward. Like Harold, Hereward was a good general, and he was both clever and brave.

After trying vainly to find a way through the marshes and fens to Hereward's camp, William decided at last to build a road strong enough and broad enough to carry his army over. So the soldiers set to work at once with stones, wood, and skins of animals, to make a strong, broad, solid road. When it was finished William's men marched over it to attack Hereward's men in their own camp, but the English fought desperately, and the Normans were driven back.

In those days people believed in witches. So William next found a poor old woman who was supposed to be a witch. He built a wooden tower, placed it on wheels, and with the witch inside, pushed it along the road, at the head of the Norman army. This poor old woman was meant to cast a spell over the English soldiers, so that they would not be able to fight any more. Of course she could really do them no harm, and Hereward and his men captured the tower and burned it up, witch and all. Again William had failed.

Hereward had brought large stores of food into the camp, and he and his men hunted wild animals, so that there was always enough to eat, although the fare was plain. But the monks who were used to living a very easy life and to having fine things to eat and drink, grew tired of fighting and of plain food, and they sent a message to William telling him of a secret way through the fens to the camp.

So Hereward who could not be conquered was betrayed.

One evening the Norman soldiers, led by the wicked monks, came stealthily through the thick woods among the marshes. In the gathering dusk they came creeping, silent and eager. Then, when they were close upon the camp, they burst with wild cries upon the unsuspecting English, and, when the sun had set, the sky was red with the flames from burning English homes.

Many lay dead, many were taken prisoners. To the prisoners William was very cruel. He put out their eyes, cut off their hands, and treated them so dreadfully that they cried aloud, "It is better to fall into the hands of God than into those of the Norman tyrant."

Hereward escaped, and with some of his bravest followers continued to fight, although all hope of freedom for England was gone. But he, too, yielded at length and bowed his proud head to the conqueror. William of Normandy was at last master of all England. He was indeed William the Conqueror.

CHAPTER XXVI

WILLIAM THE CONQUEROR—THE DEATH OF THE KING

WILLIAM was ruler of the land, but English hearts never accepted him. Norman and Englishman lived side by side, yet a wide sea of hatred kept them apart.

As he had promised, William rewarded the Norman barons and nobles who had helped him to conquer England. He gave them the lands and goods of the conquered people, so it was not wonderful that there was fierce hatred between the two races.

The Normans were greedy, and they not only took the lands which William gave them, but they forced the English to pay large sums of money too. Every high position was filled by Normans, and the English were forced to be the servants and slaves of these proud Norman masters.

The Normans talked a great deal of "right," but the more they talked of right, the more wrong they did. The very sheriffs and judges, who ought to have seen that the laws were kept and that justice was done, were more greedy than thieves and robbers, and the king was greediest of all. He made the people pay tolls and taxes until they had hardly any money left. Much of this money he took away with him to France, much he kept locked up in his strong treasure-room.

As if he had not already spoiled enough of the country in battle, William next laid waste a great part in the south, simply because he was very fond of hunting and he wanted a good hunting-ground. He turned the people out of their houses, burning and ruining whole villages in order to make a great place in which to ride and hunt. He called this place the New Forest and it is so called to this day.

Having made this forest, William also made forest laws. These laws were very cruel. If any person was found hunting or killing the deer or other wild animals, his eyes were put out or his hands and ears were cut off. So the poor people, who had been driven from their homes dared not even kill the wild animals for food.

William did not do much that was kind, but some things which he did were wise. Among the wise things was the law which he made that all lights and fires must be put out at eight o'clock at night.

Nowadays we should think it very hard indeed if all fires and lights had to be put out at eight o'clock. But in those days people used to rise very early, and go to be very early, so that it was not a great hardship. It was really a wise rule, because nearly all the houses were built of wood, and if people were careless and went to bed leaving large fires burning, the houses were apt to catch fire. In a town all built of wood, if one house caught fire sometimes a whole street would be burned to the ground before the fire could be put out.

By this wise law William made the danger of fires much less. Every night at eight o'clock a bell was rung. This bell was called "the curfew," from the French words "couvre feu" which means "cover fire."

Another wise thing which William did was to make what is called the Domesday Book, or book of judgment. This was a very big book in which a description of all the great houses and lands in the kingdom was written down, with the names of the people to whom the land and houses belonged. This book was very useful at the time, and it has been very useful since. For one thing it shows us how much land was taken from the English and given to the Normans.

When William gave the Normans land he did not give it to them for nothing. In return they had to promise to come to help the King in battle and to bring men with them. The more land they got the more men they had to promise to provide in time of war. When William wished to know how many men a certain lord would bring to fight for him, he only needed to look at his great book to see how much land he had. This plan of paying for land by fighting was called the feudal system, and it lasted in England for many years.

William spent a great deal of time in Normandy, for, though he was proud to be King of England, he loved his Norman home far better. It was in Normandy that he died.

William had been fighting with the King of France, and, with his usual cruelty, he had burned a town belonging to that king. While William was riding about among the ruins, his horse stepped upon some hot ashes, stumbled, and he was thrown to the ground. William was by this time very fat and old, and the fall hurt him so much that in a few days he died.

Only two of William's sons were with him at the time. Robert, the eldest, had quarrelled with his father long before, and was far away. But, as he lay dying, William wished to be at peace with every one. He forgave Robert and left the crown of Normandy to him. "And," he said, "although the crown of England is not mine to give away, I should like William to have it." And the son, eager to claim his father's crown, seized the great signet ring which the dying king still wore, and drew it from his finger.

To Henry, his youngest son, William left a large sum of money.

Then William and Henry hurried off to England; the one to demand the crown, the other to make sure of his treasure. The great Conqueror was left to die alone.

A strange thing happened while William was being buried. Fire broke out in the streets just as it had done when he was being crowned. The people who were carrying the bier fled, so once more the Conqueror was left alone with a few priests. They would have buried him hurriedly but, as they began the service, a young man stepped forward and stopped them. "This ground," he said, "was taken from my father by the very king whom you now wish to bury here. He has no right to the land. It is mine, not his. I refuse to allow him to be buried in it."

So even in death the Conqueror was to find no resting-place. But the priests bargained with the young man, and at last, for the sum of sixty shillings, he allowed them to bury the King in his ground.

And there the Conqueror was at last laid to rest.

CHAPTER XXVII

THE STORY OF WILLIAM THE RED

WILLIAM RUFUS, or the Red as he was called, from the colour of his hair, took the ring from his father's hand and hurried off to seize the throne of England, without waiting even till the Conqueror should die. In little more than a fortnight the crown was upon the head of William Rufus, and England had another Norman king.

But even the Norman nobles were not pleased with their new king. The Conqueror had ruled them with an iron hand, and they had hoped, when he was dead, to have some one who would be less severe. They wanted Robert, the eldest son of William the Conqueror, because they knew that he was much less harsh than William, and they thought that they would be able to do what they liked if Robert were king. So they rebelled against William the Red and asked Robert to come to England to fight for the crown.

Now the English hated to have a Norman king, but they hated the Norman nobles even more. Although William the Red was Norman he had lived in England ever since he had been about six years old. He could speak English, which the Conqueror could never learn to do, and which the Confessor had never cared to do.

So William the Red appealed to the English people. He said to them, "If you stand by me and fight for me, I will reward you. I will take away some of the heavy taxes, I will give you more liberty, and I will not allow the Norman barons to oppress you."

So the English people fought for their Norman king, and they beat the Norman nobles. Robert was obliged to fly back to France, and William the Red, with the help of the English people, sat safely on the English throne.

But as soon as he was safe, William forgot about his promises. He oppressed the people as much as ever, and they were almost more unhappy than they had been in the time of his father.

The Red King was wicked and greedy. He stole money from every one, even from the churches, and spent it on his own pleasure. Little good can be said of him except that he was fearless. Still when he was ill, and thought he might die, he became frightened because of the wicked things he had done, and promised to do better. But as soon as he was well again he forgot his fears and was as wicked as before. He was not truly a brave man, and he was very cruel.

One day William the Red went to hunt with his friends in the New Forest—that forest which his father had made by destroying so many villages. Before the hunting-party started, a man came to the King and gave him six beautiful new arrows. The King admired them very much and he gave one of them to his friend, Walter Tyrrell, who was a very good shot, saying. "The best arrows should be given to him who knows best how to use them."

It was a gay scene. The King in his rich hunting-dress rode first. His friends and servants, gayly dressed, followed. There was much talking and laughing and barking of dogs.

As they rode into the forest, the frightened deer fled before them, and soon every one was eagerly following the chase. In the many paths of the forest, the King became separated from his friends. The nobles did not notice that the King was not among them, for it often happened in hunting that a few would be separated from the others. When the hunt was over, one by one the hunting-party returned to the palace. Only the King did not return—the King and one noble, Walter Tyrrell.

What had happened?

As the shadows began to lengthen and the sun to set, the people of his household became uneasy. Who was with the King? Who saw him last?

As the question was asked, a peasant's cart came slowly up the street. It was a rough wooden cart drawn by an old white horse, led by a peasant in poor and shabby clothes.

The question was answered. In the cart the King, who so short a time before had ridden gayly away, lay dead, with an arrow through his heart.

"Who has done this?" asked the barons, seizing the peasant. "Villain, answer."

"I know naught of it, my lords," replied the man. "I was passing through the forest on my way home when I found this man lying dead as you see him. I bethought me that it was the King, so I brought him thither."

How William the Red was killed can never be known. Some people say that Walter Tyrrell, while aiming at a deer, hit the king by mistake, that the arrow struck a tree and, glancing off, pierced the king in the breast and killed him. These people think that Walter Tyrrell frightened at what he had done, fled away as fast as he could; that he fled to the seashore, got into a ship and sailed over to France.

Certain it is that Walter Tyrrell did run away that day, and did not return to England for many years. But when he came back, he vowed very solemnly that he had not done the deed and that he had not even been near the King that day when he died.

There was no sorrow for the dead king. He was hated so much that, when he was buried, no bell was rung, no prayers were said, and when some time after the tower of the church fell, people said it was because of the wickedness of William, the Red King, who lay buried there.

CHAPTER XXVIII

HENRY I.—THE STORY OF THE "WHITE SHIP"

WILLIAM THE RED died in 1100 A.D. He had no children, so his brother Henry became king after him. Henry was the youngest son of William the Conqueror. He was fond of learning and could read and write better than most people in those days, so he was called Beauclerc, which is French and means "fine scholar."

Henry's eldest brother Robert, Duke of Normandy, was still alive, and the Norman barons in England still wanted to have him for their king. So they sent over to France and asked Robert to come to fight again for the crown.

Once more the English people had to choose between the Norman king and the Norman barons. Once more they decided for the King and fought for him, even although William the Red had forgotten his promises and cruelly deceived them. For although Henry's father and mother had been Norman, Henry himself had been born in England, and the English people felt as if that almost made him English. So once more they chose to fight for the King against the barons.

Henry Beauclerc did not repay the people with promises only, as his brother had done. He gave them a written letter, or charter as it was called, in which he promised to do away with many of William the Red's cruel laws, to restore the good laws of Edward, and to lessen the power of the barons.

Later on another king gave the people a much more important charter, but in the meantime the English were very glad to get this one.

Besides giving them this charter, Henry pleased the English very much by marrying the Scottish Princess Maud, or Matilda as she was sometimes called.

Edgar the Ætheling had a sister named Margaret. She married the Scottish King Malcolm III., and this Princess Maud was their daughter, and the great-granddaughter of Edmund Ironside. When Henry married her and she became Queen of England, the English felt that the crown had come back again to their own people, and they were very glad. But the Norman nobles were angry about it. They thought Henry ought to have married a Norman lady.

Although many of the nobles were angry, Henry's marriage did a great deal of good, for other Normans followed the King's example and married English ladies so that the hatred between the two races began to disappear a little.

Thus it happened that when Robert and his barons came to fight Henry, they were met by an army of English, whose hearts were with their king and who "nowise feared the Normans." So hopeless did Robert feel it to be, that he made peace with his brother and went back to Normandy without fighting.

Then Henry punished the rebel barons by taking their lands away from many of them and banishing others. The English helped him and rejoiced at the defeat of the proud barons.

Later on Robert and Henry quarrelled again. Henry sailed over to Normandy with an army of English soldiers, defeated his brother, and took possession of Normandy. So now instead of England belonging to Normandy, Normandy belonged to England.

When Henry had been king for about twenty years a great and terrible grief came upon him. He and his son, Prince William, had been in Normandy together. Just as they were ready to return to England, a sailor came and begged Henry to honour him by using his ship. "My father Stephen," he said, "steered the ship in which your father sailed over to England when he went to conquer Harold. My father was a good sailor, and he served King William until he died. I, too, am a sailor like my father. I have a beautiful boat called the *White Ship*. It is newly rigged and freshly painted, it is manned by fifty trusty sailors, and is in every way worthy of a king. Honor me, as your father honoured my father, and give me leave to steer you to England."

"I thank you, good Master FitzStephen," said Henry, "but I have already made choice of the ship in which I intend to sail, and I cannot change. But," he added, seeing the man looked disappointed, "my son, Prince William, is with me and you may steer him and his company over the channel."

Thomas FitzStephen was very glad when he heard that, and he hurried away to tell his sailors to prepare to receive the prince.

Late in the afternoon King Henry set sail, leaving Prince William to follow in the *White Ship*. But Prince William was young and gay, and he did not feel inclined to start at once. He stayed on shore drinking and feasting and making merry with his friends. When at last he did go on board, he ordered the captain to give the sailors three barrels of good red wine with which to drink his health. So there was still further delay. As was usual in those days, priests came to bless the ship before it started, but the prince and his gay companions laughed at them, and the sailors, whom the wine had made merry, chased them away.

One of the King's friends, who had been left behind with the prince, now urged the captain to start. "Oh, there is no hurry," said FitzStephen, "my beautiful *White Ship* has sails like the wings of a bird. She skims over the water swifter than a swallow. We can easily overtake the King and be in England before him."

At last they started. The deck was crowded with fine ladies and gay gentlemen. These ladies and gentlemen had many servants, so that, together with the sailors, there were about three hundred people on board the ship.

The sails were set, the sailors bent to the oars, and to the sound of song and laughter the gay ship left the harbour, skimming over the waves like a beautiful bird, as the captain had said.

It was a clear and frosty winter's evening. The red sun had sunk and a silver moon shone brightly. All was merriment and laughter when, suddenly, there was an awful crash. The ship seemed to shiver from end to end and then stand still. The next minute it began to sink. It had struck upon a rock.

One fearful wail of agony rose from the hearts of three hundred people, breaking the stillness of the night. Far away over the sea Henry hear that cry. "What is it?" he asked, straining anxious eyes through the darkness.

"Only some night bird, sire," replied the captain.

"Methought it was some soul in distress," said Henry, still looking back over the sea, anxious he knew not why.

On the *White Ship* all was terrible confusion. Without losing a moment FitzStephen thrust the prince into the only small boat, and bade the sailors row off. He at least must be saved, though all the rest should perish.

The prince, hardly knowing what had happened, allowed the sailors to row away from the sinking vessel. But suddenly a voice called to him, "Ah, William, William, do you leave me to perish?"

It was the voice of his sister Marie.

William was careless and selfish, but he loved his sister. He could not leave her. "Go back," he said to the sailors, "go back, we must take my sister too."

"We dare not, sire," replied the boatmen. "We dare not, we must go on."

"You dare not," cried the prince, "am I not the son of the King of England? Obey me."

The prince spoke so sternly that the men turned the boat and went back to the sinking ship.

As the boat drew near, the Princess Marie, with a cry of joy, leaped into her brother's arm. But, alas! many others, eager to be saved, crowded into the little boat. The sailors tried in vain to keep them back, the little boat was overturned and the prince was drowned.

The *White Ship* sank fast, until only the mast was seen above the water. Clinging to it were two men—all that were left of that gay company. One of these men was a noble called Geoffrey de l'Aigle. The other was a poor butcher of Rouen, called Berthold.

As they clung there, a third man appeared swimming through the waves. It was the captain, FitzStephen.

"What of the prince?" he asked.

"The prince is drowned," replied Geoffrey.

"Ah, woe is me!" cried FitzStephen, and throwing up his arms, he sank.

Hour after hour the two men clung to the mast. They were numbed with cold and perishing from hunger. Again and again, as long as they had strength, they called aloud for help. But there was no one to hear. The bright stars twinkled overhead and the moon shone calmly, making paths of shining silver over the still water. But no voice answered their cries.

All through the terrible long night the noble and the butcher talked and tried to comfort each other. But towards morning the noble became exhausted. "Good-bye, friend," he whispered to Berthold, "God keep you. I can hold out no longer." Then he slipped into the water, and Berthold was left alone.

When the wintry sun rose, Berthold, faint and benumbed, was still clinging to the mast. He was the poorest of all those who had sailed in the beautiful *White Ship.* While the others had been dressed in silk and satin and velvet, his coat was of sheepskin, and perhaps that helped to save him for the rough skin kept out the cold and wet far better than a coat of satin could have done.

It was beginning to grow light when three fishermen, passing in their boat, caught sight of something floating in the water. The rowed near to see what it was, and found the poor butcher almost dead from cold and hunger.

The fishermen lifted him into their boat and took him home. When they had warmed and fed him, and he could speak again, he told his dreadful story.

Alas, what news to carry to England! There was mourning and tears among the nobles when they heard it, for almost every one among them had lost a son or a brother.

But who should tell the King? No one dared. The nobles knew that Henry loved his son above everything on earth, so for three days, in spite of his anxious questions, no one dared to tell him the truth. When alone they wept for their dear ones, but in presence of the King they put away their tears and tried to smile and jest as usual.

At last one of the nobles, taking his little son by the hand, and whispering to him, "Go, tell the King," gently pushed the child into the room where Henry was sitting.

The little boy felt frightened and shy at finding himself alone with the stern King, although he hardly understood how terrible a tale he had to tell. Half sobbing with excitement and fear, he knelt before Henry and stammered out the story.

As Henry listened, his hands clutched his robe, his lips moved, but no sound came. Then suddenly he fell senseless to the floor, and the little boy, now quite frightened, burst into loud sobbing.

At the sound of the fall the nobles rushed into the room. They lifted the King and placed him upon a couch. He lay there with white face and closed eyes. When he opened his eyes again there was a look in them that no one had seen before; his face was lined and drawn with sorrow, and no one ever saw him smile again.

Henry had no other son, but he had a daughter who was called Matilda, as her mother had been. He resolved that this daughter should be queen after he was dead.

In those days it was thought strange for a country to be ruled by a woman, and the haughty Norman nobles hated the thought of it. But Henry was so strong and stern that he forced them to promise that Matilda should be queen. How they kept that promise you shall hear.

After Prince William's death, Henry spent a great deal of his time in Normandy. He was there when he died. It is said that his death was caused by eating too many lampreys. Lampreys are fish something like eels.

Henry was very fierce and stern, but he was wise, and in those days it was necessary for a king to be stern in order to keep the strong barons in check. He loved justice so much that he was called the Lion of Justice. He took the side of the English people against the Norman barons, and the English repaid him by being true to him. We read of Henry that, "Good he was and mickle awe was of him. No man durst misdo with other in his day. Peace he made for man and deer."

Peace he made and peace he loved, so that he was called the "peace-loving king."

Kneeling beside King Henry, as he lay dying, the Archbishop of Rouen prayed, "God give him the peace he loved."

CHAPTER XXIX

THE STORY OF KING STEPHEN

HENRY I. died in 1135 A.D., and the barons, instead of keeping their promise to him and making his daughter queen, chose his nephew Stephen to be their king. Stephen was the son of Adela, William the Conqueror's daughter.

The barons chose Stephen for several reasons. They were so proud that they hated the thought of being ruled by a woman, and that woman, too, not even a Norman. For you remember Matilda's mother was a great-granddaughter of Edmund Ironside, and as she had been born in England and lived a great part of her life there she was far more English than Norman.

Matilda's husband was Geoffrey, Count of Anjou. He was also called Geoffrey Plantagenet, because when he went into battle he used to wear a sprig of yellow broom in his helmet, so that his friends might know him when his face was covered with his visor. The Latin name for broom is *planta genista*, and gradually it came to be pronounced Plantagenet.

Although Geoffrey was French he was not a Norman, and the Normans looked upon him as quite as much a stranger as an Englishman, and they did not wish to be ruled by him, as would happen if his wife Matilda were made queen. Besides this, the barons knew that Stephen was kind and gentle, and they thought he would be a king who would allow them to do just what they liked.

And so he did. Stephen was too gentle to rule the wild barons. Some one stern and harsh was needed to keep them in check, and Stephen was neither. He allowed the barons to build strong castles all over the country. These castles had dark and fearful dungeons, which were used as prisons. There such deeds of cruelty were done by the barons that the people said the castles were filled, not with men, but with evil spirits. "God has forgotten England," they said. "Christ sleeps and His holy ones."

Not even at the time of the conquest had there been such misery in England. Then there had been one stern ruler who had forced every one to bend to his will. Now each baron set himself up as a king and tyrant. His castle was his kingdom, where he tortured and killed according to his own wicked will. Stephen was a courteous knight and gentleman, but during the nineteen years of his reign there was only lawlessness and sorrow in England.

When the barons made Stephen King of England, Matilda and her husband Geoffrey fled to Normandy. But there, too, the barons rebelled against them and chose Stephen for their duke.

Then David, the King of Scotland, gathered an army and came to fight for his niece Matilda.

Ever since the days of the Romans, the Scots and English had been enemies, and the Scots were still almost as wild and fierce as they had been then. They marched through England as far as Yorkshire, doing dreadful deeds of cruelty as they went.

At a place called Northallerton a great battle was fought. It was called the Battle of the Standard because the sacred banners of four saints were hung upon a pole, which was fixed to a cart, and round this the English gathered their forces.

The Scots were fiercely brave, but they wore no armour, and, although they rushed to battle with splendid courage, they could not break through the line of steel-clad Normans, nor stand against the arrows of the English. So they were defeated, and David could not help Matilda as he had meant to do.

Later on Matilda came back from France, and, until the death of Stephen, England was filled with civil war. Civil war means war within a country itself—the people of that country, instead of fighting against a foreign nation, fighting among themselves. This is the most terrible kind of war, for often friends and brothers fight on different sides, killing and wounding each other. In this civil war those who wished Matilda to be queen fought against those who wished Stephen to remain king.

For a time Matilda's army was successful, but she was so proud and haughty that she soon made enemies even of those who had at first fought for her. Then came a time when she was shut up in Oxford, while the army of Stephen lay around. The King's soldiers kept so strict a watch that no food could be taken into the town, and no person could escape from it. This is called a siege. The people in Oxford began to starve, for they had eaten up all the food they had, and Stephen's soldiers took good care that no more was allowed to be taken into the town. It was the middle of winter. The river Thames was frozen over. Snow lay everywhere around. The cold was terrible, and the people had no wood for fires.

At last Matilda could bear it no longer. She made up her mind to run away. One night four figures dressed in white crept silently through the streets of Oxford. They reached the gate. In silence it was opened, for those guarding it knew who the white-clad figures were. One by one the figures passed through. Out into the snow-covered fields they crept, moving softly and swiftly unnoticed by Stephen's soldiers. It was Matilda and three faithful knights. They had dressed themselves in white so that they might pass unseen over the snow. There was no bridge over the river, but the frost was so hard that they crossed upon the ice and so got safely away.

Although Matilda fled, the war still went on until at length her son Henry landed in England, determined to fight for the crown. But Stephen was weary of war, and all the land longed for rest. So listening to the advice of a wise priest, Stephen and Henry made peace.

Their first meeting was on the banks of the Thames where it runs still as a little stream. They stood one on one bank, and one on the other—Stephen a broken, ruined man, worn and aged with wars and troubles, Henry young, handsome, and hopeful. And there they made a treaty called the Peace of Wallingford. By this treaty it was agreed, that Stephen should keep the crown while he lived; that he should acknowledge Henry as his adopted son; that Henry should reign after the death of Stephen; and that the dreadful castles which Stephen had allowed the wicked barons to build and which they used as dark and horrible prisons, should be destroyed.

So the land had rest. Soon afterward Stephen died, and in 1154 A.D. Henry came to the throne amid the great rejoicing of the people.

CHAPTER XXX

HENRY PLANTAGENET—THE STORY OF GILBERT AND ROHESIA

HENRY II., as you know, got his name Plantagenet from his father, Geoffrey of Anjou, who used to wear a piece of *planta genista* in his helmet. He was the first of several kings ruling England who were all Plantagenets.

Henry II. was only twenty-one years old when he began to reign, and, like his grandfather, Henry Beauclerc, he reigned thirty-five years. Like him, too, he did much to draw the English and Norman people together.

The misrule and confusion of the reign of Stephen had been so great, that Henry had to work very hard to bring his kingdom into order again. He not only worked hard himself, but he made other people work too. It is said of him that he never sat down, but was on his feet all day long.

The first thing Henry did was to send away all the foreign soldiers who had come to England to help Stephen and Matilda in their wars. Next he made the barons pull down their castles in which they used to do such dreadful deeds of cruelty. He told them they must live in ordinary houses and not in fortresses which could be turned into fearful prisons and places of torture.

The barons were very angry; but like his grandfather, Henry Beauclerc, Henry II. was stern, and forced people to obey him.

These are only a few of the things which he did, for the reign of Henry II. was a great one. To help and advise him in his work, Henry chose a man called Thomas à Becket.

Thomas à Becket's father was called Gilbert, and his mother Rohesia. Gilbert was a London merchant, and when he was young he had made a pilgrimage to the Holy Land, as was common in those days.

At that time Jerusalem was in the hands of people called Saracens. They were pagans and hated the Christians and they treated very badly those who came to visit the sepulchre of Christ.

While Gilbert was on his pilgrimage, a rich Saracen seized and put him in prison, saying he should not come out until he had paid a great sum of money.

This Saracen had a beautiful daughter. Rohesia, for that was her name, had seen the handsome young Englishman before her father put him in prison, and she felt sorry for him. She used to come to the little window of his cell to speak to him, and to bring him things to eat and drink.

Night after night she came, and they whispered to each other through the bars of the little prison window. There was no one to hear, and only the stars and the moon to keep watch. All day long Gilbert used to wait impatiently until night came, when Rohesia would creep quietly to the window, and he would hear her whisper, "Gilbert, Gilbert," and she would slip her little hand through the bars and touch his.

Rohesia could speak no English, but Gilbert could speak her language, and he taught her to say his name. She learned to say London too, and knew that that was where he lived.

Gilbert and Rohesia grew to love each other very much, and all the day seemed long and dreary until night came and they could whisper to each other through the prison bars. But one night Rohesia came breathless and pale. "Gilbert," she whispered, "Gilbert, my father is asleep, and I have stolen the keys. I will unlock the door. You are free."

Gilbert hardly believed the good news until he heard the key turn in the lock. Then the door swung open and he knew that he was indeed free. He took Rohesia in his arms and kissed her, promising that he would never forget her. "As soon as I get back to England, I shall send for you," he said. "You must come to me, and we shall be married and never part any more."

Then Gilbert went away and Rohesia was left all alone. She felt very sad after he had gone, but she comforted herself always by remembering that he was going to send for her, and that then they should be together and happy ever after.

Gilbert arrived safely in England, but he forgot all about the beautiful Saracen maiden and his promise to her. He had so many things to do when he got back to London that the time for him went very quickly. But for Rohesia the time passed slowly, slowly. Day after day went by. In the morning she said, "To-day he will send." In the evening she wept, and said, "He has not sent."

At last she could bear the waiting no longer, so she set out to try to find Gilbert. She knew only two words of English, but she was not afraid. She travelled all through the land until she reached the seashore. There she said, "London, London," to every one whom she met until at last she found a ship that was going there. She had not much money, but she gave the captain some of her jewels, and he was kind to her and landed her safely in London.

London in those days was much smaller than it is now, but Rohesia had never seen so many houses and people before, and she was bewildered and frightened. Every one turned to stare at the lovely lady dressed in such strange and beautiful clothes, who kept calling "Gilbert, Gilbert," as she passed from street to street.

Gilbert was sitting in his house when suddenly he heard his name. He knew the voice, yet he could hardly believe his ears. Could it indeed be Rohesia? In a flash he remembered everything; the dark little prison; the lovely Saracen girl; his love for, his promise to her. He ran to the door and opened it quickly. The next minute Rohesia was sobbing in his arms. Her long journey was ended. She had found Gilbert.

As Gilbert held Rohesia in his arms, he found all his old love for her had come back. So they were married and were happy. They had a little son whom they called Thomas. He grew up to be that Thomas à Becket, who was King Henry's great chancellor and friend.

I must tell that some people say that this story of Gilbert and Rohesia is only a fairy tale. Perhaps it is.

CHAPTER XXXI

HENRY PLANTAGENET—THE STORY OF THOMAS À BECKET

KING HENRY was very fond of Thomas à Becket. They used to work very seriously, but when work was done they would play together like two boys.

The chancellor took care of the King's great seal, looked after the royal chapel, and had many other duties. He was a very important person, lived in splendid style, and dressed magnificently. In fact, his house and servants were richer and grander than those of the King. Many of the nobles sent their sons to serve in the chancellor's house, and the proudest were glad to wait on him and to try to please him.

Every day a great number of people dined with the chancellor. Sometimes the King would come in from riding, in the middle of dinner, jump over the table with a merry jest, and sit down among the guests.

Many stories are told of the fun the King and the chancellor used to have together. One day, while out riding, Thomas and King Henry met an old beggar, shivering and in rags.

"It would be a good action to give that poor man a coat," said the King.

"It would indeed," replied the chancellor.

"Then give him yours," and the King laughingly seized the cloak which Thomas was wearing.

It was a beautiful new cloak of silk and fur, and Thomas did not wish to lose it. So he held it tight, while the King tugged hard to pull it off. Neither would let go until, between struggling and laughing, they both nearly fell off their horses.

The courtiers watched and laughed too, but at last the King succeeded in getting the cloak and flung it to the beggar. Thomas was not very pleased, but he had to make the best of it and go shivering for the rest of his ride. The poor beggar went away greatly delighted with the King's joke.

Once Henry sent Thomas with a message to the King of France. Thomas took so many soldiers and servants in glittering dress, so many horses and carriages with him, that the people came out of their houses to stare at him wherever he passed.

"Who is it?" every one asked.

"The Chancellor of England," was the reply.

"Only the chancellor," cried the astonished people. "What must the King be, if the chancellor is so grand?"

Henry worked hard, and with the help of his chancellor improved many things in England. He found that the Church and the clergy, like everything else, had grown very unruly and disorderly. He determined to put them in order, and Thomas à Becket he thought would be the best man to help him. Thomas had been brought up as a priest, and King Henry resolved to make him Archbishop of Canterbury and head of all the clergy in England.

But Thomas was gay and worldly. He loved fine clothes and rich food. "I do not want to be Archbishop of Canterbury," he said to the King.

"You must be," said the King.

"Then we shall quarrel," said Thomas.

"Why?" said the King.

"Because if you make head of the Church I shall work for the Church and not for you. We shall no longer be friends, but enemies," replied Thomas.

But King Henry did not believe Thomas when he talked like this and, in spite of all he could say, he made him Archbishop of Canterbury.

As soon as he became archbishop, Thomas changed his way of living. He gave up his fine house and fine clothes and his great number of servants. He began to wear coarse, rough clothes, lived in a little narrow cell, ate very plain food and drank only water.

It is difficult to understand why he did this. Perhaps he thought that the Primate of all England, as the Archbishop of Canterbury is called, ought to be a very holy man, and he knew no other way of becoming holy, for in those days if a man fasted and went barefoot and wore coarse clothing it was thought that he must be a saint.

Thomas now wrote to the king and told him that he must find another chancellor, as he could not be archbishop and chancellor too. This was a great surprise and grief to the King. In those days it was nothing unusual for one man to be archbishop as well as chancellor. Henry had expected Thomas still to be chancellor and still to help him. He had merely made him primate so that he should help him more.

But that was only the beginning of the troubles.

The Bishop of Rome, whom we call the Pope, said that he was the head of the whole Christian Church, and that no one could be made a bishop in England without his consent. Henry said that he, the King, was the head of the English church, and he would make what bishops he chose. Thomas, instead of siding with the King, sided with the Pope, so they quarrelled, as Thomas had warned Henry that they would.

In those days some of the clergy had grown very wicked. Instead of leading good lives, and being an example to others, they led bad lives. Priests and clergy who did wicked things were not judged by the same courts as other people. They were judged by a bishop's court. Now a bishop's court had no power to order any very severe punishment. If a priest killed a man, the worst that could happen to him would be that he would be beaten—not very hard—and have only bread and water to live on for a few days. Many wicked people became priests simply that they might be able to do as much wrong as they liked, without being punished for it.

Henry wished to put an end to this, so he said that all people who did wrong must be tried by the same judges, whether they were priests or not. But Thomas à Becket would not agree. Clergymen had always been judged by a bishop's court, he said, and by a bishop's court they should continue to be judged.

So the King and the primate quarrelled worse than ever, till the quarrel grew so fierce, and the King so angry, that Thomas fled over the sea to escape from him.

After a time Henry forgave Thomas and he came back to England, but almost at once he again began to quarrel with the King. This time Henry lost all patience and, in a burst of anger, he exclaimed, "Are there none of the idle people who eat my bread that will free me from this quarrelsome priest?"

Henry was angry, and did not really mean what he said. But four knights heard, and thinking to please their king they took ship (for Henry was in Normandy at this time), crossed the sea to England, and rode to Canterbury. Arrived there they went to the archbishop's house. They found him almost alone. With angry words they told him that he must either promise not to quarrel with Henry or he must leave England.

"I shall do what I think is right," replied Thomas. "If the King tells me to do things which I think are wrong, I will not obey him. I am the servant of God. God is higher than the King; I shall obey Him."

This answer enraged the knights, and more angry words were spoken. Then they went away, telling Thomas to beware, for they would come again.

"You will find me here," replied Thomas proudly. "Never again will I forsake my people."

All the archbishop's friends, and the monks and priests who lived with him, were very much afraid. They felt sure that these angry knights meant to do something dreadful. They begged Thomas to leave his house and take refuse in the cathedral, but he would not. "I said they would find me here," he replied to all entreaties.

The day passed. The time for evening service came. Then only did Thomas consent to leave his house and go into the cathedral, for, said he, "It is my duty to lead the service." The priests tried to hurry him, they tried to drag him along quickly, but Thomas would not hasten. He walked slowly and solemnly, having the great cross carried before him as usual. He feared no man.

When at last he was safe within the cathedral, the priests wished to lock and bar the doors. But Thomas forbade them. "This is not a fortress but the House of god, into which every one is free to enter. I forbid you to bar the doors," he said.

The priests were in despair. They loved their archbishop, they knew that he was in danger, but he would not try to save himself.

Even as he spoke there was a great noise without. The door burst open, and the four knights, dressed in complete armour and carrying drawn swords in their hands, rushed into the cathedral.

The frightened people fled in all directions. The archbishop was left almost alone. Only three remained with him—his cross-bearer and two other faithful friends.

In the dim twilight which filled the cathedral it would have been easy for Thomas to escape. But he would not go. "I told them that they should find me here," he said again to the monks who tried to drag him away.

Even as it was, the knights could not find him. In the gathering darkness they clanked and clanged through the great church, seeking him.

"Where is the traitor?" called one of them.

No one answered. Only the word "traitor" echoed again through the silence.

"Where is the archbishop?" he called again.

"I am here," answered the voice of Thomas à Becket out of the darkness. "I am here; no traitor, but a servant of God. What do you want?"

They stood before him, four armed knights against one unarmed priest. Yet he was not afraid.

"Will you be at peace with the King?" asked the knights.

"What I have done I shall continue to do," replied Thomas.

"Then die."

The knights seized him and tried to drag him out of the cathedral, for they feared to kill him in a holy place.

But Thomas would not go. He held tightly to a pillar. His cross-bearer, still holding the cross, threw one arm round the archbishop, trying to protect him.

The knight who had first spoken struck at Thomas. The cross-bearer received the blow upon his arm, which dropped to his side broken. The next stroke fell on Thomas à Becket's defenceless head.

In a few minutes all was over.

"In the name of Christ, and for the defence of the Church, I die willingly," said Thomas, and spoke no more.

Then the knights, fearful of what they had done, fled, leaving the dead archbishop alone in the dark, silent cathedral.

CHAPTER XXXII

HENRY PLANTAGENET—THE STORY OF THE CONQUEST OF IRELAND

WHEN Henry heard of what had happened to Thomas à Becket, he was very sorry; but strangely enough he had no power to punish the four knights; their sin was a sin against the Church, and they could only be tried by a bishop's court. The bishop's court punished them by sending them on a pilgrimage to the Holy Land. So Thomas à Becket, in quarrelling with the King, had protected his own murderers. But perhaps their punishment was very real, for they were forsaken and shunned by all their friends. No one would speak to them, nor eat with them, and at last they died in misery and loneliness.

All England was filled with horror at the dreadful deed. The people had loved Thomas when he was alive, now that he was dead they called him a saint. From far and near they came as pilgrims to his grave, over which a splendid shrine, glittering with gold and gems, was placed.

Nearly four years later the King himself came as a pilgrim to show his sorrow and repentance. He rode on horseback to Canterbury but, as soon as he came within sight of the cathedral, he got off his horse and walked barefoot, wearing only a shirt, and carrying a lighted candle in his hand, until he reached the shrine.

For a whole day and night, having nothing to eat or drink, he knelt in prayer before the grave. For a still greater punishment, he made the monks beat his bare back with knotted cords.

All this show of sorrow could not bring back the great archbishop, who had been murdered in consequence of a few words spoken in anger. But it pleased the Pope, who was very angry because Thomas à Becket had been killed. He blamed Henry, and would scarcely believe that he had not told the four knights to do the wicked deed. In those days the Pope was very powerful indeed. Even kings stood in awe of him, and Henry was glad to make peace with him by any means in his power.

Until now, in this book, we have spoken only of England, although England is but one of the countries which form the United Kingdom. Each of these countries has a history of its own, but it would be too difficult to tell all the stories in one book, so I shall tell only the story of each country after it has been joined to England.

There are four countries in the United Kingdom,—England, Scotland, Ireland and Wales. Of these, England and Ireland were the first to be joined together. This happened in the reign of Henry II., in 1172 A.D.

England, you remember, had at one time been divided into seven kingdoms, and in the same way Ireland was still divided into four, and the kings of these four divisions were always fighting with each other.

Now, one of these kings, who was called Dermot, came to Henry and asked for help against another of the Irish kings. Henry promised help if King Dermot would acknowledge him as "over-lord." This, King Dermot said he would do. Henry was very glad to fight with the Irish, because he knew it would please the Pope, and perhaps make him forget about the death of Thomas à Becket. The Pope was angry with the Irish, because they would not pay him some money to which he thought he had a right.

Henry first sent some Norman knights over to Ireland, and then went himself. There was a good deal of fighting, but in the end Ireland was added to England, and ever since, the kings of England have been lords of Ireland too, although many years passed before they could be said really to rule there.

Henry's great reign closed in sorrow. His sons did not love him, and they rebelled and fought against him. They were encouraged in this by their mother, who was not a good woman.

Two of Henry's sons died before him, both of them while fighting with their father. Two others called Richard and John were kings of England after him.

John was Henry's favourite son. He was the only one who had not rebelled against him. But when the King lay very ill the nobles came to tell him that John, too, had rebelled. This last sorrow broke Henry's heart. Crying out, "Ah, John, John, now I care no more for myself, nor for the world," he turned his face to the wall, and died.

Henry was a very rich king, for, besides being King of England and lord of Ireland, he was ruler over more than half of France. Later you will hear how one of his sons lost all these French possessions.

CHAPTER XXXIII

THE STORY OF RICHARD CŒUR DE LION

"This King Richard, I understand,
E'er he went out of England,
Let make an axe for the nonce,
There with to cleave the Saracen's bones,
The head in soothe was wrought full weel,
Thereon was twenty pounds of steel."

THE country where Christ was born, lived, and died is called Palestine. The capital of that country is Jerusalem. From that far-off country the story of Christ was carried all over the world.

Many listened to the story and were glad, but the country where he lived fell into the hands of the Saracens and Turks who neither believed in nor loved Christ. When people, for the love of Christ, went the long, long, journey to Palestine, in order to see for themselves the Holy Sepulchre, these Saracens and Turks ill-treated them, and insulted their religion.

At last a monk, called Peter the Hermit, went through Europe, preaching and calling upon all Christians to fight for the city of their Lord. If they truly loved Christ, he said, they would deliver His grave from the hands of the Saracens. At his call Christian people rose, eager to show their love, and journeyed to Palestine; but the way was long and difficult, and few reached the capital.

The people, however, were not disheartened, and the following year a great army set out which did reach Jerusalem, and after much fighting the Holy Sepulchre was taken from the Turks.

Later on the Turks took it back again, and so, for nearly two hundred years, with times of peace between, Christians and Turks were at war.

These wars were called crusades, which means, wars of the cross. The word comes from the Latin word *crux*. They were called crusades because the people who fought in them were fighting for the place where Christ died upon the cross. As a badge or sign, they wore a cross upon their armour or clothes.

Many kings and princes joined these wars. King Henry II. had been making ready to go to Palestine when he died. His son Richard I., who was king after him, made up his mind to go as soon as he was crowned.

Richard had not been a good son. He had helped to make his father's last days unhappy, but when his father was dead he was sorry for what he had done, and he punished the people who had helped him to rebel, instead of rewarding them as they had expected. Richard was very brave as his name, Cœur de Lion, which means Lion-hearted, shows. He was a great soldier, he loved to fight, he loved to have adventures. So instead of staying at home and looking after his kingdom as he ought to have done, he went far away to Palestine to fight.

And his people were proud of their king and glad to have him go, for they knew that he would make the name of England famous wherever he went, although Richard himself was really hardly English. He had indeed been born in England, but he had lived nearly all his life in France, and he did not know nor care much about the English people.

Richard Cœur de Lion came to England to be crowned. He sold everything he could in order to get money for the crusade (for wars always cost a great deal of money), and then he sailed away.

But first he chose two bishops to rule the country while he was gone. One was a very old man, and the other, William Longchamps, was a Norman. He could hardly speak a word of English and he treated the people so badly that they hated him and soon rebelled.

Now Richard's younger brother, John, wanted to be King of England, so he encouraged the people to rebel. Then he began to rule, but the unhappy people soon found that John was no kinder than William Longchamps. Indeed he was rather worse, for John wanted the kingdom for himself, and Longchamps, although proud and haughty and cruel to the people, was at least true to his king.

John and his Norman friends oppressed the people, and the hatred between English and Norman, to which Henry II. had done so much to put an end, flamed up again. Many of the English left their homes, or were driven from them, and the land became full of robbers and outlaws.

One of the most famous of these outlaws was Robin Hood. He lived in Sherwood, a forest which at that time covered a great part of the centre of England. He was the head of a large band and so powerful was he that he was called the King of Sherwood. And indeed his followers loved and obeyed him as they would have done a king.

Robbers as a rule are not men to be admired, but these were wild times, very different from ours, and Robin had been forced to become a robber through the wickedness of the rulers of the land. Among his own band he kept such good order, that in Sherwood women and children could wander safely, where it was dangerous for haughty knights and wicked priests to go. Robin's rules were strict, and those who would not obey them were driven out of the band of Merrie Men, as his followers were called.

"But, look ye, do no husbandman harm,
That tilleth with his plough,
No more ye shall the good yeoman
That walketh by green wood shaw;
Nor no knight, nor no squire,

That will be good fellow.
These bishops and archbishops
Ye shall them beat and bind;
The high sheriff of Nottingham
Hold him in your mind."

The sheriff of Nottingham was Robin's greatest enemy. Many times he tried to catch Robin but he never succeeded.

In those days bows and arrows were used in battle instead of guns, as gunpowder had not been invented. Bows and arrows were also used for hunting wild animals. The English archers were the most famous in the world, and Robin Hood was the most famous archer in England. He could split a willow wand, and hit a mark which another man could hardly see.

Robin and his men lived in caves in the forest, shooting the King's deer for food and getting money by robbing the rich knights and priests who travelled through the Green Wood. But they never hurt nor robbed the poor people, indeed Robin used to help many of them. The common people loved him, although the rich, and great barons and nobles hated him.

Far away in Palestine news of the wicked things which John was doing reached Richard, and he felt that it was time that he should go home again. He had not succeeded in what he had set out to do. He had not won Jerusalem from the Turks. But he made a truce with their great leader, Saladin. A truce means that the people who have been fighting do not make peace for good and all, but that they promise not to fight against each other for some arranged time. Saladin and Richard made a truce for three years, during which time Saladin promised that no harm should be done to the pilgrims who came to the Holy Sepulchre.

Richard set sail for home, but his heart was in the Holy Land. Tears filled his eyes as its shores grew dim in the distance. Stretching out his hand, as if in prayer, "Blessed land," he cried, "farewell. To God's keeping I commend thee. May He give me life that I may return to deliver thee from the hand of the unbeliever."

As Richard sailed homeward, storms arose and his ship was wrecked upon the shore of Austria. Nearly everyone was drowned, but the King and a few of his knights escaped.

While in Palestine, Richard had quarrelled with the Duke of Austria, and he knew that it would not be safe to travel openly in this land. So the King and his knights disguised themselves as merchants, hoping in that way to pass safely on their journey.

But they had many adventures, and more than once were nearly discovered. At last Richard was left with only one knight and one little page. When they arrived at the large town near which the Duke of Austria lived, Richard and the knight lay hidden, while the page went into the town to buy food. They had been travelling for several days without daring to enter a house, and all the food they had was finished, and they were both weary and hungry.

Richard, like many brave and reckless people, was neither thoughtful nor careful. He gave the page a large sum of money and allowed him to go into the town carrying the King's gloves in his belt.

In those days only very rich people wore gloves, and Richard's were beautifully embroidered with silk and gold, such as only kings and princes wore. The page had often before bought food for his master, and he went fearlessly into the market-place to get what was needed. But when he handed the merchant a large piece of gold in payment, the man looked sharply at him.

"Who is your master?" he asked.

"My master is a rich merchant called Hugh," replied the boy. "He is returning from a pilgrimage to the Holy Land."

"Merchant, indeed," said another man. "Look at his gloves."

A third plucked them from his belt. "Merchant indeed," he too cried. "These are king's gloves. Who is your master, boy?"

"I have told you," replied the page steadily, "he is a merchant called Hugh."

But the townspeople would not believe that. They beat and tortured the poor lad. Still he would not tell.

Then they dragged him before the duke with whom Richard had quarrelled in Palestine. He was more strong and cruel than the others, and at last forced the page to confess that his master was Richard Cœur de Lion, the King of England.

Then Leopold, Duke of Austria, was very glad. He hated Richard with a great hatred. He sent soldiers to the King's hiding-place, seized him, and put him in prison.

Duke Leopold kept Richard prisoner for some time, and then he sold him to the Emperor of Germany for a large sum of money. The Emperor of Germany also hated Richard, so he, in his turn, put him into prison.

Then the Emperor wrote to the King of France telling him that the King of England was safely imprisoned in one of his strong castles. And King Philip of France was glad, for he, too, hated Richard, and had been helping Prince John stir up the English people to rebellion. When Prince John heard about it, he was glad too. So a great many people rejoiced that Richard Cœur de Lion was in prison.

CHAPTER XXXIV

RICHARD CŒUR DE LION—THE STORY OF HOW BLONDEL FOUND THE KING

RICHARD COEUR DE LION, who loved to be free, who loved to fight and ride and hunt, to do great deeds of strength and daring, hated to be shut up in a dark and narrow prison.

Yet he did not despair. He loved, too, to laugh and sing, and he made friends with his gaolers, wrestling and fighting with them, and astonishing them by his great strength. And when he was weary of that, he would sing to them or write poetry.

But sometimes he was sad.

Although nearly all the poetry which Richard wrote has been lost, one mournful little song which he made in prison is still left. It was written in French, for Richard, you remember, was almost French, and could speak very little English.

Here it is in English words:—

"No captive ever sings so sweet a strain
As he who weareth not the prisoner's chain,
Yet song may glad his days of weariness;
Friends fail me not, but shame for them I fear.
If I, for lack of gold, this vile duresse
Sustain another year.

"Well know my knights and servants every one,
English, Poitevin, Norman, or Gascon,
That to no comrade would I help refuse,
But I would spend my wealth till he were free;
And this I say, yet them I not accuse
For my captivity.

"True it is said, and I have learned it sore,
Dead folk no lovers have, nor captives more,
But if to save their wealth here I do lie,
Disgrace and scorn shall unto them be still,
And if I suffer, more they suffer will,
Though I be left to die."

Prince John felt that nothing now stood between him and the throne of England. He told the people that the King was dead and would never come back again. He seized the royal castles and what gold and jewels he could find belonging to the King in England. But the English would neither believe nor follow John.

Meanwhile Blondel, a minstrel or singer who loved King Richard, took his harp, and, wandering from castle to castle, sought his master through all Germany. For the Emperor kept secret where he had imprisoned Richard. Wherever Blondel heard of some unknown prisoner, there he stopped and sang a song which Richard and he had made and sung together.

Again and again Blondel sang this song, but no answering voice ever came from any of the grim castle walls. At last one evening, weary and almost hopeless, he began to sing beneath the walls of a castle called Trifels.

"O Richard! O my king!
Thou art by all forgot,
Through the wide world I sadly sing,
Lamenting thy drear lot.
Alone, I pass through many lands
Alone, I sigh to break thy bands.
O Richard! O my king!
Thou art by all forgot,
Though the wide world I sadly sing,
Lamenting thy dread lot."

Blondel's voice was sad and broken, his heart was heavy, and he could scarcely sing for tears. But hardly had he finished the first verse when, from a window high above him, another voice took up the tune and sang:—

"The minstrel's song
Is Love alone,
Fidelity and Constancy,
Though recompense be none."

The voice rang out clear and full and strong. Blondel knew and loved it. It was the voice of Richard Cœur de Lion. Blondel leaned his head against the rough stone of the castle wall and wept for joy. He had found his King.

Back to England the minstrel went with his great news, and when the English people heard it, they were glad. But the Emperor would not set Richard free until the people paid a large sum of money called a ransom. The land had already been made very poor through the wars and robberies of John, but the English people wanted their king so much that they denied themselves almost everything in order to raise enough money. When they had gathered the money they sent it to the Emperor, and Richard was at last set free.

As soon as he was out of prison, Richard hurried to England. He must have been glad to see the white cliffs of his own land again. He had been away four years, and fourteen months of that time he had been shut up in a dark and lonely prison.

The people were so glad to see their King again that, poor though they were, they had such grand decorations and rejoicings that a German knight who came home with Richard was quite astonished. "Had my lord the Emperor known," said he, "how rich a country England still was, he would have demanded yet more money."

Richard set himself at once to bring order into the kingdom. Most of the people were on the side of the King, and Prince John soon submitted to him. Their mother, Queen Eleanor, begged Richard to forgive his brother.

"I forgive him," said Richard, "and I hope I shall as easily forget the wrong he has done me as I know he will forget my pardon." He knew that John was not really sorry, and would rebel again as soon as he had a chance.

Richard remained in England only a few months, and then he went to France. There he spent the rest of his life, chiefly fighting with the king of that country.

But Richard left a good and wise man to rule in England, and the people were happier, although they had to pay heavy taxes in order to help Richard in his French wars. This was very unfair, as these wars did England no good. But as long as the kings of England had possessions in France, the English had to pay for French wars. So it was a good thing for England when at last all the French possessions were lost.

Richard was killed in France in 1199 A.D., while besieging a castle called Chaluz. He was riding round the walls with one of his captains, looking for the best place of attack, when a young archer put an arrow to his bow, and saying, "Now, God speed my arrow," let it fly.

The arrow hit Richard in the shoulder. The wound was not a bad one, but doctors in those days were not very clever, and the doctor who drew out the arrow-head did it so badly that the wound was made much worse.

In a day or two it became so bad that Richard felt he was going to die. But he swore that he would first take the castle and kill the archer who had caused his death.

The castle was taken, and Richard, in his terrible wrath, hanged all the soldiers except the archer. He was kept for some more dreadful death.

Richard was lying in great agony when the young archer was brought before him. "Villain," said the King, looking fiercely at him, "what have I done to you that you should kill me?"

The young man drew himself up, and looking proudly at the King, and not in the least afraid of his angry frown, replied, "With your own hand you killed my father and my two brothers. Kill me, torture me if you will. I am glad to die, having rid the world of one who has wrought so much ill in it."

Then there was silence between these two proud, brave men, as they looked each other in the eyes, the one a poor soldier, the other a dying king.

But Richard, although fierce and hasty, was generous, and, above all things, he loved courage. "Boy," he said, "I forgive you." Then turning to his captains, "Loose his chains," he added, "let him go free, and give him a hundred shillings to boot."

So Richard Cœur de Lion died. He was so brave that all Europe rang with his fame. The Saracens stood in such awe of him that when little children were naughty their mothers would say to them, "Be good now, or Richard of England will come to you," and the children would be good at once for fear of him. "Thinkest thou that Richard of England is in that bush?" a rider would say to his horse if it were startled, so great was the terror of his name.

Richard was a good knight and brave soldier, but he was not a good king. He reigned for ten years, yet only six months of that time did he spend in England. No doubt he thought it was a great and good thing to fight for Jerusalem, but how much better it would have been if he had tried to rule his own land peacefully, and bring happiness to his people.

CHAPTER XXXV

JOHN LACKLAND—THE STORY OF PRINCE ARTHUR

WHEN Richard Cœur de Lion died, his brother John, who had plotted and rebelled against him when he was alive, became King. He was called by the French John Sans Terre, which means "without land," and John Lackland by the English. He was so called because, when his father, Henry II., died, John had no kingdom left to him as his brothers had.

John was the youngest and the worst of all Henry's sons, and he was not the heir to the throne of England.

The real heir was Prince Arthur of Brittany, the son of John's elder brother Geoffrey. And now the French king, Philip, who had fought against Richard and helped John, suddenly turned round and began to fight against John because he would not let Arthur be king.

John was wicked and wily, and he easily got Arthur into his power and shut him up in prison. But John was not content with that. He greatly feared that the English people might want to have Arthur as their King, and he resolved to make that impossible.

Prince Arthur was placed in the charge of a man called Hubert, and wicked King John ordered this man to put out Arthur's eyes.

Hubert actually said he would do this cruel deed. One morning he brought two men into Arthur's room, ready to put out his pretty blue eyes with their dreadful hot irons.

Arthur was a gentle, loving boy, and he was fond of his stern gaoler, and Hubert in his own rough way was fond of the little prince. Now he felt sad and sick at heart at the thought of what he had to do.

"Are you ill?" said Arthur. "You look so pale. I wish you were a little ill so that I could nurse you and show you how much I love you," he added.

When Arthur spoke to him so kindly the tears came into Hubert's eyes. But he brushed them away and determined to do what the King had commanded.

"I am not ill, but your uncle has commanded me to put out your eyes," he said roughly.

"To put out my eyes! Oh, you will not do it, Hubert?"

"I must."

"Oh, Hubert! Hubert! how can you?" said Arthur, putting his arms round Hubert's neck. "When your head ached only a little I sat up all night with you. Now you want to put out my eyes. These eyes that never did, nor never shall, so much as frown upon you."

"I have sworn to do it," said Hubert sadly.

"Oh, but you will not do it! You will not! You will not, Hubert?" and so

Arthur begged and prayed till Hubert could resist no longer, and he sent the wicked men with their dreadful red-hot irons away.

But Hubert was afraid that King John would be angry because his orders had not been obeyed, so he told him the cruel deed had been done, and that Prince Arthur had died of grief and pain.

Then wicked King John was glad. But the people both in France and England were very sad when they heard this news. Every one mourned for the young prince. All through the land bells were tolled as if for a funeral.

There was so much anger against John, and so much sorrow for the prince, that at last Hubert told the people that what he had said was not true, and that Arthur was still alive. Then every one was glad. Even King John was glad at first because many of his nobles had told him plainly that he would find no knight to follow him to battle, nor to guard his castles at home, if he had really killed his little nephew.

But King John's heart was black and wicked, and he could not rest while he knew that Prince Arthur lived. So one dark night he came to the castle in which his nephew was kept prisoner.

After that night no one ever saw Prince Arthur again. Next morning when the sun shone in at the narrow window where he used to sit it shone into an empty room. For Arthur's poor little body was lying at the bottom of the Seine, with a great wound in his heart made by his wicked uncle's cruel, sharp knife.

CHAPTER XXXVI

JOHN LACKLAND—THE STORY OF THE GREAT CHARTER

THE French barons soon grew weary of John and his misrule, and they all leagued against him. They fought and conquered him, and he had to fly from Normandy which, with all his other French possessions, was lost to him forever.

But although he was no longer Duke of Normandy, Count of Anjou, Lord of Touraine and Maine, John was still King of England, and to England he returned to rob and oppress the people.

The wise man, called Hubert Walter, who had ruled England during the last years of Richard Cœur de Lion, now died. He had been Archbishop of Canterbury, and John was very glad when he died, as he was one of the few men who kept him from doing just as he liked.

John chose a friend of his own as the next archbishop, but the monks of Canterbury chose some one else. Both these men went to the Pope to ask him which of them ought to be the archbishop. Henry II., you remember, had quarrelled with Thomas à Becket over this very point, because, he said, he had the right to choose the English bishops, and the Pope had nothing to do with it.

The Pope said that neither of these men should be archbishop, and he chose another man altogether, called Stephen Langdon.

Stephen Langdon was a very good man. In fact no better archbishop could have been chosen. But John was furiously angry when he heard that his friend was not to be allowed to be archbishop, and he banished Stephen Langdon from the country.

Then the Pope was very angry with John and told him that, if he did not allow Stephen to come back at once, he would lay England under an Interdict.

Interdict comes from a Latin word which means "to forbid." The Pope meant that he would forbid any religious service of any kind to be held in England.

John did not care. He meant to have his own way. So did the Pope. John would not give in and the churches were closed. No bells were rung, no services were held. People could not be married, little babies could not be christened, dead people could not be buried. Cobwebs and dust filled the churches, weeds choked the graveyards.

It was a sad and gloomy land.

Still John did not care. Then the Pope excommunicated him. Excommunicate is another Latin word and means that John was put out of union or companionship, not only with the Church, but with every human being.

The Pope told the people that John was no longer king and that they need not now obey him. They were forbidden to eat or drink with him or to serve him. Whatever he did was wrong. In fact he had lost all rights as a man and as a Christian. He might be looked upon as a wild animal. Any one who chose might kill him.

Still John did not care. He laughed at the Pope.

Then the Pope told the King of France that he would be doing a good and Christian act if he conquered John and took possession of England.

The French king was only too pleased to have a good excuse for invading England, and he began at once to prepare to fight.

Then suddenly John grew frightened and gave way. He had found out that not only the Pope and the French were against him, but the Scotch, the Irish, the Welsh, and even the English were all ready to fight. He was alone in the world, hated and despised by all. So powerful was the Pope in those days.

From being insolent and scornful, John now became meanly humble and did a shameful thing. The Pope sent a messenger to England, and John, kneeling before this messenger, took the crown from his head and gave it to him.

The Pope's messenger kept the crown for five days and then he gave it back to John. But he did not give it to him as the free King of England. He gave it to him telling him that henceforth he could wear it only as the servant of the Pope, and that he must promise always to do as the Pope commanded.

The English people felt sad and ashamed that their King should be under the Pope like this, but John did not care, for the Pope was now his friend. And John knew that the Pope could be as powerful a friend as he had been an enemy.

One good thing at least followed. The Interdict was taken from the land. Once more church bells rang, hymns were sung, and the silent gloom passed away.

Another good man who had helped to protect the people from John now died. When John heard of it he was very glad. "At last I am really King of England," he cried, for he thought that there was no one else in all the land to hinder him from being as bad and cruel as he wished.

But he was mistaken. Stephen Langdon, the man whom the Pope had made Archbishop of Canterbury, turned out to be the people of England's best friend.

You remember that King Henry I. had granted a Charter of Liberties to the people. That charter had been broken, set aside and forgotten. Stephen Langdon and the barons now drew up another charter which they determined to make John grant to them. This charter was much the same as that of Henry, only it gave still greater liberty to the people. It is called the

Magna Charta or Great Charter. Magna means "great."

The charter is very long and some of it you would find difficult to understand, but I will tell you a few of the things in it, for the Magna Charta is the foundation of all our laws and liberty.

"No free man," it says, "or merchant or peasant shall be punished a great deal for a very little fault. However bad they may have been we will not take their tools or other things by which they earn their living, away from them."

"No free man shall be seized, or put in prison, or have his goods or lands taken from him, or be outlawed or exiled, or in any way brought to ruin, unless he has been properly judged and condemned by the law of the land."

"To no man will we sell, or deny, or delay right or justice."

These things seem to us now quite natural and right, so you can imagine what evil times these were when the King was unwilling to grant such liberty to his people.

But King John was very unwilling to grant it. When he first read this charter he was furiously angry. "Why do they not ask for my kingdom at once?" he cried. "I will never, never grant anything that will make me a slave of the people."

But the Church and the barons and the people were all against John. Agree he must. Yet he kept delaying, from Christmas till Easter, from Easter till midsummer. Friend after friend deserted him, till at last he found that the whole country had risen against him like one huge army, and he had only seven knights left who were still true to him.

The angry barons would no longer be put off. They forced the King to meet them at a little place on the Thames called Runnymede. The barons and their army camped on one side of the river, the King and his friends on the other. On a little island between, they met and talked, and there, on 15th June 1215 A.D., the Great Charter was sealed with the king's great seal.

The King was sullen and angry. At the last he would have refused to set his hand to the seal, but Stephen Langdon stood beside him and the stern barons around. Then he found that he had to bend his will to that of the people.

John not only sealed the charter, but he agreed that twenty-four barons should be appointed to see that he kept the promises which it contained. He agreed only because he was compelled, because the barons stood there in bright armour with sharp swords and fierce looks, because he knew he had no friend to stand by him and help him to resist.

When the meeting was over, and John went back to his palace, his anger was terrible. He threw himself on the floor foaming with passion. "They have given me four-and-twenty over-lords," he screamed. "I am no king with four-and-twenty over-lords." He cursed the barons and the people with terrible curses. He tore and bit the rushes with which the floor was covered. He gnashed his teeth, growling and snarling like a wild animal mad with rage.

Yet this charter, against which John fought so fiercely, was nothing new; the laws and promises it contained were the laws and promises of Edward the Confessor, of Alfred the Great. But they were also the laws and promises which the foreign kings of England had broken and trampled on ever since William the Conqueror had won the battle of Hastings.

Many copies of the great charter were made, and these copies were sent to cathedrals and other safe places to be taken care of. This was done so that the people throughout all the land should know of their liberties, and if one copy were lost or destroyed, there should still be others. It is nearly seven hundred years since Magna Charta was sealed, yet one copy still remains. It is yellow and stained, but we treasure it greatly for the memory of what it was and is to us. It is kept safely in London, in the British Museum. Some day you will go there and look at it.

John sealed the Magna Charta because he had no choice, but he never meant to keep the promises it contained. And he did not keep them. He sent to France for soldiers, and when they came he made war on his own people. He asked his friend the Pope for help, and the Pope helped him by excommunicating all the barons, by laying London under Interdict, and by telling him that he need not keep his promises.

But the people of England said that this was a matter with which the Pope had nothing to do, and so they paid no attention to him. The church bells rang; there was preaching, praying, and singing in the churches, and people were married, and buried, and christened as usual. The Pope was very angry, but he could do nothing.

Then, as John still went on his wicked way, the people sent to France and asked Louis, the son of the King of France, to come to fight against John, promising to help him and to make him King of England.

Louis came, but there was little need for him to fight, as very shortly John died. While crossing the Wash to meet Louis, he, his army and all his treasure were overtaken by the tide. John himself was nearly drowned, and his crown, his jewels and the baggage of the army were lost.

A few days later John died. Some say that he died of anger and grief, others that he was poisoned, others that his death was caused by eating a great many raw peaches and by drinking a quantity of new cider too greedily.

No king of England has ever been so bad as John. He was a bad son, a bad brother, a bad king, and a bad man. Yet out of his wicked reign great good came to the English nation.

The loss of Normandy, which was caused by John's cruelty, proved to be a blessing to England. Norman lords no longer came to England expecting to fill the best places in the land. French was spoken less and less, until only a few French words remained, which we still use, and which now form part of the English language. The hatred between Norman and English died out, because the differences disappeared, and the Norman barons became English barons.

In the reign of Stephen the barons, you remember, were fierce and wicked, and oppressed the people in terrible ways. In the reign of John, the barons had become the champions of the people, and took up arms for them against a wicked king.

When the barons forced John to grant the Magna Charta, they fought, not for themselves, as barons and Normans, but for the whole English people. For the first time since the Conquest the people of England acted as one people. The Norman had disappeared. England was England again. She had conquered the Conqueror.

> *"This England never did (nor never shall)*
> *Lie at the proud foot of a conqueror,*
>
> . . . .
>
> *If England to itself do rest but true."*

CHAPTER XXXVII

HENRY III. OF WINCHESTER—THE STORY OF HUBERT DE BURGH

WHEN King John died, the anger of the barons died too, and, although he was only nine years old, they chose his son Henry to be their King. "His father was wicked," said the barons, "but the prince has done us no wrong. Why should we be angry with him?" So they crowned Henry, and told Louis to return to his own country.

But Louis was angry that, having been brought from France and promised the crown of England, he should be told to go away again. He would not go. So there was fighting once more.

Louis sent to France for men, and a great fleet of ships, filled with soldiers, came sailing to England.

Long ago, you remember, Alfred the Great had seen how much better it would be to stop the Danes from landing at all, and he built ships and fought them at sea.

Now a brave man called Hubert de Burgh saw the same thing. When he heard that more Frenchmen were coming, he said, "We will never let them land. We will fight and conquer them at sea." So under his command a brave little English fleet sailed out from Dover to meet the great French fleet.

And the English conquered the French, as Hubert had said they would. The wind was blowing from the English to the French, and the English threw quicklime in the air, which was blown into the eyes of the French and blinded them. The English archers then poured arrows among them while their quick little ships crashed with their pointed prows against the great French vessels, piercing holes in their sides until the water rushed in and they sank. The English were altogether so quick and fearless that the French were no match for them, and their fleet was utterly destroyed.

On land, too, the English beat the French, and Louis, seeing that his cause was lost, went back to France.

Henry III. was too young to rule, so Hubert de Burgh was made Regent. He was a good Regent, but his work was hard, for, after the wickedness and misrule of John, the kingdom was in a bad state.

But in spite of his good and wise teacher Henry grew up to be neither good nor wise. Listening to the advice of evil friends, he treated Hubert very badly and at last obliged him to fly for his life.

One night while Hubert was sleeping quietly, he was suddenly awakened by a friend. "Fly, my Lord Hubert," he cried, "stay not a moment. The King has sent his soldiers to take you. I have ridden hard, but they are close behind me. You have not a moment to lose."

Hubert got out of bed and, not even waiting to dress, fled with bare feet and only a cloak round him to the nearest church. There, with his hand upon the cross, he waited in the dark and cold.

Hubert fled to a church for sanctuary or safety. When any one was hunted by his enemies, if he ran into a church, reached the altar steps and laid hold upon the cross, no one dared to hurt him. This was called "taking sanctuary."

It was considered a dreadful and wicked thing to kill any one in sanctuary. Yet, you remember, the knights killed Thomas à Becket on the steps of the altar in Canterbury Cathedral.

Hubert waited in the cold and silent church until, with the first grey streaks of dawn and the first early twitter of the birds, he heard the distant tramp of feet and the clatter of swords and armour. Nearer and nearer came the sounds till at last a knight, followed by three hundred armed men, dashed into the church.

"Hubert de Burgh," said the knight, "In the King's name I command you to leave this holy place. Give yourself into my hands, that I may take you before the King to answer for your misdeeds as a rebel and traitor."

"Nay," replied Hubert, "to my King have I ever been true, but he has listened to false friends who would take my life. Here have I sought God's safety. Here will I remain."

"That shalt thou not do," cried the knight, fiercely. "On, men, and seize him!"

Then the armed men rushed forward, forced Hubert from the altar, and carried him out of the church.

"He is indeed a mighty man and strong," said the knight, when he saw how Hubert struggled. "He must be fettered, or we shall never carry our prize to London."

Near the church stood a smith's forge, and the smith, who had been already aroused by the noise, was ordered to light his fire and make fetters for the prisoner.

Soon the red fire glowed in the grey morning light, and the ring of hammer and anvil was heard.

"For whom do I made these fetters?" asked the smith, as he paused in his work.

"For the traitor and rebel, Hubert de Burgh," replied the knight.

"What!" cried the smith, throwing down his hammer, "for Hubert de Burgh. That will I never do. Hubert de Burgh is no rebel. He saved us from the French, he gave us safety and peace. Some one else may do your evil deeds. No iron of mine shall ever fetter such noble hands."

"Fool!" cried the knight, drawing his sword, "do as I command you or die."

"I can die," replied the smith calmly. "Yes, kill me, do with me what you like; I will never make fetters for Hubert de Burgh."

When the smith spoke like this, the knight began to feel rather ashamed, but he would not let Hubert go, both because he hated Hubert, and because he feared the King. So he and his followers bound Hubert with a rope, set him upon a horse, and took him to the Tower of London.

When the Bishop of London heard what had happened, he was very angry. Being a brave man he went straight to the King.

"My liege," he said to him, "have you heard how your soldiers have broken the peace of holy Church and have dragged Hubert de Burgh from sanctuary, casting him into prison?"

"I know that the rebel and traitor, Hubert de Burgh, is now in prison," replied Henry.

"Hubert de Burgh is no rebel," said the bishop, "and if he were, the soldiers have still no right to drag him from the safety of the Church. Let him go back, or I shall excommunicate every man who has had to do with it."

Very unwillingly the King allowed Hubert to go back to his place of safety. But he sent soldiers to dig a trench round the church and round the bishop's house which was close to it. There the soldiers watched day and night so that Hubert might not escape, and so that no food might be taken in to him.

But in spite of the strict watch kept by the soldiers, Hubert's friends found means to send him food, and for many days he lived in the church. Then still closer watch was kept and, at last, thinking it a disgrace to die of hunger, Hubert left the church of his own accord, and gave himself up to the King's soldiers, who at once carried him off to the Tower of London.

There he was kept for some time, but at last Henry, who was not really cruel, although he was weak and foolish, set him free. After that, Hubert lived quietly in his own home, and took no more part in the ruling of the kingdom.

CHAPTER XXXVIII

HENRY III. OF WINCHESTER—THE STORY OF SIMON DE MONTFORT

KING HENRY III. married a French lady called Eleanor. She brought a great many friends and relatives from France with her. Soon all the best places at court were given to these French people, just as they had been in the time of Edward the Confessor and of William the Conqueror.

These strangers did very much as they liked. They set aside the Great Charter and, when the English barons complained, the French nobles sneered at them. "What are your English laws to us?" they said. "We are far greater and more important than you. Such laws are made for English boors. We will not keep them unless we choose."

This treatment was not to be borne, and at last the English rose in rebellion and forced the King to send away His French favourites.

It would take too long to tell of all the quarrelling and fighting there was in this reign. Henry broke the Great Charter over and over again. No fewer than ten times did he sign it and each time, as soon as he had got what he wanted, he broke the promises he had made. But in spite of this, the power of the people was growing stronger.

Henry spent a great deal of money, far more indeed than he ought to have done. But he could not wring gold from the people as William the Conqueror had been able to do. He had to ask the barons to give it to him, and they would not grant it until he promised something in return.

Henry did indeed wring money from the Jews. They were the richest and the most despised people in the country, and Henry, although he was not usually cruel, was very cruel to them. One Jew who refused to give Henry money was put into prison. Every morning his gaoler came and pulled out one of his teeth, till at last the poor man could bear the pain no longer and he gave the King what money he wanted.

The bishops and barons grew tired of broken promises and such unkingly acts, so, when next Henry asked for money, a great council was called, to which all the barons and bishops in England came.

There was a great deal of talking and it seemed as if nothing would come of it. But the barons told Henry very sternly that he had not acted as a king ought. He had constantly broken his promises and only if he now solemnly swore to the Charter would they give him money.

Then Henry answered, "It is true. I am sadly grieved that I have acted as I have done. I will try to do better." But when he tried to blame some of the bishops and barons, they sternly said, "Our lord King, we will not talk of what is now past, but of what is to come."

Then all the bishops and the archbishops, dressed in their splendid robes and carrying lighted candles in their hands, walked in solemn procession to the great royal hall at Westminster. There, in presence of the King and all the barons, they solemnly excommunicated every one who should in the future take away in any degree the freedom of England. The words they used were very grand and terrible. The King as he listened held his hand over his heart. His face was calm and cheerful and he looked as if he never had tried, and never would try, to take away his people's liberty.

When the solemn sentence was finished and the deep voice of the archbishop died away in silence, all the bishops and the archbishops threw down their lighted candles, crying, "May all those who take away our liberties perish, even as these lights perish."

The bells were then rung joyfully, the candles were again lighted, and King Henry, standing among his people, spoke,—"So help me God, all these promises will I faithfully keep, as I am a man, a Christian, a knight and a crowned and anointed king."

Thus once more the Great Charter was solemnly signed and sealed. But in spite of this ceremony, Henry did not keep his promises. He listened to evil friends, who told him that if he did, he would not be king, nor even lord in England, but the subject of his people.

Now there arose a great man called Simon de Montfort, Earl of Leicester. For many years he had been the faithful friend of King Henry, whose sister he had married. Henry sometimes heaped favours upon him, sometimes quarrelled with him, just as he was pulled this way or that by his friends.

When Simon de Montfort first came to England the barons did not like him. "Here is another Frenchman," they said, "who comes to eat our bread and take away what belongs to us." But Simon soon showed that, if he was French in name, he was English at heart.

As Henry continually broke his promises, Simon took the side of the barons and the people, and Henry feared him as he feared no other man.

One day Henry went for a picnic on the Thames. He had rowed from his palace at Westminster some way down the river, when a thunderstorm came on, and he was obliged to take refuge in Simon's house, near which he was passing. As he arrived there the thunderstorm began to clear.

"There is nothing to fear now, my lord," said Simon, as he ran to meet the King.

"I fear the thunder and lightning," replied the king, "but I fear thee more than all the thunder and lightning in the world."

"My lord King," replied the earl sadly, "it is unjust that you should fear me who am your faithful friend. I have ever been true to you and yours and to the kingdom of England. Your flatterers are your enemies. Them you ought to fear."

Led by Simon, the barons forced Henry to hold a council at Oxford to draw up new laws for the better ruling of the kingdom. The wonderful thing about these laws was that they were written in English. Ever since the Conquest, the laws had been written in French or Latin, but at last English laws, for English people, were again written in their own language.

But Henry did not keep these new laws any better than he had kept the old ones. The patience of the people came to an end and there was war, the King's army fighting against Simon de Montfort, Earl of Leicester, and his followers. This was called the Barons' war, and it ended in a great battle at Lewes in which the King was defeated.

After this battle it was really Simon de Montfort who ruled the country. Henry was indeed still king in name, but both he and his son, Prince Edward, were Simon de Montfort's prisoners.

It was Simon de Montfort who laid the foundation of what is now our Parliament. Up to this time only bishops and barons had been allowed to come to the meetings of the council. Simon, however, now chose two knights from every shire or country, and two citizens from every city, and sent them also to the council to speak for the people and to tell of their wants. Now, too, the great council began to be called Parliament, which means "talking-place," for it is there that the people come to talk of all the affairs of the kingdom.

Unfortunately the barons could not long agree among themselves. Prince Edward escaped from Simon and joined the discontented barons, and there was another battle between the prince's men and Simon's men, in which Simon was killed.

The people had loved Simon, and now they sorrowed for his death, and called him a saint, and Sir Simon the Righteous. He is also called the Father of the English Parliament.

Although Prince Edward fought against Simon de Montfort, he had been his pupil, and had learned much from him, and he was growing into a wise prince. He now helped to make peace, and when peace again came to the land Prince Edward, like so many other princes and kings, joined a crusade and went to fight in the Holy Land.

In 1272 A.D., while his son was still in that far-off country, King Henry died, having reigned fifty-six years. His reign had not been a happy one for England, yet good came of it, for his very weakness made the people strong, and out of the troubles of his reign grew our freedom of speech and our power to make for ourselves the laws under which we have to live.

CHAPTER XXXIX

HENRY III.—THE STORY OF THE POISONED DAGGER

IN far-off Palestine the army of the crusaders lay encamped before the town of Acre. The air was hot and stifling, the sun seemed a ball of fire hung in the still blue sky. Having put off his heavy armour for the sake of coolness Prince Edward lay within his tent, wearing only a long, loose robe of linen. He lay idle, thinking perhaps of the mighty deeds which his great-uncle, Richard Cœur de Lion, had done in this same place, eighty years before; wondering, too, if he would be able to do as great things.

Presently the curtains of the doorway parted. "My lord prince," said a soldier, bowing low, "the Emir of Jaffa hath sent his servant yet again. He craves to be admitted to your presence."

"I will receive him," replied the prince, and the soldier once more left the tent.

Edward had been fighting with the Emir of Jaffa, but now, pretending that he wished to become a Christian, this Emir sent daily messages and presents to the prince. And the prince, noble and honest himself, believed the Emir to be honest too.

In a few minutes the curtains of the doorway parted once more and the Emir's dark slave crept in. He bowed himself to the ground, then, kneeling humbly before the prince, drew out a letter.

Edward took the letter and, as the prince read, the slave crouched on the ground watching him with his bright dark eyes. Then slowly, slowly his brown hand crept to the belt of his white dress. So slowly it crept that it seemed hardly to move.

Suddenly, as quick as lightning, a keen bright blade flashed in the air and fell. But Edward, too, was quick and strong. He threw up his hand and caught upon it the blow which had been aimed at his heart. Then, springing from the couch, he overthrew the slave, and placing his foot upon the man's neck, wrenched the dagger from his grasp. In another moment the slave lay still and dead upon the sand. At the noise of the struggle, several frightened servants came running into the tent, and one of them, seeing the slave upon the sand, seized a stool, and dashed his brains out.

"Foolish man," said Prince Edward, "see you not that the slave is already dead? What you do is neither brave nor honourable, but the action of a coward."

Prince Edward's wound was slight, but the dagger had been a poisoned one. When his wife, the beautiful Princess Eleanor, heard of it, she hurried to her husband's tent. Before those about her knew what she meant to do, she knelt down and, putting her lips to the wound, sucked it. It was said that if the blood from a poisoned wound was sucked at once after the wound was made, the wounded person would not die. It was a brave thing for Princess Eleanor to do, for she might herself have died. But she loved Edward so much that she was willing to risk her own life. Yet the wound grew worse, and it seemed likely that Edward would die.

He was very calm and brave, and did not fear death, but tried to comfort his friends and servants, for they were all very sorrowful.

But the princess sat beside him weeping, and would not be comforted. Then, calling for parchment and ink, Prince Edward wrote down all that he wished to be done with his money and lands, after he was dead. This was called making his will.

Now a clever doctor came to the prince and said, "I think I can cure you, only you will have to suffer a great deal of pain."

"Do what you think best," said the prince, "and cure me if you can."

Then the princess threw herself upon him, crying bitterly, and would not let any one touch him. "I know you only want to hurt him more," she sobbed, "I cannot bear it."

But Edward gently put her away, "Hush, hush," he said, and gave her into his brother Edmund's arms.

"Do you love your lord and brother?" asked the doctor, turning to Edmund.

"Ay, that I do," replied he.

"Then take this lady away, and do not let her lord see her again until I tell you."

So Princess Eleanor was led away weeping.

"Ah, weep, lady," said Edmund gently. "It is better that you should weep than that all England should mourn."

But England did not mourn, for the doctor was clever, and in less than a fortnight Prince Edward was again quite well.

The false Emir sent messengers to Edward to say that he was sorry that the prince had been wounded, and was glad that he was better. But Edward no longer trusted the Emir. He looked gravely at the messengers. "You bow before me," he said, "but you do not love me, therefore go."

And they were allowed to go in peace. Although Edward's soldiers longed to be revenged upon them and kill them, the prince would not allow it.

After this Edward did not stay long in Palestine. He heard that his father was ill, so he made a ten years' peace with the Sultan, as the king of the Turks is called, and sailed back to England. On his way home he heard of his father's death. He knew that that meant he was now King of England, but he was very sad, for Edward had loved his father, although he could not help knowing that in many things he was foolish and untrustworthy.

CHAPTER XL

EDWARD I.—THE LITTLE WAR OF CHALONS

IN the days when knights wore armour and fought with sword and lance, they used often to play at war, as if they had not real fighting enough.

These mock wars were called tournaments. They took place in a great open space or plain, which was called the lists. The knights, dressed in full armour, with painted shields and waving plumes, met each other and fought as they would in battle. Each wore the badge of his lady-love in his helmet. Generally the weapons which they used were blunted, so that they could not hurt each other much, but sometimes the weapons were sharp, and the mock fight ended in wounds and death.

Round the lists were seats where fair ladies and great princes sat to watch the tournament. Each knight was eager to do great deeds, so that he might win the praise of the beautiful ladies who looked on. When the jousting, as it was called, was over, the fairest lady placed a crown of bay leaves on the head of the victor. This crown was prized more than if it had been of gold and gems, and each knight did his best to win it. It was thought that no knight could show his love and reverence for his lady better than by jousting and tilting in her name.

As Edward travelled home to England he passed through France, and near to a little town called Chalons. When the count of that place heard that the great English prince was passing through his land, he sent a message asking that they might meet in a tournament with a thousand knights on either side, lance for lance.

Far and wide Edward was known as a brave and courteous warrior, and although his knights whispered that the Count of Chalons had no love for the prince and meant to do him harm, Edward accepted the challenge, as such a message was called. Indeed it seemed to him that he was in honour bound to do so, for it was counted unknightly to refuse a challenge. Great preparations were made, and on a fair day in May the plain of Chalons was gay with knights on horseback, and lovely ladies and people of all ranks in holiday dress, crowding to see the tournament.

The earth seemed to shake as Edward and his thousand splendid and brave English knights thundered over it. But the Count of Chalons came to meet them, not with one thousand men as had been agreed, but with two thousand.

Yet the English had no fear, and the tournament began. It was soon seen, however, that it was no friendly trial of strength, but a fight of bitter hate.

The count rode again and again at Edward, until his lance was splintered in his hand. Then throwing away the shaft, he seized the prince round the neck, and tried to drag him from his horse.

This, according to the rules of the tournament, was a mean and unknightly thing to do. Edward sat his horse like a rock, and, great though the strength of the French count was, he could not move him. Then suddenly Edward spurred his horse, it sprang forward, and the count, who still clung tightly to Edward, was pulled from his saddle and fell to the ground with a fearful crash.

Enraged at such unknightly behaviour, Edward leaped down and beat with the shaft of his lance upon the armour of the fallen count, heeding not his cries for mercy. As of a hammer upon an anvil, blow after blow fell, until at last the rage of the prince was spent, and he allowed the count to rise.

The count then offered his sword to the prince in token of submission, but Edward turned from him in scorn. "Nay, sir knight," he said, "this day have you proved yourself no true knight. My servants may receive your tarnished sword, I shall not touch it." So the count was obliged to give up his sword to a common soldier, which, for a true knight, was the deepest disgrace.

Meanwhile the English archers outside the lists, seeing that the French knights far outnumbered the English, and that there was no fair play, shot with their arrows at the horses of the French. Many of them fell dead, dragging their riders to the ground, where they lay helpless, trampled upon alike by friend and foe. Then the French foot-soldiers joined in the fight, and the tournament became a battle.

The English were far outnumbered, but even so they had the best of it. They took many of the French knights prisoners, making them pay large sums of money for their freedom. The common soldiers they slew because, they said, "they were but rascals and of no great account." So fierce a tournament was this that, ever after, it was called "The little war of Chalons."

CHAPTER XLI

EDWARD I.—THE LAWGIVER—THE STORY OF THE FIRST PRINCE OF WALES

SOON after "The little war of Chalons," Edward reached England. The people welcomed him with delight, and he and his beautiful queen, Eleanor, were crowned at Westminster Abbey with great splendour.

Since the days of Alfred no king had been received with such joy and love, for the people felt that Edward was truly and indeed an English king.

We think now that such names as Henry, Richard, and John are English names. But they were not known in England until after the Conquest, when they were brought into England by the French. For more than two hundred years the kings of England had borne French names, and had indeed been Frenchmen. But Edward was a Saxon name. The King had been born and had lived nearly all his life in England, he spoke the English language, and he loved his people and his country, which no king of England since Harold had truly done. Not only did Edward love his people, but he longed for their love in return, and tried to be a good king.

The feasting and rejoicing at the coronation continued for a fortnight. Many large new buildings had to be made to hold all the guests. The streets were hung with silk and embroidery. Rich men scattered handfuls of gold and silver to the people. Fountains ran with wine instead of water. For the coronation feast alone there were needed three hundred and eighty cattle, four hundred and thirty sheep, four hundred and fifty pigs, eighteen wild boars, two hundred and seventy-eight flitches of bacon, and twenty thousand fowls. Never had there been such feasting and grandeur in England.

The King of Scotland came to the coronation, and with him a hundred knights. When they got off their horses they let them go free, and any one who caught them might keep them. Seeing this, and not wishing to be outdone, the King's brother, Edmund, and three other nobles came each with a hundred knights riding upon splendid horses and, leaping down, they, too, let them go free for any one to have who would.

Edward was crowned King of England, Lord of Ireland, and Duke of Aquitaine. Aquitaine was all that remained of the great French possessions of Henry II. But Edward longed to rule over the whole island of Britain; he wanted to be Prince of Wales and King of Scotland as well as King of England.

You remember that hundreds of years before this, when the Saxons came to Britain, they gradually drove the Britons out before them, until they took refuge in the mountains of Wales. There they remained, speaking the ancient British language and having very little intercourse with the English, but often fighting with them. And the kings of England, ever since the days of Edward the Confessor, had from time to time forced the Welsh to own them as over-lords.

When Edward came to the throne he sent for Llewellyn, Prince of Wales, to come to do homage; that is, to own him as over-lord. Llewellyn would not come. Six times did Edward send. Still Llewellyn refused.

This made Edward very angry and, hearing that a beautiful lady was coming from France to be married to Llewellyn, he seized her and kept her prisoner in London. He then sent messengers to the Prince of Wales, telling him that he should have his bride when he had done homage, and not till then. Llewellyn, instead of submitting, was furiously angry. He raised an army and marched against Edward. But brave little Wales could not do much against great England. The Welsh were soon defeated and scattered, and their prince starved into submission in his castle on Snowdon. But as soon as Llewellyn did homage to Edward as over-lord, the king acknowledged him as Prince of Wales, and not only let him have his bride but made a great wedding-feast for her and gave her many presents. So there was peace.

But peace did not last long.

In the days when Arthur was king, Merlin, his wise councillor, had foretold that when money should be round, a Prince of Wales should be crowned in London. Before the time of Edward I. there was very little money of any kind. When the people wanted to give change, they took a large piece of money and cut it into two or three or four pieces, just as they liked. This of course made it easy to cheat with money, for, when a coin was cut up, it became difficult to know whether it really was a coin or not.

Edward made a law forbidding people to cut coins into pieces, and he had pennies and small silver coins made, in order that people could give change. So money was round, instead of being all sorts of shapes as it had been.

The Welsh thought that the time of which Merlin had spoken had now come, and they began to fight with the English, hoping to conquer them and to see Llewellyn crowned in London.

But the Welsh were again defeated, and this time Llewellyn was killed. In the cruel fashion of those days his head was cut off and sent to London. There it was crowned with a silver crown and carried through the streets on a spear, and at last it was set upon the Tower, wreathed with willow. Then the English laughed unkindly, saying that the prophecy was fulfilled.

Sad and overcome, the Welsh once more owned England's king as lord, but, when the barons came to do homage to Edward, he promised to give them a Welsh prince as ruler, one who had been born in Wales, and who could neither speak French nor English. On the day appointed, when the barons gathered to do homage to this new ruler, Edward appeared before them carrying in his arms his little baby son, who had been born at Caernarvon Castle only a few days before. He was truly a prince who could neither speak French nor English, nor indeed any other language.

This little prince was named Edward, like his father. Ever since that time, the eldest son of the King of England has been called the Prince of Wales, and England and Wales have formed one kingdom.

CHAPTER XLII

EDWARD I.—THE HAMMER OF THE SCOTS

WHEN Edward had joined Wales to England, he longed more than ever to gain possession of Scotland. It seemed, too, as if he might succeed in doing this, for the King of Scotland died, and the heir to the throne was a little princess called the Maid of Norway.

Edward I. arranged with the people of Scotland that this princess should marry his son Edward, Prince of Wales, and in that way England and Scotland would be peaceably joined together. But unfortunately, on her way from Norway to claim the crown of Scotland, the princess died. So Edward's hopes of joining the two countries together in that way were at an end.

After the death of the Maid of Norway, twelve Scottish nobles claimed the crown, and, as they could not agree as to who had really the best right to it, they asked Edward, who was known to be a wise and just man, to settle the question.

Edward said that a man called John Balliol had the best right to the crown of Scotland, and John was accordingly crowned at Scone, the town where all the kings of Scotland were crowned.

But before Edward said that John was the real heir, he made him promise to own the King of England as over-lord.

Edward had no right to demand this homage, and John Balliol had no right to give it. But John did give it. Perhaps he thought, if he did not, Edward would choose some one else.

The Scots had always been a warlike people, and, ever since the days of the Romans, they had fought with the people in the south part of the island, and had tried to take away part of their land. At last it had been agreed between the kings of England and Scotland that the Scots should be allowed to keep part of the north of England, on condition that they did homage for that part, just as the Norman kings of England did homage to the King of France for Normandy and their other French possessions. But the King of England had no more right over Scotland than the King of France had over England.

The people of Scotland were very far from agreeing to John Balliol's bargain with Edward, and in less than a year quarrels began, and war followed. Edward marched into Scotland with a great army, and although the Scots were in the right and fighting for their freedom, Edward was the stronger, and the Scots were defeated.

Edward, thinking he had conquered the Scots, went back to England, taking with him the crown and sceptre of Scotland, and also the "Stone of Destiny" on which the Scottish kings sat when they were crowned. This stone was supposed to be the very stone which Jacob used as a pillow when he slept in the wilderness and saw the vision of the ladder up to heaven, with the angels going up and down upon it. The Scots prized this stone very highly, and it had been prophesied that wherever it was, there the kings of Scotland would be crowned.

"Unless the fates are faithless found,
And prophet's voice be vain,
Where'er this monument is found,
The Scottish race shall reign."

Edward took the Stone of Destiny to Westminster, and there it remains to this day, and it is always used when the kings of Britain are crowned.

Besides taking these treasures away, Edward caused many of the old Scottish records to be destroyed, hoping in that way to make the people forget their freedom. But all this only made the Scots more determined not to submit to the King of England. Their weak king, John Balliol, had been driven from the throne, but other brave leaders arose, and wars between England and Scotland continued until Edward died in 1307 A.D.

Edward died while on his way to fight once more against Scotland. He was within sight of its blue mountains, and he died knowing that its people were still free, and that his dearest wish was not fulfilled. The disappointed king begged his son to go on with the war, to carry his bones with the army, and bury his heart in Scotland.

But Edward II. did not do as his father wished. He turned back to London, and Edward I. lies buried in Westminster, where you may still see his grave with these lines upon it in Latin: "Here lies Edward I., the Hammer of the Scots, 1308. Keep troth."

Edward I. has many names: Edward of Westminster, because he was born there; Edward Longshanks, because he was very tall and his legs were long and thin; Edward, the Hammer of Scots, because of the many battles he fought with them; but the name by which it is best to remember him is Edward, the Lawgiver. He earned this name by the many wise laws which he made. Although his people were not always pleased with these laws at first, they generally came to see that they were just and good.

Edward was a great soldier and a valiant knight, but it was because he loved England and made good laws, because he was a true man and kept his word, that his people loved him, and mourned for him when he died.

"All that are of heart true,
A while hearken to my song
Of douleur that death hath dealt us new
That maketh me sigh and sorrow among;

Of a knight that was so strong
Of whom God hath done His will:
Methinks that death hath done us wrong
That he so soon shall lie still.
"All England ought to know
Of whom that song is that I sing;
Of Edward, king that lieth so low,
Though all the world his name did spring
Truest man in everything,
And in war wary and wise
For him we ought our hands to wring,
Of Christendom he bare the prize.
"Now is Edward of Caernarvon
King of England in his right,
God never let him be worse man
Than his father, not less of might.
To hold his poor man to right,
And understand good council,
All England to rule and direct
Of good knights there need not him fail.
"Though my tongue were made of steel,
And my heart smote out of brass,
The goodness might I never tell
That with King Edward was.
King, as thou art called conqueror,
In each battle thou hadest the prize;
God bring thy soul to the honour
That ever was and ever is
That lasteth aye without end,
Pray we God and our Lady
To that bliss Jesus us send."

CHAPTER XLIII

EDWARD II. OF CAERNARVON—THE STORY OF KING ROBERT THE BRUCE AND BOHUN

WHEN Edward, the first Prince of Wales, was young, he had a French friend called Piers Gaveston. Piers was tall and handsome and gay, but he was wicked. He led the prince into all kinds of mischief until at last King Edward I. put his son in prison for a time, and banished Piers from the kingdom.

When Edward lay dying he begged his son never to bring Piers back again. The Prince of Wales promised, but, as soon as his father was dead, he broke his word and sent for Piers. Edward II. made Piers Earl of Cornwall, and married him to a great lady. Then leaving him to rule England the King crossed to France to marry the beautiful Princess Isabella.

The English barons were very angry at again having a foreigner to rule. They hated Piers, and Piers laughed at and insulted them. He called them all sorts of names, such as "the Jew," "the actor," "the black dog," and "the hog."

Piers made Edward II. do many wicked things. The King filled the court with bad and foolish people like himself, sending away the wise men who had helped Edward I. to rule.

At last the hatred of the barons grew so fierce that they forced Edward to send Piers away, and when after a time Edward brought him back, they seized him and put him to death.

Edward was very angry with the barons for killing Piers, and he was sad too, for he had really loved his friend. He was too weak a king, however, to punish the barons, so he was obliged to pretend that he forgave them. But he did not become a better king, even after his favourite was dead.

Meanwhile the Scots were fighting against the English, and driving them out of Scotland. A king, called Robert the Bruce, was now upon the throne, and under him the Scots fought so bravely that soon the English had lost all the Scottish towns which they had, except Stirling. The castle of Stirling was strong, and the English soldiers within it brave. But the Scots were brave too, and determined, for they were fighting for their freedom and their country. At last the governor, feeling that he could hold out no longer, promised to yield the castle on 24th June 1314 A.D., if before then no help came to him.

When Edward II. heard that Stirling was in danger, he at last roused himself. He gathered a great army of English, Irish, Welsh, and French, barons and men of high degree, with their servants and followers—a hundred thousand men in all. Such a splendid army as now marched over the border had never before been seen in Scotland.

As they passed through the country to Stirling, fear filled the hearts of the women and children. They thought of their husbands, and fathers and brothers who were gathered at Stirling to meet this great army, and wept for them as lost.

The whole of Robert the Bruce's army numbered less than forty thousand men, and they were neither so well drilled nor so well armed as the English. But King Robert was a great soldier and a wise general. He knew that he could only hope to defeat the English by using his brain as well as his sword and battle-axe. Therefore he chose the position of his army with great care. In front there lay marshes, through which the English would have to ride in order to reach the Scots, who were drawn up upon the dry plain beyond. Where the ground was firm, Bruce made his men dig pits about three feet deep. These pits were filled with twigs and branches of gorse, and the turf was then laid over them again, so that from a distance it seemed like a firm and level plain.

On one side of King Robert's position rose the steep castle hill, and on the other flowed the little stream called the Bannock. Only from the front could the English attack, and the front was guarded by pits and marshes.

Not till the 23rd of June, the very day before the governor had promised to give up the castle, did King Edward appear and camp opposite the Scottish army.

When King Robert heard that the English were near he drew up his army in battle array ready to fight, although he did not expect to do so that day.

Randolph, Earl of Moray, the nephew of King Robert, was given charge of a small body of horsemen, and told that he must stop any of the English who might try to get into Stirling. For it might have been very bad for the Scots had the English been able to take a strong position there.

The Scottish leaders stood watching the advance of the English, when King Robert's eye caught the gleam of armour away to the east. Turning to his young nephew he said, "Ah, Randolph, a rose has fallen from your crown." By this he meant that Randolph had missed a chance of making himself famous. For a party of English horsemen were quietly stealing towards Stirling, and Randolph, who had been told to prevent this, had not noticed.

Too ashamed to reply Randolph called to his men and dashed upon the English. They turned and charged Randolph so fiercely that Douglas, another of the Scottish leaders, begged to be allowed to go to his help.

"No," replied King Robert, "let Randolph win back the honour which he has lost, or die. I cannot risk the whole battle because of a careless boy. Leave him."

So Douglas waited and watched. It seemed to him as if the little company of Scotsmen were being swallowed up by the English horsemen.

Then Douglas could bear it no longer. "My Lord King, I pray you, let me go," he said. "Randolph and his men are sore pressed. I cannot stand idly by and see him die." And scarcely waiting for permission Douglas rode off.

But, as he came near to Randolph, he saw that the English were giving way. "Halt," he called to his men. "Randolph has no need of our help. We will not take the honour from him." And without striking a blow, he and his men turned and rode back to the King.

Soon the English horsemen were seen flying from the field, and Randolph, joyful and victorious, returned to his place. He had recovered the rose which had fallen from his crown.

Meanwhile the rest of the English army was steadily advancing. King Robert the Bruce, mounted upon a little brown pony and wearing a gold crown upon his helmet, rode up and down in front of his army, watching everything, commanding and encouraging. His armour was light, and for a weapon he carried only a battle-axe.

Seeing King Robert so lightly armed, an English knight, called Sir Henry de Bohun, thought he would earn a great name for himself and win the battle at one blow. So setting spurs to his horse he rushed upon the King at full speed.

As the full-armed knight came thundering along on his great war-horse, King Robert, sitting firmly on his little pony, waited calmly. When Bohun reached him, when the sharp point of the spear almost touched his armour, Bruce suddenly made his pony spring to one side. The knight flashed past him. Quick as lightning Bruce turned, rose in his stirrups, and lifting his battle-axe high in the air, brought it crashing down upon the helmet of Bohun. Head and helmet were split, and without a groan Bohun fell dead to the ground, while his riderless horse galloped wildly away.

Cheer upon cheer rose from the Scottish ranks and the nobles crowded round their King, glad yet vexed with him. "My lord, my lord, is it well thus to risk your life?" they said. "Had you been killed, our cause were lost."

But the King paid no heed to them. "I have broken my good axe," was all he said, "I have broken my good axe."

CHAPTER XLIV

EDWARD II. OF CAERNARVON—THE STORY OF THE BATTLE OF BANNOCKBURN

AFTER the death of Bohun there was no more fighting that day. The sun soon set, and during the short summer night the two armies lay opposite each other, silently waiting for the dawn.

When day broke, the whole plain was astir. Trumpets sounded, drums beat, and as the English army advanced, they seemed to roll onward like mighty waves. "No hand but God's can save us from so great a host," said the Scots. And, as a holy abbot with bare feet and head passed along the lines to bless them, they knelt in prayer.

"See," cried King Edward, "they kneel! they ask for mercy!"

"True," replied the knight to whom he spoke, "they ask for mercy, but from Heaven, not from us. These men will conquer, or die on the field."

The fight began and long and fiercely it raged. The Scottish horse scattered the English archers, and the English horse fell into the pits which Bruce had caused to be dug. The English army was already in confusion when suddenly, over the brow of a neighbouring hill, there appeared what seemed to them another Scottish army.

Then the English fled. Blind with fear they rode, hardly knowing where. Many were drowned while trying to cross the river Forth, others fell over the rocky banks of the Bannock till the stream was choked with the dead.

The new army which had so frightened the English was no army at all, but only the servants and camp-followers whom Bruce had separated from the soldiers and sent to wait behind the hill. They had grown tired of watching and doing nothing, so they tied cloths on to poles for banners, armed themselves with sticks, and came to join the fight. They came just at the right time, for the English, already beginning to feel that the battle was lost, fled before this new host.

Edward, although he was no coward, fled too. He went first to Stirling, but the Governor would not let him stay there. "Have you forgotten, my lord," he said, "that to-morrow I must yield up the castle to the King of Scots? If you remain here you will become his prisoner."

So Edward rode south, attended only by a few knights. One brave man rode with the King until he thought he was safe, then drawing rein, "Farewell, my liege," he said, "I am not wont to flee," and turning he rode back, and fell fighting with his face to the enemy.

The King fled on, and he had need to flee fast. For, when it became known that he had left the field, he was hotly pursued as far as Dunbar, which was still in the hands of the English. From there he went in a little fishing-boat to Berwick and so reached England and safety.

"So eagerly he was pursued,
They got to him so near,
He was on point of being ta'en,
But got into Dunbar.
"To Berwick in a fishing boat
They sculled him away,
While to be kept from wrath of Scots
He earnestly did pray."

Upon the field many of England's noblest men lay dead, many were wounded, many taken prisoner. So much spoil fell into the hands of the Scots, and so much money was paid to them as ransom for their prisoners, that it was said that Scotland became rich in one day. Scotland became not only rich but free in one day, for if the battle of Bannockburn did not quite end the war, it showed what Scotsmen loving their country could do, and in the dark days which were still to come they never again despaired.

The battle of Bannockburn is the greatest battle ever fought on Scottish ground. It is great not because so many noble men fell upon the field; but because at one blow it made the Scots free.

Beaten and angry Edward returned to England, and the rest of his life was dark and miserable. He ruled so badly that at last the nobles put him from the throne, and crowned his little son, who was also called Edward.

Edward II., King no longer, was sent as a prisoner from castle to castle. No one loved or cared for him, and each new goaler treated the poor, fallen King worse than the last, till one night terrible shrieks rang through the castle in which he was imprisoned. In the morning Edward II. was found dead. He had been murdered.

CHAPTER XLV

EDWARD III. OF WINDSOR—THE STORY OF THE BATTLE OF SLUYS

WHEN Edward III. was made king in 1327 A.D., he was only fourteen. He was too young to rule, and the power was really in the hands of his mother, Queen Isabella, and of a man called Roger Mortimer, Earl of March. Both the Queen and the Earl were wicked, so it was a sad time for England. There was fighting with Scotland, fighting with France, sorrow and misery at home.

When Edward was eighteen he resolved that he would no longer be king in name only. He took the Earl of March prisoner, tried him for the wicked thing he had done, and condemned him to death.

Queen Isabella he shut up in a castle, and would not allow her to rule the kingdom any more. But he gave her money to spend, and he went once every year.

King Edward then really began to reign. He made peace with France, and, I am sorry to say, war again with Scotland. But after fighting there for some time he left Scotland, and began to fight again with France.

The war which now began is called the "Hundred Years' War," because it lasted, with times of peace between, for a hundred years. It began because Edward said that he had a right to be King of France as well as King of England. He said this was so because his mother, Queen Isabella, was the sister of King Charles IV. of France, who had died, leaving no son to succeed him. But the French had a law by which women were not allowed to wear the crown, so Edward had really no right to it. He could not receive from his mother what had never been hers. King Philip VI., who now had the crown, would, of course, not give it up, so a fierce and bitter war began.

The first great fight was at sea. Edward sailed from England with a fleet of about three hundred ships. As he came near to Sluys, a town in Flanders, he saw such a number of masts that it seemed as if a forest had come sailing out to sea.

"What ships are these?" said King Edward to the captain of his vessel.

"They are the ships of the King of France," replied the captain. "They have oftentime plundered your coasts. They lately burned the town of Southampton and took your good ship the *Christopher.*"

"Ah, I have long wished to meet them," replied the King. "Now, please God and St. George, we will fight them; for in truth they have done me so much mischief, I will be revenged upon them if possible."

Edward's wife, Queen Philippa, was at Ghent, and Edward had many ladies on board who were going to join her there. So he arranged his vessels with great care, for he knew that the French had far more men and ships than he had. He put the ladies in the safest place, and guarded them carefully with a large body of archers and soldiers.

As the sun and wind were both against Edward, he lowered his sails and moved round so that the sun should be behind him. The French seeing this thought that he was afraid, and that he was running away. They had been waiting for the English in strong battle array. All their ships were fastened together with heavy chains so as to make it impossible for the English ships to break through their lines. Seeing the English flee, as they thought, the French unfastened the chains and made ready to pursue.

As the royal standard floated from the masthead the French knew that the King of England was with his fleet, and they hoped to take him prisoner. They filled the *Christopher*, the ship which they had taken from the English, with trumpeters and drummers and, to the sound of music and shouting, sent it to attack the English.

But the English won their own ship back again, and amid great cheering manned it with Englishmen once more.

The battle was fierce and terrible. The English were often in great danger, for the French were much the stronger, but when the battle was over there were very few Frenchmen left, and most of their ships were sunk or destroyed.

It was such a dreadful defeat that no one dared tell the King of France about it.

At last his court fool told him.

In those days great people always had some one near to amuse them by making jokes, and by laughing at everything. He was called a fool, although sometimes he was very wise and witty. But because he was called a fool he was allowed to say what he liked, and no one was angry with him.

"The English are great cowards," said the French king's fool to him one day.

"Why so?" asked the King.

"Because they have not the courage to jump into the sea and be drowned, like the French at Sluys," replied the fool.

In this way King Philip was told of the loss of all his ships, and his anger was so terrible that even his fool fled from him in fear.

CHAPTER XLVI

EDWARD III. OF WINDSOR—THE STORY OF THE BATTLE OF CRECY

SIX years after the battle of Sluys another great battle was fought between the French and English at a place called Crecy. Edward had been marching through France for some time, when he heard that King Philip was close behind him with an army of one hundred and twenty thousand men. He himself had only twenty thousand men, but he resolved to camp where he was, on a rising ground near the little French village of Crecy, and there conquer or be conquered.

On Saturday, 26th August 1346 A.D., Edward rose very early. He divided his army into three parts. One part he gave in command of his young son Edward, the Black Prince. Prince Edward took his name from the black armour which he always wore, and at this time he was only seventeen years old.

Having divided his army, King Edward, carrying a white wand in his hand and mounted upon a pony, rode slowly through the ranks, talking to the soldiers and encouraging them. He looked so cheerful and spoke so bravely, that the soldiers cheered him as he passed among them, and if any of them had felt afraid, they took heart again.

Then Edward gave orders that the men should have breakfast sitting on the ground where they were, each man in his place. So the men took off their helmets and, laying their weapons down, ate and drank as they sat upon the ground.

The King himself went to a windmill near by, and there waited and watched for the French to arrive.

When at last the French came in sight, it was about three o'clock in the afternoon. Then each man of the English rose, put on his helmet, took his weapon in his hand, and stood waiting.

King Philip meanwhile told four knights to ride quickly forward and bring back news of the English army. The English saw these knights, and saw, too, that they had come to spy, but they took no notice of them, and let them return to King Philip.

"My lords, what news?" said he, as they rode back to him.

The knights looked at each other in silence, each waiting for the other to speak first.

"Come, my lords, what news?" said the King again.

Then the bravest of the knights said, "I speak, my lord King, as you desire, and I hope that my companions will tell you if they think that I say wrong. The English are encamped in a strong place. They are well-fed and rested, and are waiting for you. Our soldiers are hungry and weary with the long march. My advice is that you halt here, let the soldiers rest to-night, and to-morrow they will be fresh and able to conquer the English."

"I thank you, my lord," replied Philip, "it is good advice and shall be followed." Then turning to his generals, "Go," he said, "command a halt."

Two generals rode off, one to the front, the other to the rear, calling out as they went, "Halt banners, in the name of God and St. Denis."

The soldiers in front halted as they were commanded, but those behind would not do so. "We shall not halt until we are as far forward as the others," they said, and they marched on. When they overtook the soldiers in front, these, feeling themselves being pushed forward from behind, moved on too, and neither the King nor the generals could stop them.

They marched on until they came close to the English. When the soldiers in front saw that they were near the English they fell back, hut those behind still pressed forward so that the confusion was great. The roads behind the French army were filled with peasants and country people armed with sticks and stones. These peasants made a great noise, and shouting "kill, kill," were eager to be at the English. They mixed with the army, and made the confusion worse still.

In a few minutes all order was lost, and King Philip, seeing that there was no help for it, decided to begin the battle at once. Beside, as soon as he saw the English, his anger against them rose so that he longed to be fighting them.

"Forward, archers, and begin the battle, in the name of God and St. Denis," he cried.

The archers advanced, shouting fiercely, in order to frighten the English.

But the English stood still. Not a man moved so much as a finger.

Again the French archers shouted.

Still the English never moved.

With a third fierce yell the French archers shot.

Then the English archers made one step forward, raised their bows, and shot arrow after arrow till it seemed as if it snowed.

When the French archers felt these terrible arrows pierce their arms, breast, head, and legs, even through the armour which they wore, they threw down their bows and fled.

These archers were not Frenchmen, but Italians, whom Philip had hired to help him in his war with the English, and when he saw them throw down their bows and run away he was dreadfully angry. "Kill these cowards," he shouted, "they do but stop the way and are of no use." So the French horsemen dashed upon the flying archers, who, having thrown down their bows, had no other weapon, and killed as many as they could, while the English poured arrows upon archers and horsemen alike.

It was a terrible battle, and to make it seem still worse, there was an eclipse of the sun and a thunderstorm while it was going on. The sky became black, thunder roared, lightning flashed, and rain fell in torrents. Great flocks of crows flew over the field caw-cawing, in such a fearful manner, that even the bravest felt afraid, and thought something dreadful was going to happen.

At this battle, too, cannon were used for the first time. Gunpowder had been invented only a short time before, and people did not yet know what a terrible thing it would become in battle. The English had four cannon. They were made of wood bound round with iron, and although perhaps they did not kill many people, they at least frightened the French, who already had so much else to make them afraid.

Meanwhile the Black Prince was fighting gallantly with his part of the army. But the French about him were so fierce that his knights began to fear for his safety. So a messenger was sent to the King, who was watching the battle from the windmill.

"Sire," said the messenger, "we entreat you to send help to the Prince, your son."

"Is my son dead?" asked the King.

"No, sire, thank God."

"Is he wounded?"

"No, sire, but he is in danger. The French are fierce about him and he is in need of help."

"Then, sir," replied the King, "if my son is neither dead nor wounded, go back to those who sent you. Tell them not to send again to me this day. Tell them that if they do I shall neither come nor send help so long as my son is living. Tell them that I command them to let the boy win his spurs, for I wish the glory of the day to be his. God will guard him."

The knight returned and told the others what the King had said, and they were sorry that they had sent any such message, and resolved to fight to the last.

Edward said that he wanted the Prince to win his spurs. By that he meant that he hoped he would do such brave deed that he might be made a knight. When any one was made a knight he received a pair of golden spurs. So when a man did a great deed worthy of a knight he was said to have "won his spurs."

The King of Bohemia was with the French army, and his son Charles was fighting for Philip. The King himself could not fight because he was blind. When he heard that the day was going against the French, he asked where his son was.

"We know not," replied the knights who were round him. "Doubtless he is in the thickest of the fight."

Really he had fled from the field, but these gallant knights would not grieve their brave old king by telling him so.

"I, too, would strike a blow," said the blind king, "Lead me into the battle." The knights fastened their horses together with the King of Bohemia in the middle, so that they might not lose him in the crowd of soldiers, and dashed into the fight. When the day was over they were all found dead together, the King still in the middle of them, and their horses still bound to each other.

In those days a knight always had a crest and motto, called a device, painted upon his shield. The crest of the King of Bohemia was three feathers and his motto was *Ich dien*, which is German and means "I serve." The arms of a fallen foe belonged to the conqueror. So when after the battle the Black Prince was made a knight, he took the motto and the crest of the King of Bohemia for his own. It has been borne ever since by the eldest son of the King of England. And that is why the Prince of Wales has a German motto.

When night fell and the terrible noise and clamour of fighting ceased, the French were beaten, and their king had fled from the field. The King of England came down from the windmill where he had remained watching the fight. He had not struck a blow, nor put on his helmet all day; not because he was a coward, but because he wanted the Black Prince to have all the praise of the victory. There, on the battle-field, he took his son in his arms and kissed him. "Dear son," he said, "God give you strength to go on as you have begun. Bravely and nobly have you fought, and you are worthy to be a king. The honour of the day is yours."

The prince bowed before his father. "I do not deserve any praise," he said, "I have only done my duty." But he had shown himself so brave that his father made him a knight. He was one of the first knights of the Order of the Garter, a new Order which Edward III. founded, and the King can bestow upon any one. You shall hear why it was called by this name.

King Edward III. loved the stories of Arthur and his knights of the Round Table. He made a new Round Table and tried to bring back those knightly days, and to make his knights and gentlemen courteous and gentle. One day, at a ball, Edward picked up a lady's garter. Some one laughed rudely, but Edward turned to him and said, "Honi soit qui mal y pense," which is French and means "Evil be to him who evil thinks." "Soon," he added, "you shall see this garter set so high that you will think it an honour to wear it." And so when he founded a new order of knighthood he made it the Order of the Garter, and to this day great men are proud to wear it. It was founded on St. George's day and the ornament which the knights of the Garter wear is called the George.

CHAPTER XLVII

EDWARD III. OF WINDSOR—THE STORY OF THE SIEGE OF CALAIS

FIVE days after the battle of Crecy, Edward began to besiege the town of Calais. He did not fight, for the fortifications were so strong that he knew it would be useless. He made his men build a ring of wooden houses round Calais, in which they could live until the people of the town were starved into giving in.

When the Governor of Calais saw what Edward was doing, he gathered all the weak, poor, and old people, who were not able to fight, and sent them out of the town. He did this so that there would be fewer people to feed, and therefore the food they had in the town would last longer.

King Edward was surprised to see all these people leave the town, and he asked them what it meant, "We have no food nor money, and cannot fight," they replied, "so the Governor has sent us away."

Then Edward, instead of making them return into the town, gave them a good dinner and some money, and allowed them to go safely through his camp, to the country beyond.

For nearly a year Calais held out bravely. Day after day the people hoped that the King of France would come with his army to help them. But day after day passed and no one came. "We have eaten everything," wrote the Governor to Philip, "even the cats, and dogs, and horses, and there is nothing left for us but to die of hunger unless you come soon. You will get no more letters from me, but if you do not come, you will hear that the town is lost and all we who are in it also."

At last one morning, the watchman on the walls saw the gleam of spears, and heard the drums and trumpet-call of the French army.

When the good news was told, the joy in Calais was great. Pale and thin from want of food, hardly able to walk or stand, the people yet crowded to the walls. Oh, what joy! At last they would be free! The king had not forgotten them.

But the day passed. There was no movement in the French camp. No battle-cry was heard, no sounds of war. "To-morrow," said the men of Calais sadly, "to-morrow the king will fight. To-morrow we will open our gates to our victorious army."

But the next day and the next passed by, while the King of England strengthened his camp, and the King of France talked of peace.

Then one morning the sun shone upon the army of Philip of France, with its gay banners and glittering spears, as it turned and marched away, without having struck one blow for the town and its brave defenders.

Calais was left to misery and tears. All hope was lost. "Our king has forsaken us," said the people sadly.

When the Governor saw that there was indeed no hope, he mounted upon the walls, waving a white flag. King Edward saw the signal and sent two of his knights to talk with the Governor.

"Are you willing to give up the town?" they asked.

"Yes," replied the Governor, "we have kept the town well and truly for our king, but now we can hold out no longer. We have nothing more to eat, and we are all perishing of hunger. I will yield the town and castle, with all its riches and treasures, if King Edward will grant us our lives."

"Nay," replied the knights, "our noble King will not accept these terms. You and your people have been too stubborn in resisting him, and have cost him to much. You must give yourselves up, freely and entirely. Whom he pleases he will set free, whom he pleases he will put to death."

"These terms are too hard," replied the Governor, "we have only done our duty, we have fought for our King and master, as you have for yours. We know the King of England is noble and generous. It cannot be that he will deal so hardly with us. Go back, I entreat you, and beg him to have pity."

So the two knights rode back and told King Edward what the Governor had said.

But Edward was stern. "I will listen to no conditions," he said. "What! am I to wait twelve months, and then have the saucy rascals make conditions? No, let them yield themselves entirely into my hands."

But Edward's knights were so full of admiration for the noble men of Calais, and they begged their King so earnestly to be merciful, that at last he gave way.

"My lords," he said, "I cannot hold out against you all. Go back to the Governor; tell him to send to me six of the chief men of Calais. They must come dressed in their shirts, with bare heads and feet, with ropes round their necks, and with the keys of the castle and town in their hands. These six shall be mine to do with what I will. The rest shall go free."

One of the knights who had before spoken to the Governor, now returned and told him what the King had said.

"I beg of you," said the Governor, "to wait until I have spoken to the townspeople. It is they who must give the answer."

"I will wait," said the knight.

The Governor left the walls, and going to the market-place told the bellman to ring the great bell. At the sound of it all the people of Calais, both men and women, hurried to the town hall. They were full of wonder and hope. They knew something great must have happened. "What is it?" they asked, "what is it?"

When the people were all gathered together the Governor stood up among them and spoke. He told them of all that he had said and done, and what a hard answer the King of England had returned.

When he had finished speaking, the men groaned and the women wept. They were all worn with suffering and hunger. For weeks and weeks they had not had enough to eat, and they could no longer bear the pain of it. But, where would six men be found brave enough to give their lives for the others? Even the Governor who, all through the terrible year, had encouraged and cheered the people, now lost heart. Hiding his face in his hands he, too, burst into tears.

For a few minutes there was dreadful silence, broken only by low sobs. Then a brave man called Eustace de St. Pierre stood up. He was one of the richest and most important men of the town.

"Friends," he said, "it would be a great wrong to allow so many people to die if in any way it could be prevented. I have such faith and trust in God that I pray He will not forget me if I die to save my fellow townsmen. I offer myself as the first of the six."

When Eustace had finished speaking, the people crowded round him. They fell at his feet, they kissed his hands, they thanked and blessed him. Then, amidst the sobs and cries of the people, another and another man rose, till six of the richest merchants of Calais stood together, ready to die for their friends.

With ropes round their necks, with bare feet and heads, and carrying the keys of the town in their hands, these six brave men walked through the streets, followed by the townspeople, who wept and sobbed and blessed them as they went.

The Governor, who was hardly able to walk, rode before them, mounted upon a poor, little thin pony. When they came to the gates of the town, he commanded them to be opened, and the gates, which for a whole year had opened neither to friend nor foe, now swung wide. The Governor passed out and, with bent heads, the six men followed, feeling that they were saying farewell for ever to their beloved town. Then the heavy gates were closed again behind them.

The Governor led the way to the outer wall where the English knight still waited. There he stopped.

"As Governor of Calais," he said, "I deliver up to you these six citizens. I swear to you that they are no mean men, but the richest and greatest of our town. I beg of you, gentle sir, out of the goodness of your heart, to pray the King that he will not put them to death."

"I cannot answer for what the King will do," replied the knight, "but this I swear to you, I will do all that is in my power to save them."

Then the barriers were opened, the six brave men passed out, and the Governor slowly and sadly returned to the town.

The knight at once brought the six men of Calais to the King's tent. There they fell upon their knees, presenting the keys of the city to him. "We are yours to do with what you will," they said, "but, noble King, pity our misery and spare us."

The King looked at them darkly. He hated the people of Calais, not only because they had held out against him for so long, but because they often fought with his ships at sea and did them much damage. So, instead of listening to the prayers of the brave men, he ordered their heads to be cut off.

All the lords and knights round him begged him to have mercy, but he would not hear. The knight who had brought the men from Calais, begged hardest. "All the world will say that you have acted cruelly, if you put these men to death," he said. "They come of their own free will, and give themselves into your hands in order to save their fellows. Such a noble deed should be rewarded, not punished."

But the King only waved his hand, as if to say that he did not care what all the world said, and ordered the headsman to be sent for.

Then Queen Philippa fell upon her knees beside him, weeping. "Ah, my dear lord," she said, "I have never before asked a favour from you, but now I beg you, by the love you have to me, let these men go."

The King looked at her in silence, and tried to raise her from her knees, but still she knelt, and still she begged for the lives of these brave men.

"Ah, lady," said Edward at last, "I would you were anywhere but here, for I can refuse you nothing. Take the men. They are yours. Do with them as you please."

Then there was rejoicing indeed. The Queen led the men away to her own rooms. She ordered clothes to be given to them, and made a great feast for them. They had not had such a dinner for many months. When they were clothed and fed Queen Philippa sent them away, each with a large sum of money.

So ended the siege of Calais.

CHAPTER XLVIII

EDWARD III. OF WINDSOR—THE STORY OF THE BATTLE OF POITIERS

NINE years passed and the quarrelling between France and England still went on, and in 1356 A.D. the English, under the Black Prince, gained another great victory over the French. Philip, the King of France, had died, and his son John now reigned. He came against the English with such a great army that the Black Prince, rather than fight, offered to set free all the prisoners he had made, to give up all the French towns which he had taken, and to promise not to fight against the French for seven years.

But that did not satisfy King John. He demanded that the Prince and the whole English army should give themselves up as prisoners.

The Black Prince refused even to think of such a thing. Then King John said that he would be satisfied if the Prince and one hundred of his best knights gave themselves up. Again the Black Prince refused, and he and his men prepared to fight, and to win or die.

"My men," said the Prince, "we are only a very small body compared with the army of the French. But numbers do not always bring victory. Therefore fight manfully, and, if it please God and St. George, you shall see me this day act like a true English knight."

The Prince posted his army very cleverly. Only narrow lanes led to the place he had chosen, behind the hedges of which his archers were hidden. As the French knights rode down the lanes, the English archers shot so fast and well that the knights knew not where to turn, and soon the lanes were filled with dead and dying men and horses.

The English shouted "St. George," the French "St. Denis," and fiercely the battle raged. But, in spite of their bravery and their numbers, the French lost the day, and both King John and his son were taken prisoner.

They were led before the Black Prince, who received them very kindly, and treated them as friends rather than as prisoners. When the evening came, and supper was served, the Prince made the French king and his son take the most honoured places at table, and, instead of sitting down to eat with them, he himself waited upon them.

King John begged the Black Prince to sit down to supper with him, but he would not. "It is honour enough for me," he said, "to serve so great a king and so brave a soldier."

After the battle of Poitiers, the Black Prince remained in France for some time, then he set out for England, taking King John with him.

When King Edward heard that they were coming, he gave orders to the people of London to make the city bright and beautiful in honour of the King of France. So the houses were decked with flags and wreaths of flowers, and the people, dressed in their holiday clothes, marched through the streets in gay crowds, cheering the King of France and their own brave Prince.

King John was mounted upon a beautiful white horse, and beside him rode the Black Prince on a little black pony. It seemed as if the Prince wanted to do everything in his power to make King John forget that he was a prisoner.

But, in spite of all the kindness shown to him by King Edward and the Black Prince, John found the months during which he was kept a prisoner and unable to go back to his own dear land long and weary. At last, after four years, Edward made peace with France for a time, and set King John free on condition that he paid a large sum of money.

King John returned to his own land, but as he could not find enough money with which to pay Edward, he came back to prison, like an honourable man, and died in England.

All these wars in France had cost a great deal of money. The English people were proud of their King and Prince, and glad that they should win so many battles, and make the name of England famous; but the people had to pay for these wars. They had to pay tax after tax, and their poverty and misery grew greater year by year.

It is true the King could no longer tax the people how and when he liked, for the power of Parliament grew stronger and stronger. It was only through Parliament that the King could now get the money he required, and whenever they gave it to him they made him promise something in return. In this way, as the power of Parliament grew, the power of the King became less, and the country became really more free. But the poor, who were robbed of nearly all their money, found it difficult to understand this. So many men had been killed in the wars that there were too few to do all the work of the land. There were still slaves in England at this time, and when these slaves saw that there were not enough people to do the work, they rebelled and refused to work without wages. Other people joined them, and so there was war between rich and poor.

Besides poverty, a terrible sickness called the Black Death fell upon the land. Thousands upon thousands died until there were not enough people left in the land to sow and reap and plough. The fields lay barren, no corn was grown, and the people starved. These were very unhappy times for England.

King Edward's wars still went on, and it became more and more difficult to find money for them and, instead of always winning battles, he now often lost them.

To the sorrow of every one the brave Black Prince died. His health had been broken by the terrible hardships of his long wars in France. At last he became so ill that he could no longer sit upon his horse, nor lead his soldiers in battle, and he came home to England to die. He was buried with great pomp in Canterbury Cathedral. There his tomb is still to be seen, and over it there still hangs the black armour which he used to wear, and from which he took his name of the Black Prince.

King Edward died shortly after his son, and his long reign, which had been so brilliant and glorious, ended in darkness and misery, for the people, instead of loving and admiring their King, had grown to hate him.

CHAPTER XLIX

RICHARD II. OF BORDEAUX—THE STORY OF WAT TYLER'S REBELLION

WHEN Edward III. died in 1377 A.D., his grandson, Richard, the son of the Black Prince, became king. He was only a boy of eleven, but the people already loved him for the sake of his brave father, and there was great rejoicing when he was crowned.

Like so many other boy kings, Richard was too young to reign, and the power was really in the hands of his uncle, John of Gaunt, Duke of Lancaster. The people hoped that with a new king happier times would come for them, but they were soon disappointed, and John of Gaunt was hated as Edward had been hated in his last years.

The war with France still went on, although it became harder and harder to find money with which to pay the soldiers, and the people were taxed more and more heavily.

A new tax, called the poll-tax, had been first paid in the reign of Edward III. Poll means head, and it really was a tax upon the head of every one in the kingdom over the age of fourteen. Rich people had to pay more than poor people, still it was the poor who felt the burden most.

This tax was now made three times as heavy as it had been, and the poor were driven almost to despair. Rough, rude men were sent all over the country to gather the money. These men insulted and ill-treated the people, and at last one of them behaved so brutally to the daughter of a man called Wat, that Wat struck him on the head with his hammer and killed him.

This man Wat or Walter was a tiler of houses, and from that he was called "Wat the Tiler" or Tyler. In those days people very often took their names from the work they did.

As soon as it became known that Wat Tyler had killed a tax-collector, the people of the town flocked round him. They had been ready to rise in rebellion before, and now this action of Wat decided them. They armed themselves with any kind of weapon upon which they could lay hands—sticks, rusty swords, old bows and featherless arrows—and began to march to London. Everywhere, as they passed along through towns and villages, others joined them, and men, leaving their carts and ploughs in the fields, forsook their wives and children till, when they reached London, they were a great army of one hundred thousand men.

The chief leaders of this army were Wat Tyler, Jack Straw, and a priest called John Ball.

This priest had done a great deal towards stirring up the people against their masters. He had already been put into prison three times for preaching that all men should be equal, and that it was wicked for one man to have more money than another.

"When Adam delved and Eve span,
Who was then the gentleman?"

he asked.

Many of those who had joined Wat Tyler hardly knew what they wanted. They knew only that they were miserable and poor, and they hoped that if they saw the King he would do something to make them happy. They blamed John of Gaunt for the misery they suffered, and on the road to London they stopped all whom they met, and made them swear to be true to Richard II., and never to accept any one of the name of John as King.

When they came near London they camped upon Blackheath, and sent messengers to the King begging to be allowed to speak with him.

"You need not fear," they said, "we will do you no harm. We have always respected you, and will respect you as our King. But we have many things to say to you which you ought to hear."

"Tell them," said King Richard, "that to-morrow I will meet their leaders by the river." This answer gave the peasants great joy, and they camped for the night as best they could. They had no tents nor covering of any kind, and many of them had no supper, for they had eaten any food which they had brought with them, and had no money to buy more.

The next day the young King rowed down the river to talk to the people as he had promised. But when he saw what a great crowd there was he would not land. He sat in his boat and tried to talk to the leaders as they stood upon the bank. But they were angry because he would not land, and made such a noise that it was impossible to hear anything.

"Tell me what you want," shouted the King; "I have come to hear what you have to say."

"You must land first. Then we will tell you what we want," yelled the crowd in return.

But Richard was afraid to land, and indeed the barons and lords would not allow him to do so. So after rowing up and down the river for some time, trying in vain to make himself heard by the howling, yelling crowd on the bank, he returned to the Tower, where he was living.

When the people saw the King row away they were madly angry. They had been quiet and orderly. They were so no longer. "Let us march to London," they said, "and take it."

The Mayor of London shut the city gates, but the poor people within opened them to their friends, and the yelling crowd poured into the city.

They broke into all the shops where food was sold, eating and drinking as much as they wanted. They burned and wrecked John of Gaunt's house, called the Savoy, which was the most beautiful palace in London. Other houses and some churches were destroyed, and many people were killed. The prisons were broken open, and all the prisoners set free. Yet the rioters did not steal. They burned and threw into the river the beautiful furniture and jewels belonging to John of Gaunt, because they hated him and blamed him for their misery, but they would not allow anything to be taken away. One man who was seen to steal a piece of silver was thrown into the flames, and burned alive as a punishment by his companions. "We are not thieves and robbers," they said. "We are fighting only for truth and justice."

As the day went on, the noise grew greater and greater, and when night came the rioters collected in the square in front of the Tower. There they made a terrible noise, swearing that, if the King did not come out to them, they would burn the Tower.

The King and his friends held a council together, and Richard decided that next day he would again try to speak with the people. He sent a message to them telling them to go to an open space called Mile End, and that there he would come to speak with them in the morning.

A great many of the people, when they heard this, marched to Mile End, but others refused to go away from the Tower. Next morning, as soon as the gates were opened for the King to pass out, these rioters rushed in. They killed many of the people in the Tower, and nearly frightened the King's mother, the Princess of Wales, to death.

Meanwhile, Richard rode to Mile End, and found a great company of people awaiting him there. As soon as he was near enough he spoke to them kindly.

"My good people," he said, "I am your King. What is it you want? And what do you wish to say to me?"

"We want you to make us free for ever, both ourselves and our children. We will not be slaves any longer," they replied.

"You have your wish," answered Richard. "Now go home quietly. Leave behind you one or two men from each village. To them I will give letters signed and sealed with my seal, promising what you ask."

Then the people, who really did not know quite what they wanted, set up a great shout for the King, and went back to their homes.

Richard gave orders to about thirty secretaries, who wrote the letters as fast as they could. They sat up all night to write. These letters promised freedom to all the slaves and, as soon as they were written, they were signed and sealed with the King's seal, and given to the men who waited for them.

But Wat Tyler had not been with the rioters at Mile End, and he would not agree to go home. He wanted the King to promise much more than that there should no longer be slaves in England. Next day, while he and his followers were gathered at a place called Smithfield, the King came riding by, attended only by a few friends and soldiers.

"Here is the King," said Wat, "I will go to speak to him. You must not move until I give you a signal." He waved his hand and added, "When you see me make this sign, run forward and kill every man of them, except the King. Do not kill him, for he is young, and we can make him do what we like."

Then he set spurs to his horse, and galloped towards Richard, who was waiting to see what the rebels meant to do.

"King," said Wat, "do you see all those men there?"

"Yes," replied the King, "I do. Why do you ask?"

"Because they are all under my orders," said Wat, "and have sworn to do whatever I command them."

"I have no objection to that," replied the King, and he went on to speak quietly and peaceably to Wat Tyler, but Wat was too angry to listen. Finding that he could not quarrel with the King, he began to do so with one of the gentlemen beside him.

Hot words passed between them, till Richard growing angry turned to the Mayor of London, who was also there, and told him to seize Wat Tyler.

"Truly," said the Mayor, "it ill becomes such a rascal to use such words in the presence of the King. I will pay him for it," and raising his sword he struck Wat Tyler a blow on the head. Wat fell to the ground, the King's friends closed round him, and a minute later he was dead.

When Wat Tyler's men saw him fall, they called out, "They have killed our captain. Let us slay them all," and they ran towards the King with their bows bent ready to shoot.

Then Richard did a brave thing. Forbidding any of his men to follow him, he rode alone toward the rioters, "Friends," he said, "what are you doing? I am your King. Follow me. I myself shall be your leader."

At these words many of the rioters were ashamed. Some of them at once slipped quietly away, and Richard, putting himself at the head of the others, led them out into the country.

Meanwhile some of Richard's company had fled back into London, crying, "They are killing the King, they are killing the King."

When the people heard that, many of the King's soldiers came running together, and an army marched out to the fields to meet Richard and the rebels.

As soon as he saw them, the king left the rebels and put himself at the head of his own soldiers. Several of the nobles then wished to attack the rebels, but Richard forbade them to do so. But he ordered all the letters promising freedom, which the rioters had among them, to be given up at once on pain of instant death.

As soon as the King received the letters, he tore them up in sight of the rebels. These poor people now saw all their hopes of freedom gone. Their leader, too, was dead, so not waiting for more they broke and fled they hardly knew where. Many of them returned to their homes, but John Ball and Jack Straw were cruelly betrayed by the very men they had tried to help and free. They were beheaded by Richard's orders, along with many of their followers.

The King did not keep any of his promises to the people. "Slaves you are, and slaves you shall remain," he said savagely, when the danger to himself was over. It seemed as if the rising had been in vain. But that was not so. Many masters freed their slaves, and although years passed before all were free, Wat Tyler's rebellion was the beginning of freedom for the lower classes in England. Up to this time many of the labourers and workers who were free men had been treated almost as badly as slaves, but now their condition became better.

CHAPTER L

HOW KING RICHARD II. LOST HIS THRONE

RICHARD was only a boy of fifteen when he faced the rioters at Smithfield so bravely, and afterward broke his promises so basely. It would have been better for England if he had always been brave as he was the day he faced the rioters, and never base as he was afterward.

It was not until Richard was twenty-one that he really ruled. Until then his uncles ruled for him.

"How old do you think I am, uncle?" he said suddenly to one of them at a feast.

"Your highness is in his twenty-second year," replied he.

"Then I am surely old enough to rule. I thank you for your past help, uncle. I require it no longer." And before his uncle could recover from his surprise, Richard had asked for the great seal and keys of office, and had proclaimed to the people that in the future he himself should rule. And for a time Richard ruled well. He made peace with France, and the taxes on the poor were made lighter. But this was not for long. It was soon seen that he intended to do exactly as he liked, and would take advice from no one. He banished and outlawed those who tried to keep him in check. As he was always in need of money, he seized the lands and money of these banished people, and did many other wicked and dishonest things. At last the King, who had been placed upon the throne amid so much rejoicing, came to be hated and despised.

One of the people whom Richard had banished was his cousin, Henry of Bolingbroke, the son of his uncle, John of Gaunt. Soon after Henry had been banished John of Gaunt died, and Richard, in spite of having promised not to do so, seized his land and money.

When Henry heard of this he came back to England to take possession of his own inheritance, he said, but really to try to win the crown of England. The people had always loved Henry, and had been very sorry when he was banished, and now they welcomed him back with joy, hoping that he would free them from their hated King. Henry came with only fifteen knights, but as soon as he landed, many people flocked to him.

Richard, at this time, was in Ireland, trying to put down a rebellion there. As soon as he heard that Henry was in England he hurried home. But he was too late. Henry was already master of the country.

Richard brought a large army with him from Ireland, but many of the soldiers deserted almost as soon as they landed and joined the standard of Henry.

At last, forsaken by all, in utter despair, without food or clothes, or even a bed upon which to sleep, Richard was forced to submit to his cousin.

They met at the castle of Flint in Wales. Henry knelt to Richard as to his king and kissed his hand.

"Fair cousin of Lancaster," said Richard, looking down upon him, "you are right welcome."

"My lord," replied Henry, "I am come somewhat before my time." By which he meant that he had a right to the throne after the death of Richard, but that he had not waited until then. "But," he went on, "I will tell you the reason. Your people complain that you have ruled them badly these twenty years. Please God, I will now help you to rule them better." And the poor, broken, spiritless king replied, "Fair cousin, if it pleaseth you, it pleaseth me right well."

But when Richard was left alone he burst out in furious rage, "Would to Heaven that I had killed when I might this false cousin, this Henry of Bolingbroke."

Amid the curses of his people, forsaken even by his favourite dog which left him for Henry, Richard II. was led a prisoner to the Tower of London. There he solemnly gave up his right to the crown, and Henry of Bolingbroke was made king. This was in 1399 A.D.

Richard was afterwards sent to Pontefract Castle in Yorkshire, where, it is believed, he was cruelly murdered.

CHAPTER LI

HENRY IV. OF BOLINGBROKE—THE STORY OF THE BATTLE OF SHREWSBURY

HENRY IV. knew quite well that he was not the real heir to the throne, although he tried to make people believe that he was. The real heir was Edmund Mortimer, Earl of March.

Richard II. was the son of Edward the Black Prince, who was the eldest son of Edward III. Edmund Mortimer was descended from Lionel of Clarence, who was the third son of Edward III. Henry Bolingbroke was descended from John of Gaunt, who was the fourth son of Edward III. So, of course, Edmund Mortimer had a better right to the throne than Henry Bolingbroke had. But Edmund Mortimer was only a little boy, and, like so many other little princes, he was passed over and forgotten. The people chose rather to have a strong man who could really rule, than a little boy who could rule only in name. But Henry was afraid of Edmund, and kept him a prisoner in Windsor Castle, although he was not otherwise unkind to him.

Henry had seized the throne in an unlawful manner, and he found that it was no easy matter to keep it. No sooner was he crowned than plots thickened around him, and people who had hated Richard were now sorry that they had put Henry on the throne.

The Welsh, who had been conquered by Edward I., had never been content to live under the rule of English kings, and Owen Glendower, a Welsh nobleman, now rebelled against Henry. He called himself the Prince of Wales, claiming to be descended from Llewellyn, that Welsh prince whom Edward I. had defeated and killed.

Nearly all Wales joined Owen Glendower, and although Henry went against them with a large army, he was not able to subdue them. The Welsh took several of Henry's nobles prisoner, among them Sir Edmund Mortimer. This Sir Edmund was an uncle of the young Earl of March, whom Henry kept in prison at Windsor. Henry was quite pleased that Sir Edmund should be a captive, because he was afraid that he might at some time try to put his nephew on the throne.

The Scots had meanwhile also been fighting with the English, and had been defeated by the Earl of Northumberland and his young son, who was called Harry Hotspur. He was called Hotspur because he was so quick and brave in battle.

Harry Hotspur and his father had taken the Scottish leader, Douglas, prisoner. They expected to get a large ransom from the Scots for him. But Henry said the Douglas must be given up to him. This made the Percies, as

Harry Hotspur and his father were called, very angry. They thought that, as they had taken the Douglas prisoner, they had a right to the money which would be paid for his release.

The Percies then asked Henry to send money to Owen Glendower to ransom Edmund Mortimer, for Edmund was Harry Hotspur's dear friend. But Henry refused. He did not wish Edmund to be free, because he was afraid of him. This refusal made the Percies still more angry.

The Percies had helped to put Henry on the throne, but now they became so angry with him that they were sorry that they had done so, and they turned against him.

Instead of giving up the Douglas to Henry, the Percies set him free, on condition that he should help them to fight against the King. They made friends with Owen Glendower, who set Edmund Mortimer free, and persuaded him also to join them against Henry.

When the King heard of this great rebellion, he marched with a large army to Shrewsbury, and there he defeated the Percies before Owen Glendower could come with his soldiers to their help.

King Henry had been told that some of the rebel nobles had sworn to kill him, so he went into battle in plain armour, while four or five knights went dressed like the King. These knights were all killed, Douglas himself killing three of them. "I marvel to see so many kings rise thus one after the other," he said. "I have this day slain three."

But the real king was not among them, although he was in the battle fighting bravely.

The Prince of Wales, or Prince Hal, as he was often called, was only a boy, but he did great deeds at this battle, and even when he had been badly wounded, he would not leave the field until victory for his father was sure.

Harry Hotspur was killed, the Douglas taken prisoner, and so with this one battle the rebellion was almost at an end.

Henry next marched against Owen Glendower, but still he could not subdue him. Owen fought against Henry all his life, and at last died among the lonely mountains of Wales, still free and still unconquered.

Henry IV. had a very unquiet reign; he was in constant fear of rebellion in England, and besides the Welsh, the Scots and the French were always fighting with him. But a great misfortune fell upon the Scottish king, which forced him to make peace with Henry.

The Scots and the French had always been good friends, and now King Robert III. sent his little son, James, to France to learn French. But while on his way there his ship was captured by the English, and Prince James, who was only nine years old, was taken a prisoner to London.

Henry was very glad to have Prince James in his power, for the Scots were now afraid to fight against him in case he should do some harm to their little Prince.

"If the Scots had been kind," said Henry, "they would have sent their Prince to me. I could teach him the French language as well as any Frenchman."

When the King of Scotland heard that his son had fallen into the hands of his enemy, he was so sad and afraid that he died of a broken heart.

The King's brother, the Duke of Albany, wanted to rule Scotland himself, so he was pleased that James was a prisoner, and did not try to make Henry set him free.

Although King Henry kept Prince James in prison, he allowed him to have books and teachers, who taught him many things which were afterwards useful to him, and helped him to become a good king. He also wrote some very beautiful poetry while he was in prison, so those years were not altogether lost.

CHAPTER LII

HENRY IV. OF BOLINGBROKE—THE STORY OF HOW PRINCE HAL WAS SENT TO PRISON

PRINCE HAL was clever and brave, but he was so wild and fond of fun that he was called "Madcap Hal." He spent a great deal of time with gay companions and often got into mischief.

One day a servant of Prince Hal, having done something wicked, was taken before the Lord Chief-Justice Gascoigne to be tried and punished. When Prince Hal heard about it he was very angry, and went at once to the court-house. He strode up to where his servant was standing, and turning to the officer beside him, "Take off these fetters," he said. "Let my man go free. How dare you arrest my servant?"

"My lord Prince," said Judge Gascoigne calmly, "your servant has broken the law, and must be punished by the law. If you wish to save him, you must go to the King, your father, and beg mercy from him. He can grant it if he thinks fit. Now, I pray you leave the court, and allow me to deal as I think just with the prisoner."

Prince Hal was very angry at being spoken to like this. He was so angry that he hardly knew what he was doing, and, springing forward, he struck the judge in the face.

The people in the court were dumb with astonishment and fear. What would happen next no one knew. The Prince was in such a passion that they were afraid he might kill the judge.

But Judge Gascoigne sat quite still and unmoved. "Sir," he said sternly to the Prince, "remember that I am here in place of the King, your lord and father. In his name I charge you to give up your sword. For your contempt and disobedience I send you to prison. There you shall remain until the will of the King, your father, shall be known."

At these calm, grave words, the Prince was ashamed. All his anger vanished and, taking off his sword, he bowed humbly to the judge, and went quietly to prison.

As soon as the Prince had gone, some of his servants ran to tell the King what had happened. They expected him to be very angry with the judge. But, after hearing the story, the King sat silent for a few minutes. Then he said, "I thank God that He has given me a judge who does not fear to do justice, and a son who can obey the law."

Towards the end of his troubled reign, Henry IV. was often ill, and although very unwilling to do so, he was obliged to allow Prince Hal to help in ruling the kingdom. Once, while the King was ill, Prince Hal came into his room, and finding him lying very still and quiet thought that he was dead. The crown was beside the King's bed and the Prince lifted it, put it on his own head, and went away.

But the King was not dead, and when he awoke and found that the crown was gone, he was greatly alarmed. He called to his nobles, who were in a room near, "Why have you left me alone? Some one has stolen the crown."

The nobles came running to the King. "The Prince was with you, my lord, while you slept," they said; "he must have taken the crown."

"The Prince took it?" said the King. "Go, bring him here."

When he was told that the King was not dead, Prince Hal returned at once. With tears in his eyes he knelt beside his father's bed. "I never thought to hear you speak again," he said.

And the King replied sadly:—

> *"Thy wish was father, Henry, to that thought:*
> *I stay too long by thee, I weary thee;*
> *Dost thou so hunger for my empty chair,*
> *That thou wilt needs invest thee with mine honours*
> *Before thy hour is ripe? O foolish youth!*
> *Thou seek'st the greatness that will overwhelm thee."*

"Oh, pardon me, my liege," said Prince Hal, weeping; and the King pardoned and blessed him before he died.

> *"How I came by the crown, O God, forgive,*
> *And grant it may with thee in true peace live."*

CHAPTER LIII

HENRY V. OF MONMOUTH—THE STORY OF THE BATTLE OF AGINCOURT

WHEN Prince Hal came to the throne in 1413 A.D., he gave up all his wild ways and tried to rule as a wise king should. Judge Gascoigne was much afraid that he would suffer now for having sent the Prince to prison. But Henry had a noble mind. He knew that the judge had only done what was right. So after he became king, Henry treated Judge Gascoigne as a friend, and when he gave up his judgeship it was because he was a very old man. "Still be my judge," he said, "and if I should ever have a son who does wrong, I hope you will punish him as you did me."

"Therefore still bear the balance and the sword:
And I do wish your honours may increase,
Till you do live to see a son of mine
Offend you, and obey you, as I did.
So shall I live to speak my father's words—
'Happy am I, that have a man so bold,
That dares do justice on my proper son;
And no less happy, having such a son,
That would deliver up his greatness so
Into the hands of justice.' "

Henry came peacefully to the throne, but he had no better right to it than his father had. There were many people who could not forget that, and it was not long before plots were formed. But Henry put down these plots, and then he thought of fighting with France.

You remember how Edward III. had claimed to be King of France as well as King of England, and how he did indeed conquer a great part of France. But at the end of his reign, and during the reigns of Richard II. and Henry IV., all that he had conquered had again been lost. Of the many French lands which had at one time belonged to England, only the town of Calais remained.

Henry V. made up his mind to try to win back these lands. He thought that if the plots against him became too strong, and he were driven from the throne of England, he could then still be King of France.

The eldest son of the King of France was called the Dauphin, just as the eldest son of the King of England is always called the Prince of Wales.

At this time the King of France was mad, so the Dauphin ruled. When he heard that Henry V. was coming to fight against him he sent a present of some tennis balls.

"Tell the English king," he said to his messenger, "that he is too young and foolish to claim dukedoms here. It will be better for him to amuse himself at home with these balls."

Henry laughed when he received the present and sent back this message:—

> *"And tell the pleasant prince, this mock of his*
> *Hath turned his balls to gun stones."*

Henry gathered his army and, landing in France, laid siege to the town of Harfleur. The town held out bravely for a long time, and, when at last it fell, the English army was so worn out, so many of them had been killed and wounded, that they were not strong enough to fight any more. Yet Henry did not want to return to England having only taken one French town. He resolved to march from Harfleur to Calais, and sail home from there. He would show the French that the English were not afraid of them.

So the army left Harfleur and, day after day, ragged, hungry, and worn, they marched along the weary way towards Calais. Day after day passed, but no French soldiers ever came in sight, till one evening, when they had gone about half the long journey, the enemy appeared. Even then, weary and worn though the English were, the French did not think themselves strong enough to attack, and fell back before them. But about forty miles from Calais Henry found the French army right across his path. If Calais was to be reached, the French must be beaten. And Calais had to be reached, as it was the only way home, and Henry's men were utterly weary and almost starving.

On the morning of the battle, Henry rode along the lines, cheering his poor tired soldiers. He had a gold crown upon his helmet, and the coat which he wore over his armour was embroidered with the leopards of England and the lilies of France, for already he called himself King of France and England.

As Henry rode along he heard one of his nobles say, "I would that some of the thousands of warriors, who lie idle this day in England, were here to aid us."

"Nay, replied the King, "I would not have one man more. If we win, the greater is the glory God gives to us. If we die, the less is the loss to England."

When Henry had ridden all along the lines, he got off his horse and took his place among his soldiers, with the royal standard waving over him.

The fight began, and a terrible fight it was. It seemed as if it were the story of Crecy and Poitiers over again. The French had an army ten times greater than that of the English; many of the English, too, were sick and ill, weary, ragged and half fed, and yet they won the battle.

When it was over, Henry, riding across the field, met one of the French heralds. "To whom does the victory belong?" he asked.

"To you, sire," replied the man.

"Nay," said the King, "but to God. We English made not this great slaughter. What fortress is that?" he added, "for it is fitting that the battle should have a name."

"That is the castle of Agincourt, sire," replied the herald.

"Then Agincourt shall this battle be called," said Henry. And by that name we know it.

This was one of the greatest battles ever fought between the French and English but, although the English won, the army was too worn out to do more, and so they went home to England.

But Henry soon gathered another army, and returned to France. There was more fighting till at last, five years later, peace was made, and Henry married Catherine, the daughter of the French king.

It was arranged that King Charles who, you remember, was mad, should keep the title of king while he lived, but that Henry should rule, and that when Charles died, Henry should be King of France.

But about two years after this, Henry himself died. He was only thirty-four and had reigned but ten years. He was a wise king and ruled well, yet his great battles are what we hear most of in his reign, and they brought suffering and sorrow to many of his people. Still his people loved him, and their grief at his death was great.

"Henry the fifth, too famous to live long.
England ne'er lost a king of so much worth,
England ne'er had a king until his time.
Virtue he had deserving to command:
His brandished sword did blind men with his beams:
His arms spread wider than a dragon's wings:
His sparkling eyes replete with wrathful fire
More dazzled and drove back his enemies,
Than mid-day sun fierce bent against their faces.
What should I say? his deeds exceed all speech.
He ne'er lift up his hand but conquerèd."

CHAPTER LIV

HENRY VI. OF WINDSOR—THE STORY OF THE MAID OF ORLEANS

WHEN Henry V. died in 1422 A.D., his son, who was also called Henry, was only a tiny baby nine months old. Yet the people had loved Henry V. so much that they chose that this tiny baby should be called their King. Of course a baby nine months old, who could not even speak, could not rule, so his uncle, the Duke of Gloucester, ruled instead. Queen Catherine, the baby's mother, married a Welsh gentleman called Owen Tudor, and took no part in ruling the kingdom.

For a little time things seemed to go well, but soon troubles began. Charles, the mad King of France, died about two months after the death of Henry V., and the baby Henry VI. was proclaimed King of France in his place. "May God grant long life to Henry, by the grace of God, King of France and England," cried the heralds. But the Dauphin, Charles, felt that he was the rightful heir, and he, too, called himself King of France.

The baby king of course did not know anything about what was happening, but his uncle John, Duke of Bedford, who ruled France for him, was very angry with the Dauphin and began to fight with him.

The English were so strong that at first they defeated the French armies, and the Dauphin was in despair.

The Scots had been helping the French. To stop them doing so, the English said that they would set their King free if they would promise not to help the French any more. You remember that King James, when he was a little boy, had been taken prisoner by Henry IV., and he had now been in prison for nineteen years.

While in prison James had seen a beautiful lady, from his window, as she walked in the garden of the palace. He loved her, although he had never spoken to her, nor heard her speak. James was a poet as well as a king, and he wrote some beautiful poetry about her.

"And therewith cast I down my eyes again,
Where as I walking saw beneath the tower,
Full secretly, new coming her to play,
The fairest and the freshest young flower
That ever I saw, methought, before that hour,
For which sudden surprise, anon did start
The blood of all my body to my heart.

"And when she walkèd had a little time
Under the sweet green branches bent,

Her fair, fresh face as white as any snow,
She turned has, and forth her way she went.
But then began my sickness and torment,
To see her go and follow not I might,
Methought the day was turned into night.

"Bewailing in my chamber thus alone,
Despairing of all joy and remedy,
Oft weary of my thoughts and woe begone,
Unto the window would I walk in haste,
To see the world and the folk who went forbye,
As for the time, though I of mirthe's food
Might have no more, to look it did me good."

As soon as James was free, he married this beautiful lady and went back to Scotland with her. But before he went the English made him pay a large sum of money in return for all that had been spent on him while he was in prison. He also promised not to help the French in their battles with the English.

So this is why the Scots could no longer fight for the French. But other help came to them. They found a great leader who brought them victory. This great leader was a woman.

In a peaceful little village, far away from the sounds of war, lived a peasant girl called Jeanne d'Arc or as we call her in English, Joan of Arc. She had never been to school. She could neither read nor write. Ever since she had been quite a little girl she had had to work hard all day long in the fields and in the house. But although she was ignorant, Joan was gentle and good, and her heart was full of love for her country.

From time to time stories of battle and loss and death, were brought to the little village by sick and wounded soldiers from the battle-fields. As Joan listened to these stories, tears filled her eyes, and a great longing grew in her heart to do something for her dear country.

She spent long days alone in the fields taking care of her master's sheep. While she watched the sheep, she kept thinking and longing. "What can I do?" she said to herself. "I am only a poor, ignorant girl; what can I do for my country?"

At last it seemed to her as if the empty air around her was full of voices, which answered her question. It seemed to her that saints and angels came to her and whispered that she was chosen to free France.

"Put on the courage and the armour of a man," said the voices, "and lead the armies to victory."

When Joan told people that God had chosen her as captain, they thought at first that she was mad. But she was so earnest and so sure that at last they took her to the Dauphin.

Dressed like a man in shining white armour, riding upon a beautiful white horse, and carrying a white banner sewed with the gold lilies of France, she looked so beautiful and so good that the Dauphin and the soldiers could not but believe in her.

So this peasant girl, who knew nothing of war, who had never before worn armour, nor carried a sword, nor ridden upon a horse, took command of the army. The rough soldiers honoured, obeyed and almost worshipped her. New hope sprang up in their hearts, new strength to fight.

So full of courage were they now, that in less than a week fortune changed, the English began to lose and the French to win. Joan's first fighting was at Orleans, which had been besieged by the English for some months. Joan beat the English and drove them away, and because of that she was afterwards often called the Maid of Orleans. Battle after battle was fought, town after town was taken from the English, until about two months from the time Joan began to fight, the French were so completely victorious that the Dauphin was crowned at Rheims.

It was a very splendid sight. The church was crowded with knights and nobles and rejoicing people, but no one rejoiced more than the Maid of Orleans. Dressed still in her beautiful white armour, holding her white banner in her hand, she stood beside the Dauphin as the crown was placed upon his head and he was proclaimed King of France instead of the little English King Henry VI.

Then when all was over Joan begged to be allowed to go home again to tend sheep once more and to be with her brothers and her sisters. "They would be so glad to see me," she said, "my work here is done."

But the King would not let her go. The English still remained in the country and fighting still went on. So Joan, as she was not allowed to go home, went on fighting too. But one sad day, during a battle, she was wounded and taken prisoner by the English.

The English were very glad of this, because they thought that she was a witch. In those days people still believed in witches and were very much afraid of them. The English thought that no one who was not a witch could have done the wonderful things Joan had done. After being kept in prison for nearly a year, Joan, young, beautiful, and good though she was, was burned as a witch because she had freed her country. The English did not do this wicked deed but, what was almost as bad, they allowed their friends, the Burgundians, who were French, but who had been fighting on the English side, to do it.

After this the English proclaimed Henry VI. King of France at Paris. But it was only an empty show, for he was not really King of France. Fighting still went on, but the English lost more and more till at last they had lost all the lands they had ever held in France. In 1451 A.D., only the town of Calais remained to them, and the Hundred Years' War, begun by Edward III. in

1340 A.D., came to an end.

While these things were happening in France, the baby King of England was growing up to be a man. And a very weak man he grew to be. He was pulled this way and that among his many advisers who ruled the country and quarrelled among themselves.

The lords made the King marry a French lady called Margaret of Anjou. She was very strong-willed and it was really she, more than King Henry, who ruled.

The country was in a very unhappy state. The long wars with France had cost a great deal of money and a great many lives. The people were heavily taxed in order to pay for the wars. The men who were taken away for soldiers very often never came home again. There were not enough people in the country to do the work, and famine, disease, and all kinds of misery followed.

At last the people rebelled, just as they had rebelled in the time of Richard II. under Wat Tyler. This time their leader was called Jack Cade.

It all happened very much as before. The rebels marched to London and camped upon Blackheath. A battle was fought in which the King's men were defeated. Then Jack Cade and his followers were promised what they asked. Many of them afterwards went home quietly, but Jack Cade himself was killed.

This rising lasted only a few weeks, but another struggle which lasted thirty years soon began. This struggle was called the Wars of the Roses.

CHAPTER LV

HENRY VI. OF WINDSOR—THE RED ROSE AND THE WHITE

YOU remember that Henry IV., who took the crown from Richard II., was descended from John of Gaunt, Duke of Lancaster, the *fourth* son of Edward III. But there was some one who had a better right to the throne. That was Edmund Mortimer, who was descended from the *third* son of Edward III. Now in the time of Henry VI. there was still living a descendant of Edmund Mortimer. He was called Richard, Duke of York.

The Wars of the Roses began because Richard claimed to be the rightful heir to the throne. At first Richard said he only wanted to be made protector of the kingdom because he saw how weak and easily led the King was. It seemed indeed as if the King needed a protector, for he was not only weak and foolish, but at times he was quite mad and unable even to speak for days. The Duke of York hoped that if he was protector during Henry's life, the people would make him King after Henry died.

The people would very likely have agreed to this had not a little son been born to Henry. This little son was called Edward, and many of the nobles turned from the Duke of York for his sake. Although Henry was quite unfit to rule, they hoped that his little son would grow up wise and good and more like his grandfather, Henry V.

So some of the nobles sided with the Duke of York and others with the King, and the quarrelling between them became very bad. Many at first were afraid to speak out and say openly on which side they were, but soon the quarrel grew to be so bitter that not only the nobles but the whole nation took sides.

One day while walking in the Temple gardens in London with some other nobles, Richard, Duke of York tried to persuade them to join his cause. "Ah," he said at last, "I see you are afraid to speak out. Well, then, give me a sign to show on whose side you are."

"Let him that is a true-born gentleman,
And stands upon the honour of his birth,
If he supposes that I have pleaded truth,
From off this brier pluck a white rose with me."

Saying that he pulled a white rose which grew on a bush near and stuck it in his cap.

Then the Duke of Somerset sprang forward and, tearing a red rose from another bush, said:—

"Let him that is no coward, nor no flatterer,
But dare maintain the party of the truth
Pluck a red rose from off the thorn with me."

Then one after another all the nobles who were there plucked red or white roses. Those who were for Lancaster, that is the King, because he was descended from John of Gaunt, Duke of Lancaster, wore red roses in their caps; those who were for the Duke of York wore white roses in theirs. And ever after, during all the years that the wars lasted, red and white roses were the sign or badge of the two parties, and the wars were called the Wars of the Roses.

The first battle was fought at St. Albans in 1455 A.D. The White Rose won this battle and King Henry was taken prisoner. The Duke of York treated Henry very kindly, and, as he became quite mad for a time, the duke ruled the country.

The next year, however, the King recovered from his madness. He sent the duke away, and once more ruled the kingdom himself, or rather it was the Queen who ruled, for she was very fond of power, but did not care in the least to do what was best for the people. So she was greatly hated, and it was not long before war again broke out.

This time, too, the White Rose was successful. Queen Margaret fled to Scotland with her little son, and Henry was again taken prisoner.

The Duke of York now claimed the throne in earnest. He entered London in great state. Trumpets were sounded, the sword of office was carried before him, and he was followed and surrounded by a train of soldiers and servants. He rode straight to Westminster, where Parliament was sitting, and did not pause until he reached the House of Lords. There he marched up to the throne and laid his hand upon the cloth of state with which it was covered, as if he meant to show that he had taken possession of it. But he did not sit on the throne.

He stood for some time in silence looking at the empty seat, keeping his hand still upon the cloth. Then turning he looked at the nobles, as they crowded before him. Still silent he stood wondering and as if asking himself, "Are they glad or sorry to see me?"

Then in the silence the Archbishop of Canterbury stepped forward. "My lord duke," he said, "will you come to see the King?"

The Duke of York drew himself up proudly. "I cannot remember, my lord archbishop," he said, "that there is any one in this kingdom who should not rather come to me than I go to him." Then he turned and boldly sat upon the throne.

Sitting there, the duke made a long speech to the lords. He reminded them that Henry IV. had taken the crown by force, and tried to show that he, the Duke of York, had a better right to the throne than Henry VI.

"Therefore," he said, "according to my just and free title I have and do take possession of this royal throne and, with God's help, I shall keep it for His glory, my own honour, and the good of all my people."

When the duke had finished there was a deep silence. The lords sat as if struck dumb. In their astonishment they seemed afraid even to whisper or utter one word.

"It is good," said the duke at last, "that you should think well of what I have said," and rising he went away, not very pleased at their silence, yet not quite displeased either.

He went to the royal palace, took possession of Henry's own rooms, and lived there more like a king than a duke.

Left to themselves, the lords and the commons, after a great deal of talking, decided that while Henry lived he should still be called King, but that the Duke of York should be protector, and that when Henry died the duke should be the next King.

Henry, who was weak and idle, was quite satisfied with this. So was the duke, for he was a wise man who really love his country. He meant to rule well, and hoped in this way to become King without further fighting. But Queen Margaret was very angry. She loved to rule and she hated the Duke of York, and she would not be ruled by him nor have her son set aside for him. She came from Scotland, where she had been hiding with her little boy and gathering an army, fought another battle with the Duke of York and his followers.

It was a terrible battle. This time the Red Rose won, and the Duke of York himself was taken prisoner.

After the battle was over the Red Rose soldiers set the duke on a little mound. They crowned him with bulrushes and then knelt before him crying, "Hail king without rule! Hail king without heritage! Hail duke and prince without people or possessions!" and after this cruel mocking of a helpless prisoner they cut off his head.

The wicked Queen Margaret laughed with joy when she saw it and, to mock the dead man still further, she placed a paper crown upon the head and stuck it upon the walls of York.

One of the duke's sons, a pretty boy of only twelve, was killed too. He was trying to run away with his tutor when he was caught by one of the Red Rose soldiers.

"Oh please, please do not kill me," sobbed the boy, the tears running down his cheeks, "I do not want to die." But the soldier had a cruel heart and would not listen. Dumb with fear, the poor little boy fell upon his knees, holding up his hands to beg for mercy. But the soldier had no mercy. "Your father killed mine," he cried, "I will kill you." So the poor little boy died.

Queen Margaret had no mercy either. She seemed mad with revenge.

She killed as many of the White Rose nobles as she could, and the White Rose cause seemed lost.

But although Richard, Duke of York, was dead, he had a son called Edward, who now became duke and the head of the White Rose party, and more terrible battles were fought.

The people hated the Queen for her cruelty and her wickedness. She had no money with which to pay her soldiers, so she allowed them to plunder, and they too were hated and feared wherever they went. The gates of London were closed against them, the people refusing to give them even the plainest food.

But Edward of York was young, brave, and handsome, and, when he came to London with his army, the people threw open the gates to him welcoming him as their King.

Then the Bishop of Exeter, standing up among the great crowds who had gathered to meet him, reminded the people of all the cruel wrongs which they had suffered during Henry's reign. "Will you have him still to rule over you?" he asked.

"No! no!" shouted the people. "No! no!"

"If you will not have Henry, whom will you have?" asked the bishop. "Will you serve, love, honour, and obey Edward, Earl of March and Duke of York, as your only King and sovereign lord?"

"Yes, yes," shouted the people. "King Edward, King Edward, long live King Edward!"

So with shouting and cheering and clapping of hands the people chose Edward of York to be their King.

CHAPTER LVI

EDWARD IV.—THE STORY OF QUEEN MARGARET AND THE ROBBERS

IT was in 1461 A.D. that the people chose Edward IV. as their King, and so there were two kings in England—Henry VI. the head of the Red Rose, and Edward IV. the head of the White Rose party.

There could be no peace in the country so long as there were two kings each claiming the throne, so, without waiting to be crowned, Edward marched to meet the Red Rose army and to fight for the crown.

On a cold, bleak day in March the two forces met at Towton in Yorkshire, and fought amid a wild storm of wind and snow. For ten hours the battle raged. The white snow was stained and the river which flowed near ran red with blood, till it seemed as if the earth and the sky had taken sides with the red and white roses. Never since Hastings had such a terrible battle been fought on English ground.

The White Rose was victorious. Henry's cause seemed utterly lost and he and his wife and their little son fled to Scotland.

If Henry had been left to himself he would have given up fighting for the crown, for he loved quiet and peace. But Queen Margaret loved power and would not rest until she had again won the kingdom. She got help from the French king and in three years was back in England once more.

But Edward and the great Earl of Warwick, who had helped to put Edward upon the throne, were too strong for Margaret, and she was utterly defeated.

Without a single friend or servant, Margaret and her little son, who was now about eleven years old, fled into the forest to hide. The night came on, it grew dark, and they lost their way among the winding paths. Hungry and tired, they did not know which way to turn. Afraid to stop, afraid to go on, starting and shrinking at every sound, they clung to each other trembling.

Presently they heard men's voices and saw the glimmer of a fire. Margaret whispered to her little son to be very, very still, as they crept near to find out who these people were, whether friends or enemies.

Hidden by the trees, the Queen and her little boy came quite close to the fire and stood listening and watching.

In a few minutes they found out that these men were robbers. Holding the Prince tight by the hand, Queen Margaret made ready to run away. But suddenly one of the robbers looked towards them. He saw the glitter of jewels in the firelight. With a cry he made a spring at the Queen and, in spite of her screams and struggles, she was dragged into the circle round the fire.

"Ah, ah, what have we here?" cried one robber.

"A fine prize, truly," said another.

"Here is gold enough," said a third, roughly pulling at the chain round Margaret's neck. "Come, lady, we will have all these things," he went on, pointing to her jewels.

The Queen began to take off her rings and jewels, for she was very much afraid. But one robber pushed the other aside. "Let be," he said, "the prize is mine. I took her."

"Nay, nay, share and share alike."

"It is mine, I say."

"I took her, I say, it is mine."

So the robbers began to quarrel fiercely about the treasure, and while they quarrelled, Margaret took the Prince in her arms and ran away.

Where she ran she did not know. On and on she went, stumbling through the dark forest. At last, breathless and weary, unable to go another step, she sank down on a grassy bank. Scarcely had she done so when another robber appeared.

Seeing no escape, Margaret went towards this robber putting the little Prince into his arms, "Friend," she said, "take care of him, he is the son of your true King."

The hard, rough man, accustomed only to murder and rob, felt sorry for the poor, tired lady and her little boy. He held the Prince in his arms saying, "Lady, I will not hurt you. Come with me and I will show you where you can rest safely."

The robber led the Queen and Prince through the forest till he came to his secret cave. There he fed them and kept them safe for some days, and at last took them to the shore, where they found a ship in which to sail over the sea.

But King Henry was not so fortunate. He escaped and hid in various places for nearly a year, but he was discovered at last and taken prisoner to London.

As he rode a prisoner into the city, he was met by the Earl of Warwick, and the poor unfortunate King was made to ride through the streets like a common criminal, with his feet tied under his horse. Then he was shut up in the Tower of London.

CHAPTER LVII

EDWARD IV.—THE STORY OF THE KING-MAKER

EDWARD IV. now felt quite sure of the throne, and he married secretly a beautiful lady called Elizabeth Woodville. When this marriage became known, the Earl of Warwick was very angry, because he thought the King should have married some one more great and powerful.

The Earl of Warwick himself was so great and powerful that he was called the King-maker, and he had done much to make Edward king.

Edward soon acted in many ways which displeased the earl, and they quarrelled, and plots were formed to drive Edward from the throne. Among the people who plotted against him was the Duke of Clarence, King Edward's own brother.

At last the Earl of Warwick became so angry with Edward that he took him prisoner, and shut him up in a castle called Middleham. So there were two kings in England, both of them prisoners.

The King-maker, having made and unmade the King, now ruled the country himself for a year. He really had intended to make the Duke of Clarence king, but he found that even he was not powerful enough to do that.

In about a year's time Warwick set Edward free again and, strange to say, they made up their quarrels, and were friends once more.

But in a very short time they again quarrelled; so badly this time that the Earl of Warwick, who had fought so hard for the White Rose of York, forsook it and joined the Red Rose of Lancaster. He went to France, where Margaret and her son were, and offered to help them to conquer England and placed Henry again on the throne.

So one morning Edward awoke to hear the Red Rose war-cry, and two friends, running into his room, begged him to fly. "For," they said, "even in your own army we know not who is true and who is false, many like Warwick having turned traitor."

Hardly waiting to dress, without money or armour, Edward threw himself upon his horse and rode as fast as possible to the coast. There he found some ships, and with a few friends and two or three hundred faithful soldiers, he sailed over to Holland.

They were very poor, had no money nor goods nor indeed anything except the clothes they wore. Edward, who had one day been King of England, Wales and Ireland, found himself the next a homeless, penniless wanderer. And Warwick, in little more than a week, had deposed the King whom he had helped to set on the throne, and had place Henry VI. once more there.

Henry was brought out of prison and dressed in beautiful robes, and, riding upon a splendid horse, was led through the town, while the people cheered and shouted, "God save the King! Long live King Harry!" Did he remember that the last time he rode through the same streets it had been as a wretched prisoner, bound and disgraced by the very man who now set him again on the throne? And did he remember that the people, who now cheered, had then cursed and laughed at him?

Although Henry was once more on the throne, he could not rule. He was like a wooden doll in the hands of a clever man such as the Earl of Warwick, and it was the earl and the Duke of Clarence who ruled.

Henry would have been far happier had he been left alone to his books and prayers. He loved peace, yet he was made the cause of war by the proud and powerful men and women around him.

Edward had been obliged to fly from the country penniless and almost friendless, yet he did not despair. He persuaded the Duke of Burgundy to help him, and soon returned to England with and army.

No sooner had he landed than people began to flock to him. By the time he reached Barnet, near London, he had a large army. Many who had joined Warwick now forsook him and returned to Edward, among them Edward's own brother, the Duke of Clarence, who brought twelve thousand men with him. There seemed to be no faith nor loyalty in those days. It was hard to know who was friend and who was foe.

At Barnet, on Easter Day, 14th April 1471 A.D., another terrible battle was fought. What made it more terrible was that it was begun and ended in a thick mist. In the white dimness, which wrapped both armies, it was difficult to know the Red Roses from the White, and indeed at one time the Red Roses fought against themselves. King Edward's men wore a golden sun embroidered upon their coats. The Duke of Oxford's men, who were fighting for King Henry, wore a golden star. In the mist the Red Rose soldiers, mistaking the star for the sun, attacked the Duke of Oxford's men, thinking that they were King Edward's men, and killed many of them.

From dawn to midday the battle raged. Then the Earl of Warwick's army broke and fled, leaving the White Rose victorious. The great King-maker was found dead upon the field, and Edward IV. was once more King.

On the very day of this battle Queen Margaret and her son, who was now about eighteen, landed in England. They had hoped to find Warwick victorious, and Henry on the throne. Instead they found Warwick dead, his army shattered, and Edward on the throne.

But Margaret was as bold as ever. She marched through England, gathering soldiers as she went, and at Tewkesbury another great battle was fought. Here again the Red Rose was utterly defeated, and Margaret and her son were taken prisoner.

Prince Edward was led before King Edward. The King looked fiercely at the young and handsome Prince. He hated him more than he had ever hated his poor, weak, gentle father.

"How dare you come into my kingdom to stir up my people to rebellion?" he asked.

"It is not your kingdom, but my father's," replied Prince Edward proudly. "You are a traitor. I should sit where you are. You should stand before me as a subject."

Then King Edward, pale with rage and hate, struck the boy in the face with his steel-gloved hand. The Dukes of Clarence and Gloucester, the King's brothers, dragged the Prince away and stabbed him to death.

Queen Margaret was put in prison, and a few days later King Henry died mysteriously in the Tower of London. Many people thought that he was murdered by King Edward's brother, Richard, Duke of Gloucester.

At last it seemed as if all Edward's enemies were either dead or in prison, and that he might really rule in peace. The Red Rose party was for the time utterly crushed; some of the great nobles even were seen barefoot in rags, begging for bread from door to door.

Edward never quite forgave his brother, the Duke of Clarence, for having, at one time, sided with Warwick. Clarence, too, was jealous of the Queen Elizabeth and her relatives, many of whom had the chief posts at court, so he quarrelled with them and with his brother the King.

At last, an old wizard prophesied that some one whose name began with "G" would bring about the death of King Edward and the ruin of his house. The Duke of Clarence was called George, and King Edward made the prophecy and excuse for shutting him up in the Tower. He never came out again.

It is supposed that he was murdered, some say by being drowned in a cask of wine by the order of his brother, the Duke of Gloucester.

Edward IV. died in 1483 A.D. He was brave, but cruel and revengeful, handsome but wicked, caring little for the happiness of his people, and his reign was dark with many battles and murders. He had ruled for twenty-two years, during twelve of which King Henry still lived.

CHAPTER LVIII

EDWARD V.—THE STORY OF THE KING WHO WAS NEVER CROWNED

WHEN Edward IV. died, his eldest son was only thirteen, but the people willingly chose him to be King.

The young Prince of Wales, now Edward V., was living at Ludlow Castle with his uncle, Lord Rivers, when the new of his father's death was brought to him. He at once set out for London, accompanied by his uncle and some gentlemen.

On the way he was met by another uncle, Richard of Gloucester, who was a wicked, hard-hearted man. He sent Lord Rivers and his friends to prison, and himself took charge of the young King.

Edward was very fond of Lord Rivers, and was afraid of his ugly uncle Richard. He cried when Lord Rivers and his friends were taken away from him. That did no good, but the poor little King was only a boy, and he did not know what else to do.

When the Queen heard of what happened, she was so frightened that she ran away from the palace in which she had been living, taking her daughters and her other little son, who was called Richard, with her. She ran to Westminster Abbey and there took sanctuary, as Hubert de Burgh did, you remember, many years before, in the days of Henry III.

The Duke of Gloucester had the young King in his power, but he was not satisfied with that. He wanted to have Prince Richard too. Queen Elizabeth, however, would not give up her little boy, who was only ten years old. And the Duke of Gloucester, bad though he was, was afraid to take him by force, because he was still trying to pretend to be a good, kind uncle to the little boys.

At last the duke sent a bishop to the Queen to try to persuade her to give up her little son. This bishop said everything he could think of to make her do so, but all in vain.

"My little boy has been ill," said the Queen; "he is not well enough yet to leave his mother."

"Ah, lady," said the bishop, "it is not kind to his brother, the King, to keep him here. They should be together so that they could play with each other."

"Oh, surely some other little boy could play with the King," said the Queen. "Little boys, even if they are kings, do not ask that their playmates should be princes. I cannot, I will not, let my little boy go."

"Let him but come to me, and I will guard his life as my own," said the bishop.

At these words the Queen stood for a long time thinking silently. It seemed to her as if she must give up her boy sooner or later. It would be better to give him to this kind bishop, who would perhaps keep him safe, than to his wicked uncle.

So, taking the Prince by the hand, she led him to the bishop. "I know you are faithful and true," she said. "You are strong and powerful too, and oh, for the trust his father put in you, I now charge you, guard my boy."

Then kneeling beside her little son, and putting her arms round him, she held him close to her heart. "Farewell, my own sweet son," she said. "God give you good keeping. Let me kiss you yet once before you go, for God knows when we shall kiss together again." Then she kissed him and blessed him, and kissed him again and again, and at last, crying bitterly, put him into the arms of the bishop and turned her face from him. But, weeping as bitterly, little Richard clung to her and would not go, until the bishop, taking him strongly in his arms, carried him away.

The bishop led the Prince straight to his uncle, who was very glad to see him. His ugly face shone with joy as he took his nephew in his arms and kissed him. "Now, welcome, my lord," he said, "with all my heart you are right welcome."

King Edward, too, was very glad to see his brother, for they had been parted for a long time. The duke led them through the streets with great pomp, and put them into the Tower.

Now that the Duke of Gloucester had both the princes in his power he began to show his wickedness. He sent to the prison in which Lord Rivers and his friends were imprisoned and ordered their heads to be cut off, because he knew that they were the Queen's friends.

Then he called a council to arrange, he said, about the coronation. Only a very few lords were asked to this council. When they were all gathered together he came into the room seemingly very much disturbed.

"What should be done to people who try to murder me?" he asked.

At first every one was so astonished that no one spoke. Then Lord Hastings, who was a brave man, and true to the King, and the Queen, his mother, said, "If any one has tried he deserves to be punished, whoever he is."

"The Queen has tried with her sorcery," cried the duke, "and others have helped her." And pulling up his sleeve, he showed his arm which was all puckered and withered.

In those days it was believed that people had power to hurt their enemies by saying wicked words and rhymes, and wishing evil to them. It was thought that people could even kill others who were quite far away, and who they could not even see nor touch. This was called sorcery. Of course, it was a very foolish belief, and every one knew that the Duke of Gloucester's arm had always been withered up, but when he said that the Queen had done it by sorcery, no one dared to contradict him.

There was silence in the hall till Lord Hastings said, "If the Queen has done this—"

"You answer me with ifs and ands," cried the duke, "you are a traitor. A traitor, I say," and with that he struck with his hand upon the table.

Immediately soldiers rushed into the room.

"Seize him," he said, pointing to Lord Hastings, "cut off his head."

"My lord," said Hastings, "I am no traitor."

"You are a traitor!" yelled the duke, "and, by Heaven, I will not dine till I see your head cut from your body. Obey your orders," he added, turning to the soldiers.

Lord Hastings was hurried away, and, without being allowed to defend himself, without a trial of any kind, he was made to lay his neck upon a rough plank of wood which happened to be at hand, and his head was at once cut off. So another of the King's friends was dead.

The Duke of Gloucester next made a clergyman, called Shaw, preach to the people and tell that the little princes were not really the sons of King Edward IV. and his Queen and that, therefore, they had no right to the throne of England.

"Our true King," said this wicked clergyman, "is Richard, Duke of Gloucester."Then he waited, expecting every one to cry out, "King Richard! King Richard!" But there was not a sound. The people stood as if they had been turned into stone. Pale and trembling they went away to their homes, wondering what would happen next. The clergyman, too, went home. He was so ashamed to have preached such a wicked sermon that he never again showed himself to the people, and died soon after.

The Duke of Gloucester was very angry and disappointed when he heard of the bad success of his wicked plans, but he did not give them up. He again gathered a lot of people together, and this time his friend, the Duke of Buckingham, talked to them. The Duke of Buckingham said much the same things as the clergyman had said. When the people heard these wicked lies for the second time, they began to whisper among themselves, till it seemed as if a swarm of buzzing bees filled the hall. But not a single person shouted, "King Richard!"

Then some of the duke's servants and friends came into the hall, and they shouted, "King Richard! King Richard! Long live King Richard!" but the cries sounded very feeble, for they came from only a few.

The Duke of Buckingham, however, pretended that all the people had shouted for King Richard. He thanked them, and he and his friends went to the Duke of Gloucester and told him that the people had chosen him as their King, and were cheering and shouting for King Richard.

Richard then pretended to be very unwilling to take the crown, and only consented to do so after a great deal of persuasion. This was all a part of his wickedness and cunning.

Richard was crowned with much splendour and grandeur. And poor little King Edward, who had never been crowned at all, and who had only been called King for a few weeks, was kept shut up in the Tower of London.

CHAPTER LIX

RICHARD III.—THE STORY OF THE TWO LITTLE PRINCES IN THE TOWER

WHEN Edward was told what his uncle had done, he was very sad and very much afraid. "Oh," he said, "I hope my uncle will not take my life as he has taken my kingdom." From that day he became sorrowful, and did not seem to care about anything. He did not even trouble to dress himself properly.

Richard took away all the little Princes' servants and left them only one man, called Black Bill. He was rough and rude, but even he loved the gentle little boys and tried to comfort them, for, shut up in one room with nothing to do, the days seemed very long and dreary.

But although Richard was King, he could not be happy. He could not forget the little Princes in the Tower. As long as they lived, he knew that some day the people might drag him from the throne and make one of them King instead. So he determined to kill Edward and his brother.

King Richard sent a message to the Governor of the Tower telling him to kill the Princes. But the Governor refused to do the wicked deed. Richard, however, could always find men bad enough to do what he wanted.

He sent a bad man now to the Governor of the Tower, commanding him to give up the keys of the Tower for one night. The Governor was forced to obey the King, but he did so with a sad heart.

That night the little Princes went to sleep with their arms round each other's necks, each trying to comfort the other. They lay together in a great big bed, happy in their dreams, with tears still wet upon their cheeks.

As they slept two men crept softly, softly up the dark stair. Quietly they opened the door and stole into the room. They stood beside the bed, hardly daring to look at the two pretty children in case the sight might soften even their hard hearts, and they would be unable to do the cruel deed. Then they seized the clothes and the pillows and pressed them over the faces of the little boys. They could not scream, they could not breathe. Soon they lay still, smothered in their sleep.

Then these wicked men took the bodies of the two little Princes, threw them into a hole which they had made under the staircase, covered them over and fled away. There the bodies were found many years later.

Now that Richard had murdered the rightful King and his brother, he was no happier. Terrible dreams came to him at night so that he could not sleep. By day he thought that people were ever ready to kill him, and his hand was almost always on his dagger. The people hated him and he knew no rest nor peace. He tried to make good laws so that the people might forget his wickedness. But it was no use. They hated him in spite of all he could do.

Plots against Richard soon began. Even the Duke of Buckingham, who had helped him in his wickedness, and put him on the throne, turned against him.

The people longed for another King, and their thoughts went out to Henry Tudor, Duke of Richmond.

You remember that Queen Catherine, the widow of King Henry V., married a Welsh gentleman called Owen Tudor. This Henry Tudor was her grandson and he was also descended from John of Gaunt. He belonged to the House of Lancaster and had fought for the Red Rose.

Henry of Richmond was at this time living in France, but he now gathered an army and came over to England. But before he came Richard had already fought the Duke of Buckingham. He defeated him, took him prisoner, and then cut off his head. When Henry heard that, he went away again.

But he soon came back. This time as soon as Henry landed, people flocked to him. Noble after noble deserted Richard and joined the Red Rose party.

In 1485 A.D. a great battle was fought called the Battle of Bosworth Field. This was the last of the Wars of the Roses, and in it King Richard was killed. He fought well, for, although he was small and deformed, he could fight. His horse was killed under him, but he still fought on foot. In the middle of the battle Lord Stanley left the King, and, with all his followers, joined Henry Tudor. Seeing that the battle was lost, some of his nobles begged Richard to fly, but he would not. "I will die a King," he said, and so he fell in the thickest of the fight. As he fell, the crown which he had worn over his helmet rolled away under a hawthorn tree. There it was found by Lord Stanley who set it upon Henry's Tudor's head and, on the battle-field with the dead and dying round, the soldiers shouted, "King Henry! King Henry! Long live King Henry!" The place is still called Crown Hill to this day.

Richard III. had reigned two years, two months and one day. "And it was twenty-six months and twenty-four hours too long," said a man who lived about that time, and who tells his story.

CHAPTER LX

HENRY VII.—THE STORY OF A MAKE-BELIEVE PRINCE

WITH Henry Tudor a new race of kings began to reign in England.

For more than three hundred years the kings of England had been Plantagenets. Henry II. was the first of the Plantagenets, and he took his name from Geoffrey of Anjou who used to wear a piece of *planta genista* in his cap. With Richard III. the last of the Platagenets died, for Henry VII., though a Plantagenet on his mother's side, was a Tudor on his father's side, and it was from his family that Henry took his name.

The Tudors were Welsh and claimed to be descended from the ancient British princes who, you remember, were driven into Wales when the Saxons took possession of England.

The Battle of Bosworth Field was the last of the Wars of the Roses. Henry Tudor, who was the Red Rose Prince, married Elizabeth, the daughter of Edward IV. and sister of the little princes who were murdered in the Tower. She was the White Rose Princess, but by marrying Henry she became the Red Rose Queen, and the differences between the House of Lancaster and the House of York, between the Red Rose and the White, ought to have been quite forgotten.

But Henry himself could not entirely forget these quarrels which had been so bitter. There were many people in England who still belonged to the White Rose party. Although they had hated Richard they were not pleased to see a Red Rose king upon the throne. So Henry VII. was hardly crowned before rebellions against him began.

Soon after Henry VII. was crowned, a handsome boy and a priest landed in Dublin. This boy called himself the Earl of Warwick. He was, he said, the son of that Duke of Clarence, brother of Edward IV., who was murdered in the Tower by being drowned in a cask of wine. The priest, he said, was his tutor. Ever since the death of his father, the Earl of Warwick had been kept a prisoner. But now, he said, he had escaped in some wonderful manner.

The simple Irish people believed this story. They knew nothing of Henry and had no reason for either hating or loving him. But they did love the House of York, for the Earl of Warwick's grandfather had at one time governed Ireland in the name of the King, and, having governed well, the people remembered and loved him.

So now they welcomed this young prince with great joy. Edward, Earl of Warwick, as he called himself, was gay and young and handsome, and he gained the love of the Irish so much that they resolved to crown him King.

This was done with great rejoicing in Dublin. But they had no crown, so the priest took the golden crown from the statue of the Virgin Mary which was in the church, and put it upon the boy's head. Then, wearing this crown and dressed in beautiful robes, the new King was carried through the streets on the shoulders of a great strong Irish chieftain, while the people shouted, "Long live King Edward VI.!"

Having been crowned in Ireland, "Edward VI." thought he would next conquer England. So he sailed across the Irish Sea and landed in England with a small army of wild Irishmen and Germans.

Meanwhile Henry VII. had heard of these doings in Ireland and had not been idle. He brought the real Earl of Warwick out of the Tower where he had been kept prisoner ever since he had been quite a tiny boy. Dressed in fine clothes and riding upon a splendid horse, the real earl was slowly led through the streets of London. From the Tower to St. Paul's and back again by another way, he was led so that all the people might see him.

The young earl had spent all his life in prison. It must have been a wonderful thing for him to come out into the open streets, to see the blue sky and the houses and the trees, the great procession of soldiers and knights in glittering armour and gorgeous clothes, and the people, men, women, and children, crowding in the streets, all eager to see him. And, having been led out, having seen for once all the life and stir of the great city, the poor young prince was taken back again to his dull, quiet prison, while the King marched with his army to fight the pretended earl.

The two armies met at a place called Stoke. Very few English had joined the pretender, for they were quite sure that the earl whom they had seen riding through the streets of London was the real earl and that this one was only a make-believe. The pretender's soldiers were soon defeated, for most of them were wild Irishmen badly armed; and wearing no armour, they were no match for Henry's well-armed and well-trained soldiers.

The pretender was taken prisoner, and so was the priest who was with him. They confessed that the prince was no prince at all, but a boy called Lambert Simnel, the son of a baker. The priest who was a Yorkist, or White Rose man, hated Henry, and finding that the boy Lambert was clever as well as handsome, he taught him how to behave as a prince ought. He told him stories of the Duke of Clarence and of Richard III. so that he might pretend to be what he was not.

Henry did not kill Lambert Simnel as many kings who reigned before him would have done. Instead he gave him a punishment, which, had Lambert indeed been a prince, would have been a very dreadful one. He was sent into the King's kitchen to be a scullery boy and to help the cooks.

This boy, who had worn a crown and royal robes, who had been carried through the streets shoulder high while the people cheered him as their King, was a few days later turned into a kitchen drudge, to be ordered about by the cooks and set to do the meanest kinds of work.

But Lambert Simnel behaved himself so well that the King soon took him out of the kitchen and made him a kind of page. He had then to look after the King's falcons.

All great people kept falcons in those days. They were used for hunting, and were trained to fly up in the air to catch and kill other birds.

A great deal of time and money was spent on falcons. They had hoods of velvet and jewels, and gold and silver chains. Lambert must have found his new work much more pleasant than helping the cooks in the hot kitchens.

The priest who had taught Lambert Simnel was allowed to go free, but some of the nobles who had helped him were beheaded, and others were made to pay large sums of money.

CHAPTER LXI

HENRY VII.—THE STORY OF ANOTHER MAKE-BELIEVE PRINCE

A FEW years after the rebellion of Lambert Simnel there was another which lasted longer and was more serious.

A second handsome boy, even more handsome, gay, and princely than Lambert Simnel, landed in Ireland. He was, he said, Richard, Duke of York, the younger of the two little princes who had been smothered in the Tower, by order of their uncle Richard.

It was quite true, he said, that his brother, Edward V., had been killed, but the wicked murderers had not been cruel enough to kill them both, and he had been saved. For seven years he had been wandering about the world from place to place. Now he had come to claim his own again and take the throne from Henry.

This story was not true. The boy's real name was Perkin Warbeck, but, like Lambert Simnel, he had been taught to tell these lies by the enemies of Henry, who hoped in this way to drive him from the throne.

Although the Irish had already been deceived once, they believed Perkin Warbeck, and many people promised to help him. The French king, who was quarrelling with Henry, invited him to come to France. There he was kindly treated, and more help was promised to him. But Henry, who always avoided war when he could, made peace with France. And the French King, although he would not betray Perkin to the English king, sent him out of France.

When he was obliged to leave the French court, Perkin went to Margaret, Duchess of Burgundy. This lady was a sister of Edward IV., she hated Henry VII. So much that she was glad to hurt or annoy him when she could. She had helped Lambert Simnel, and now she welcomed Perkin as her nephew. She said that he was very like his supposed father, Edward IV., and she called him the White Rose of England.

Just as Henry had taken trouble to prove that Lambert Simnel was a false earl, now he took trouble to prove that Perkin was a false prince. He sent spies to the places where Perkin had been born and had lived till now, and made sure that he was really Perkin or Peterkin Warbeck. Then he found the two men who had killed the Princes in the Tower. They confessed to the murder, but they were not punished for it, perhaps because Henry thought they had not been so much to blame as Richard III. who had made them do it.

But in spite of all this, many people believed in Perkin. The king of Scotland—not that King who had been kept prisoner for such a long time in England—believed in him so much that he not only helped him with soldiers, but married him to his cousin, a beautiful lady called Catherine Gordon.

Like Lambert Simnel, Perkin was crowned and his followers called him Richard IV. The rebellion went on for about five years. Battles were fought now and again, but Perkin was never successful. His beautiful wife, Catherine, went everywhere with him. She at least believed in him and loved him.

At last, hearing that the men of Cornwall were angry with the King because he had taxed them too heavily, Perkin decided to try his fortune there. He landed in Cornwall, left his beautiful wife at St. Michael's Mount, where she might be safe, and marched to besiege Exeter. But the people of Exeter were true to the King and would not yield. So Perkin grew tired of besieging a town which would not yield and he marched away to Taunton.

There, hearing that Henry was coming against him with a great army, he took fright and ran away in the night.

Next morning, when Perkin's poor soldier's woke up and found that they had lost their leader, they had no heart to fight. Some of them ran away like Perkin, others gave themselves up, begging the King to forgive them. They were all gathered together in a churchyard at Exeter, their heads and their feet bare and ropes around their necks. King Henry came to a great window and looked down upon them. When the people saw him, they all fell upon their knees begging for pardon.

There were so many of them that the King could not punish all. So he spoke to them and, warning them not to rebel again, said he would forgive them all except the ringleaders who should be put to death.

Then with a great cry of rejoicing and thanks the people threw the ropes from their necks and went to their homes.

Henry sent to St. Michael's Mount for the Lady Catherine, Perkin's beautiful wife and when she was brought before him, blushing and trembling and fearful of the rough soldiers, the King felt so sorry for her that he treated her as a royal guest. He gave her a guard of honour and sent her to London to the court of his Queen Elizabeth.

There she lived for many years, loved and admired for her beauty and her gentleness. She was so lovely that she was called the White Rose of England, the name which the Duchess of Burgundy had given to her cowardly husband.

Meanwhile Perkin had taken sanctuary at a place called Beaulieu. Henry would not seize him while he remained in sanctuary, but he kept such a close watch that Perkin could find no way of escape, and at last gave himself up.

Henry would not see nor speak with Perkin, but made him ride in his train to London. When they arrived there, all the people came out into the streets to see the wonderful man who had pretended to be a prince, and who had made people believe in him for so many years.

Perkin was even more fortunate than Lambert Simnel had been. He was neither put in prison nor was he made a servant. He was allowed to live at court like a gentleman, although there were guards always with him who had orders never to lose sight of him.

Perkin might have spent the rest of his life in peace but he soon grew tired of being watched and one day he managed to run away. But he did not run very far. Henry's soldiers were too quick for him and once more Perkin gave himself up.

This time Henry punished Perkin by putting him into the stocks for two whole days, first at Westminster and then at Cheapside. He also made him read a paper aloud, in which he confessed that the story he had told was not true and that he was not the Duke of York.

In those days people were often punished by being put in the stocks. They had to sit in a very uncomfortable position with their feet through holes in a board. It was uncomfortable and painful also, and was considered a great disgrace. Little boys, and grown up people too, used to hoot and yell at those in the stocks and pelt them with mud, rotten eggs, and other disagreeable things.

After Perkin Warbeck had been in the stocks for two days Henry shut him up in the Tower. There he met the Earl of Warwick—the real earl, not Lambert Simnel.

These two prisoners were allowed to talk together, and soon they formed a plot to kill the Governor of the Tower, and escape. But the plot was found out and that put an end to Perkin Warbeck, for Henry, thinking that he was too dangerous to be allowed to live any longer, ordered his head to be cut off.

The poor Earl of Warwick was also put to death. This was a needless and cruel act, for the earl alone was too simple to harm any one. Indeed he was so ignorant of the world and the things in it, that it was said he did not know the difference between a hen and a goose.

Except for the wars which these pretenders, Perkin Warbeck and Lambert Simnel caused, the reign of Henry VII. was very peaceful. One reason for that was that Henry was greedy, and he knew that wars cost a great deal of money. Once indeed he got money from the people in order to make war against the French, but as soon as he got it he made peace and kept the money for himself. The people were very angry, but Henry as a King was far more powerful than the Plantagenets had ever been and the people had to submit.

One reason why the Tudors were such powerful kings was that, during the Wars of the Roses, nearly all the nobles were killed. The King took all the money and lands which had belonged to these dead nobles, and so he became very rich. Being rich he did not need to ask Parliament for grants of money, so the people became less powerful. Indeed during a great part of Henry's reign he called no Parliament, which shows how much he had of his own way.

About this time two very wonderful things happened which made a great difference throughout the world. One was the discovery of printing. The other was the discovery of America.

Up to the time of Edward IV. books had all been written by hand, and they were so dear that only a few rich people could buy them. But, when a clever man called Caxton brought the art of printing to England, books became cheaper, and people began to think more about learning and less about fighting.

Then Columbus discovered America. That, too, made people think less about fighting, for they gave up quarrelling about little bits of the Old World and turned their thoughts to exploring the wonders of the New World, as Columbus called the land he discovered.

CHAPTER LXII

HENRY VIII.—THE STORY OF THE FIELD OF THE CLOTH OF GOLD

LONG before Henry VII. died in 1509 A.D., all the joy and love, which the people had felt for him when he came to the throne, had faded away. He had proved to be a hard and greedy King and no one was sorry when he died.

His son was also called Henry, and he was only eighteen years old when his father died. He was gay and handsome and the people believed him to be generous and good, so there was great rejoicing when he was crowned.

Henry's Chancellor was a man called Wolsey. He was a very great man and for many years it was really he who ruled England. Wolsey was the son of a butcher. Being a clever boy he was sent to school, and afterwards to college at Oxford. There he showed himself to be so clever that people soon began to notice him, and he quickly rose from one post to another until he became chaplain to Henry VII. Henry VII. found Wolsey very useful to him. He became one of Prince Henry's greatest friends, and when Prince Henry became King, he made Wolsey Chancellor and Archbishop of York, and heaped upon him many other honours and posts, until he was almost as rich and as great as the King himself. Wolsey had most splendid houses and about five hundred servants, all of whom wore most beautiful clothes. His cook even wore a satin or velvet coat and had a gold chain around his neck.

Wolsey himself dressed most gorgeously in bright red silk or satin, and he wore gilded shoes set with pearls and jewels. Whenever he went out there was a great procession. A man carrying a mace walked first, then came two gentlemen carrying silver wands, then two of the biggest and handsomest priests that could be found, each carrying a great silver cross, then came Wolsey mounted upon a mule. He rode upon a mule because he said, being a humble priest, it was more fitting for him than a horse. But the harness and saddle were of velvet and gold, and behind him came a long train of his servants and followers on splendid horses.

Henry VIII. was fond of magnificence and show, and it pleased him to have so fine a chancellor. Henry was gay and the Chancellor was gay. If Henry were sad Wolsey would joke and laugh until the King laughed too; if Henry were merry Wolsey would be merry with him. Soon people began to see that if they wanted anything from the King, it was best to make friends with the Chancellor.

Wolsey, on the whole, made good use of his power. He was fond of learning. He saw that without learning no country could be truly great, and he founded a school at Ipswich, which was his birthplace, and a college at

Oxford. If he tried to make himself great, he also thought of England and how to make England great.

The first few years of Henry's reign were peaceful and quiet. Henry VII. had been a very rich man when he died, so Henry VIII. had plenty of money and, at first, the people were not troubled with new taxes.

Henry pleased everyone by marrying a rich and beautiful lady called Katherine of Arragon. She was a widow, having already been married to Henry's elder brother, who was called Arthur. Arthur would have been King had he lived, but he had died a few months after his marriage with Katherine. After Arthur died Henry VII. kept Katherine at the English court in the hope that his second son, Henry, would one day marry her. This he now did, although it was then, and still is, against the law for a man to marry his dead brother's wife.

However, as Henry thought it was a wise thing for him to marry Katherine, he asked the Pope to give him leave to do so. And the Pope, whom, you know, was a very powerful person, gave him leave.

In those days people were never long content to be at peace, and Henry soon began to fight with France and with Scotland. In a battle called Flodden, the Scots were defeated and their King killed, and Henry made peace with the Queen, who was his own sister. Soon afterwards he also made peace with France.

Henry then decided it would be wise not only to be at peace with France, but to make friends with the French king. So the great Chancellor, Wolsey, arranged a meeting between Francis I. of France and Henry VIII. of England. This meeting took place on a plain in France near a little town called Guisnes, and everything about it was so splendid that it was called "The field of the cloth of gold."

A palace for the English king was built so quickly that it seemed like a magic thing. It was only made of wood, but it was so painted and gilded that it shone and glittered in the sunshine like a fairy palace. Great golden gates opened into a courtyard where a fountain, sparkling with gold and gems, flowed all day with red and white wine instead of water. This fountain bore the motto—"Make good cheer who will."

The palace walls were hung inside with cloth of gold and silver, everything was rich with embroidery and sparkling with gems. Wherever possible, gold and jewels shone, the Queen's footstools even being sewn with pearls.

When the French king saw Henry's splendid palace, he did not wish to be outdone. He set up a great tent, the center pole of which was a gilded mast. The tent was lined inside with blue velvet. The roof was spangled with golden stars, and a golden sun and moon shone night and day. The outside was covered with cloth of gold, and the ropes which held it up were of blue silk and gold.

The tent looked very grand, and glittered in the sunshine like a ball of fire. But when everything was ready, a terrible wind arose which snapped the ropes of silk and gold, broke the mast, and brought the blue velvet sky, the glittering stars, and golden walls to the ground. So Francis had to content himself with living in an old castle which stood not far away, and very likely he was far more comfortable there than he would have been in his golden and blue tent.

When all was ready, King Henry and Queen Katherine sailed from England, and with them a great company of nobles, each trying to be more splendid than the other.

The two kings met on the plain near Henry's palace. They were both dressed in gold and silver cloth, and rode beautiful horses with harness of gold and velvet. While still on horseback, they embraced and kissed each other. "My dear brother and cousin," said Francis, "I have come a long way to see you. I hope you will think that I am worthy of your love and help. My great possessions show how powerful I am."

"Dear cousin," replied Henry, "I never saw prince with my eyes that I could love better with my heart, and for your love I have crossed the seas to the furthest bounds of my kingdom in order to see you."

Then the kings got off their horses and, arm in arm, walked to a gorgeous tent near by, where a very fine dinner was prepared for them.

For three weeks there were gay times. Grand tournaments were held, in which the kings fought with the knights. And the kings always won. There were balls and feasts too. Sometimes the kings and queens and lords and ladies dressed up and disguised themselves so that no one could tell who was who. This they thought was the greatest fun of all.

The English people were very fond of wrestling, and the soldiers used to amuse themselves in this way. Henry was fond of all kinds of games and sport, and one day, while watching the soldiers, he proposed to King Francis that they, too, should try a wrestling match, and laughingly laid hold of his collar.

Francis was quite pleased, for although he did not look so strong as Henry, he was very quick and wiry. Soon the two kings were struggling together, and in a few minutes Henry was lying upon the ground. He sprang up with a laugh and wanted to try again. But the nobles who stood round persuaded him not to do so. They were afraid that what had begun in fun might end in a quarrel, if Francis should again throw Henry down, for Henry had a very fiery temper.

Francis felt, too, that in spite of all the show of friendship, there was no love between the French and the English. This was hardly to be wondered at, for they had been such bitter enemies for so long a time that it was hard to forget all at once. Francis himself, however, was really generous, and wished it really could be forgotten.

One morning, Francis rose early and, without telling any of his nobles, he rode quite alone to the English camp. Henry was still in bed when King Francis came into his room and said, laughing, "My dear cousin, I come to you of my own free will. I am now your prisoner."

Henry was very pleased to see that Francis trusted him so much that he was not afraid to come quite alone like this. He sprang out of bed and threw a chain of gold round the French king's neck.

In return Francis gave Henry a beautiful bracelet, and then, laughing and joking like a schoolboy, he insisted on helping Henry to dress. He warmed his shirt, helped him to tie and button his clothes, and then, mounting on his horse, rode gayly home.

When he came near his castle he was met by some of his nobles, who were anxiously looking for him. Francis laughingly told them what he had been doing. "Sire," said one of them, "I am very glad to see you back again. But let me tell you, master, you were a fool to do what you have done. Ill luck be to him who advised you to do it."

"Well, that was nobody," replied Francis. "The thought was all my own."

In spite of the fears and jealousy of the French and English, the meeting came to an end as peacefully as it had begun. Henry sailed home again with all his gay knights, but many of them were quite ruined and penniless. They had spent all their money on fine clothes and jewels, so anxious were they to make a great display and be grander than the French.

But all this splendour and show of friendliness meant nothing and came to nothing, for Henry, both immediately before and after this meeting with Francis, met and plotted with Charles, the Emperor of Germany, who was the enemy of Francis. When war again broke out the English fought against the French as they had always done.

CHAPTER LXIII

HENRY VIII.—HOW THE KING BECAME THE DEFENDER OF THE FAITH AND HOW THE GREAT CARDINAL DIED

IN the reign of Henry VIII. the Pope was still the head of all the Christian Church although, as long ago as the time of Edward III., a man called John Wycliffe had begun to preach and teach against his rule over the English Church. Wycliffe translated the Bible from Latin into English and encouraged the people to read it. His followers were called Lollards, and they helped the people at the time of Wat Tyler's rebellion in the reign of Richard II. The heads of the Church hated the Lollards, and Henry IV., who wanted to please the priests, made a law, saying that any one who would not believe just what the Pope said he must believe should be burned to death. This was a very wicked law, and it marked the beginning of another struggle for freedom in England; that is the struggle for freedom of conscience, which means freedom to think and do what one feels to be right in matters of religion, instead of being forced to think and do as some one else says is right. For some time now very little had been heard of the Lollards, but the things which Wycliffe had taught had not been forgotten.

After printing was discovered and books became cheaper, people began to read and, in consequence, to think much more than they had done before. The more people read and thought, the more difficult some of them found it to believe just what they were ordered to believe by the Pope.

It was not only in England that this was happening, but in many other lands as well. In Germany a monk called Martin Luther, after thinking a great deal about it, decided that some things which were done in the Romish Church were wrong. He was brave enough to say what he thought and, in spite of the anger of the Pope and the priests, a great many people followed Martin Luther and left the Roman Catholic Church.

This is the beginning of what is called the Reformation. That is a long word, but it is quite easy to understand. It is made from two Latin words, *re*, "again, " and *formare*, "to form or make." It means that the people who left the Roman Church again formed or made the Church.

These people were called Protestants. The word Protestant is also made from two Latin words, *pro*, "publicly," and *testari*, "to bear witness." So a Protestant really means some one who openly and publicly bears witness or protests.

We can hardly understand how bold and brave a thing these Protestants did. Now everyone is free to believe what they think is best and right but, in those days, people who could not agree with the Pope were cruelly punished or put to death. Now, Protestant churches and Roman Catholic churches stand side by side, and we do not kill and hate each other because we worship God in different ways, but in those days nothing caused such cruel suffering and such bitter hatred.

When King Henry heard what Martin Luther had done, he was very angry. Being a clever man, and proud of his learning and knowledge about religion, he wrote a book against Martin Luther and his teaching. This book he had bound most beautifully, and then he sent it to the Pope.

With great splendour and ceremony, dressed in his most magnificent robes, and sitting upon his throne with all his priests around him, the Pope received Henry's messenger. The messenger knelt humbly presenting the book and kissing first the Pope's toe and then his cheek.

Afterwards the messenger made a long speech, and the Pope made a long speech, and so the ceremony ended.

When the Pope had read the book, he was so pleased with it that he gave the King of England a new title. He called him *Fidei Defensor*, which means, "Defender of the Faith." He wrote a letter to Henry thanking him for his book, and calling him "Our most dear son Henry, the illustrious King of England and Defender of the Faith."

Henry was very proud of his new title, and he held a solemn service in the church at Westminster, when the Pope's letter was read, and the King's new title proclaimed.

Afterwards Henry quarrelled with the Pope, but he kept the title of Defender of the Faith, and it has been borne by the kings and queens of England ever since, although the faith they now defend is no longer the faith of the Roman Catholic Church. If you look at some of the coins which we use now you will see F.D. or Fid. Def. upon them. These letters means Fidei Defensor or Defender of the Faith.

King Henry quarrelled with the Pope because he would not let him put away his wife, Queen Katherine. Queen Katherine had done no wrong, but she was some years older than Henry, and now that he had been married to her for nearly twenty years, and she was no longer young and pretty, he had grown tired and wanted another wife.

Henry was very selfish. He thought a great deal of his own pleasure and always wanted to have his own way. Years before, when he wished to marry Katherine, he had made the Pope give him leave to do so, although it was against the laws of the Church because, as you remember, she had already been married to his brother Arthur. Now Henry began to think, or pretended to think, that he had been wrong ever to marry her at all, and he tried to make the Pope say so.

Wolsey, whom the Pope had made a cardinal, tried very hard to make him say so too, but in vain. After a long time the Pope sent another cardinal to England, and a great trial was held to decide whether Henry should be allowed to put away his wife or not.

Many wise men were gathered together with the King and Queen, the two cardinals, and their priests and clerks. When the Queen's name was called she rose from her chair, but although she tried to speak, she could not. She stood a moment, then crossing the hall to where the King sat, she threw herself at his feet. "Sir," she said, "I pray you do me justice and right, and take some pity upon me. For I am a poor woman and a stranger born out of your dominion. Alas, sir, how have I offended you? I take God to judge that I have ever been your true and humble wife. I have been glad for the things which have made you glad, and I have been sorry for the things which have made you sorry. Your friends have been my friends, your enemies my enemies. I have loved, for your sake, all whom you have loved. I have been your wife these twenty years and more. If there be any just cause for the anger you have against me, I am content to depart in shame and rebuke: if there be none, then I pray you to let me have justice at your hand."

With that she rose up, and making a low curtsey to the King, she walked proudly out of the court, a most unhappy woman, but a grand and dignified Queen.

The King sent messengers after her to call her back, but she would not return. Nor did she ever again come into the court.

The cardinals and the wise men talked for a long time, but they could not decide whether Henry might be allowed to send his wife away or not. The fact was the Pope was afraid of Henry on the one hand and of the Emperor of Germany, who was Katherine's nephew, on the other, and dared say nothing.

Then Henry grew very angry and impatient, and blamed Wolsey. Perhaps Wolsey had something to do with the delay, for although he did not love Queen Katherine, and would have been quite glad to have had her sent away, he hated Anne Boleyn, the lady whom Henry now wished to marry.

Anne Boleyn hated Wolsey too, and little by little she so turned the King against his old friend that he took many of his offices from Wolsey, and in the end sent him away from court.

When Wolsey was sent away, he went to a house which he had in the country, a sad and worn-out man. He loved power, but he loved England too, and in all he had done he had thought of making England great in the eyes of the world. With his wise counsels he had done much for England, and yet the people hated him.

The nobles hated Wolsey because he was proud and haughty. They could not forget that he was a butcher's son, and yet they knew that although Henry ruled England, Wolsey ruled Henry.

The common people hated him because when Henry needed money it was Wolsey, his Chancellor, who had to wring it from the poor. So they looked upon him as the cause of all their sorrows, and there were few who mourned and many who were glad at his fall.

Henry next accused Wolsey of treason and sent for him to come to London to be tried. Worn with sorrow and sickness, the cardinal started on his journey, but when he reached Leicester he was so ill that he could go no further.

"Father, I am come to lay my bones among you," he said sadly to the abbot, who came to welcome him when he arrived at the Abbey of Leicester. It was true, for in a few days the great cardinal lay dead. "Had I served my God as faithfully as I have served my King," he said before he died, "He would not have cast me off in my old age."

CHAPTER LXIV

HENRY VIII.—THE STORY OF THE KING'S SIX WIVES

AFTER the death of Wolsey, Henry chose a wise and gentle man called Sir Thomas More to be his Chancellor.

As the Pope still refused to give Henry leave to send Katherine away, he resolved to do so without leave. He sent her away, married his new wife, Anne Boleyn, and, because the Pope as head of the Church had refused to allow him to send Katherine away, he announced that the Pope had nothing more to do with the Church of England. Henry told the people that in future they must look upon the King of England as head of the Church as well as of the State.

The Pope was very angry with Henry and threatened him with all kinds of punishments, but Henry did not care. He had done what he wished to do, and was no longer afraid of the Pope.

Soon it began to be seen how wise Wolsey had been, for now that Henry ruled without him he became a much worse King than he had been before. Some good and wise men, among them the Chancellor, Sir Thomas More, felt that Henry had been wrong to quarrel with the Pope. They would not acknowledge him as head of the Church, so Henry first put them into prison and then he cut off their heads.

The King soon tired of Anne Boleyn, and, when people told him that she was a wicked woman, he was quite willing to believe them. He put her into prison and presently cut off her head. The very next day he married another lady called Jane Seymour. This lady was good and gentle, but she did not live very long after she was married to Henry. He was very sad at her death, and for two years he did not marry any one else. At the end of that time he married a fourth lady. She was called Anne of Cleves. Henry had never seen her, as she lived in Germany, but he had seen a picture of her painted by a famous artist called Holbein. In it she looked very pretty, and Henry said he would marry her because Thomas Cromwell, who was his chief adviser at that time, told him that it would be a wise thing to do.

But when the lady came to England, Henry found that she was not in the least like her picture. She was not at all pretty; she was very clumsy and awkward and could not speak a word of English.

Henry flew into a great passion, rudely called her "a great Flanders mare" and vowed he would not marry her. He was, however, obliged to do so. He was afraid if he did not, he might have to fight the German Princes who were her friends. But in revenge he put Thomas Cromwell into the Tower, and cut off his head because he had advised this marriage.

Henry soon got rid of his new wife. He offered her a large sum of money if she would go away and let him marry another lady. Anne was quite pleased to do this. No doubt she was glad to get away with her head safe upon her shoulders from such an angry, passionate man.

About a fortnight later Henry married another lady, called Catherine Howard.

This time the King soon discovered that he had married a wicked woman. She was not any more wicked than Henry was himself, but he did not think of that. To punish her, he cut off her head and the heads of several of her friends as well.

About a year later Henry married his sixth and last wife, a lady called Catherine Parr. She was a good woman, and it is wonderful that she should have been willing to marry so bad a man, and one who was so fond of cutting off the heads of his wives. Perhaps she thought that Henry might cut off her head if she refused, and after all it was a fine thing to be called Queen of England.

Catherine Parr was clever and she managed to keep her head upon her shoulders, although Henry once thought of cutting it off, because she did not quite agree with him about religious matters.

Although Henry had quarrelled with the Pope, he did not wish England to become a Protestant country. He wished the people to remain Roman Catholics, but to look upon him instead of the Pope as the head of the Church. So he beheaded and burned the people who tried to follow the teaching of Luther, and he also beheaded and burned those who still looked upon the Pope as the head of the Church.

Yet Henry helped on the Reformation, for he gave an order that a Bible should be placed in every church, so that people might go there and read it. And as books were still very dear, these Bibles were chained to the desks in case people should be tempted to steal them away.

Henry VII. had left a great deal of money when he died, but Henry VIII. was so extravagant and reckless that he soon spent it all. He tried many ways of getting more money, and after he quarrelled with the Pope he thought of a new way.

All over England there were monasteries and convents in which men and women lived who gave up their lives to good works. They cared for the sick and poor, taught the people how to read and write, and did many other useful things. Some of these monasteries and convents were very rich, possessing land and jewels besides much money. Henry said that the people who lived in these places led wicked lives. No doubt some of them did, but many of them led good lives and brought great comfort and happiness to the poor around them. But because of the evil which some did, Henry shut up these monasteries and convents. He sent the people who had lived in them out into the fields and streets homeless wanderers, and took all their money and lands for himself.

Besides doing this Henry taxed the people very heavily, and at last they rebelled. It was a curious rabble-like army which gathered together—an army of peasants and weavers led by priests and monks carrying their sacred banners and crucifixes.

They called their rebellion "The Pilgrimage of Grace." "Who is your leader?" asked the Duke of Norfolk, who had been sent against them.

"Our leader is Poverty," they replied, "and we are driven on by Necessity."

Although the King was not well prepared, the rebels did not succeed. The Duke of Norfolk persuaded them to go home, promising them pardon in the King's name. They went home, but the following year the rebellion broke out again. This time the King's soldiers were better prepared. The rebels were defeated, many of them being taken prisoner and put to death in cruel ways.

Henry VIII. died in 1547 A.D., having reigned for nearly thirty-eight years. His reign was a great one for England, the country becoming more important among the kingdoms of Europe than it had ever been. But Henry himself was bad and selfish, and at the end of his reign at least, proved himself to be a cruel tyrant.

CHAPTER LXV

EDWARD VI.—THE STORY OF A BOY KING

HENRY VIII. had three children. They were called Mary, Elizabeth, and Edward.

Edward was the son of Lady Jane Seymour, Henry's third wife, and was the youngest of the three. But for several reasons he was made King.

Edward was only nine years old and his uncle, Lord Somerset, was made Regent or Protector. Lord Somerset was not a strong man and did not rule well. He wished to be powerful and tried to make himself King in all but name. His brother, Thomas Seymour, also wanted to rule, so there were plots and quarrels between them and between the other great nobles.

Although Henry VIII. had quarrelled with the Pope he never became a Protestant, nor did he wish the religion of the country to be changed. But Lady Jane Seymour had been a Protestant and so was her brother who was now Protector. Edward VI. had been brought up in the new religion and although he had very little power, he wanted the country to become Protestant.

But this was not the wish of the whole people. Many of them did not like the new English service which the King ordered to be used in the churches. It was like a Christmas game, they said, and they asked for the old Latin service called the Mass to which they were accustomed.

When Henry VIII. shut up the monasteries he brought great distress on the poor in many ways. He gave some of the monastery land to his friends, and these gentlemen, growing greedy, began now to add to their possessions by enclosing with fences the common lands, which before had been free to every one. The poor had been allowed to feed their cows and sheep on these common lands but now that they were enclosed by fences, the sheep and cows died from hunger, and the poor people were worse off than ever.

Those who had been turned out of the monasteries were all Roman Catholics. They were now homeless and went among the people telling them that all their sorrows were because of the change of religion. At last the people rose in rebellion, many of them hardly knowing why, but only feeling that they were very unhappy. But the rebellion was soon crushed and the ringleaders put to death.

It is told how the Provost Marshal wrote to one man, the Mayor of Bodmin, who was known to have been one of the leaders, saying that he was coming to dinner. The mayor was very glad, thinking that he was not to be punished for his share in the riots. He made ready a splendid dinner and received the provost and his friends with great politeness.

"Mr. Mayor," said the provost, "I have to hang a man in the town after dinner. Will you have a gallows set up?"

The mayor gave the order to the hangman and then they sat down to dinner. They were all very gay and merry and, when the meal was over, the provost took the mayor by the arm, saying cheerfully, "Come now, let me see these gallows."

The mayor led him to where they were set up.

"Do you think they are strong enough?" said the provost.

"Oh yes," replied the mayor, "I can assure your lordship they are quite strong enough."

"Very well," said the provost, "you shall go up and try, for you are the man that is to be hanged."

"You do not mean that, my lord, you are joking," said the mayor.

"Nay, but I do mean it," said the provost. "Up you get, you have been a busy rebel and now here is your reward."

And in spite of all he could say the poor mayor was hanged upon his own gallows.

But the people rose again and again. One of the chief rebellions was under a man called Ket. He was a tanner. A great many people gathered round him, and they camped near Norwich on a plain, in the centre of which stood a great oak tree. This tree they called the Oak of Reformation, and under its branches Ket held his Parliament and Court, deciding quarrels, making laws, and punishing wrong-doers.

Ket encouraged his followers to pull up the hedges, throw down the fences, and fill up the ditches with which the common lands had been surrounded. Otherwise they behaved in a wonderfully orderly manner. They did indeed steal sheep and cattle from the rich gentlemen round so that they might have plenty to eat in the camp. But Ket ordered his men not to hurt any honest or poor people. He called himself the King's friend, and said he fought only against the wicked lords who gave him bad advice.

For some time the Protector did nothing and Ket's army grew larger and larger. Lord Somerset was sorry for the people. He knew that they were very poor, and felt that they were badly treated. Yet he knew, too, that he ought to do something to put down the rebellion.

At last a royal herald came. Dressed in his coat embroidered with the arms of England, he stood under the Oak of Reformation and blew his trumpet, and, while the people gathered round to listen, he cried, "All ye good subjects of King Edward VI. by the grace of God, Defender of the Faith, King of England, attend." Then he told them that he had been sent to say that King Edward would pardon them all, if they would go quietly back to heir homes.

Many of them would have done this but Ket said, "No. Pardon is for rebels. We are no rebels. We are the true subjects of the King and only wish to prevent him from being evilly advised." So he would not go home.

The Protector had gathered an army, intending to make war on Scotland, and this army he now sent against Ket and his men. There was a good deal of fighting. Many people on both sides were killed, the town of Norwich was taken and retaken, but in the end Ket was defeated. He and his brother were made prisoners with many of their followers. They were put to death, and nine of the chief rebels were hanged upon the branches of the Oak of Reformation.

As time went on, the quarrelling among the nobles grew worse. The office of Protector was first taken from Somerset, and he was then beheaded. Many of the common people were sorry for this, because they believed that Somerset had really been their friend, and they loved him although the nobles hated him.

Lord Somerset was succeeded by the Duke of Northumberland. The Duke of Northumberland was also a Protestant, and he was quite as fond of power as Somerset had been, and began to make plans to get the crown of England into his hands.

Edward had never been strong, and Northumberland knew that he was not likely to live long. The next heir to the throne was Mary, Edward's elder sister. She was the daughter of Katherine of Arragon, the first wife of Henry VIII. Princess Mary was a Roman Catholic. She hated the Protestant religion as much as Edward loved it. It made Edward sad to think that, when he was dead, Mary would undo all that he had done and that England would again become Roman Catholic.

Northumberland knew this, and he persuaded Edward to make a will leaving the throne to his cousin, Lady Jane Grey. Of course Edward had no right to do this, but he did do it.

Lady Jane Grey was the great-granddaughter of Henry VII., and she was married to the Duke of Northumberland's son. She was very young, being only about sixteen, and the duke thought that if she were Queen, he would be able to do just as he liked. He tried to keep his plan secret, for he knew that many of the people wished Mary to be Queen. He succeeded so well that even Lady Jane herself did not know what he intended to do.

In 1553 A.D., soon after Edward had made his will, leaving the crown to his cousin, he died. He was a good and gentle boy, fond of books and learning. During his short reign many schools were founded. They still exist and are called King Edward Schools.

Edward was very anxious to do what was right, but like his father Henry VIII., he was also fond of his own way. Had he lived to be old enough really to reign, he might have proved to be a good King. But it is hard to tell, for while he lived he had little real power.

CHAPTER LXVI

THE STORY OF LADY JANE GREY

AS soon as King Edward VI. was dead, Northumberland, with several other nobles, went to Lady Jane Grey, and offered her the crown. They knelt to her, kissing her hand and greeting her as their Queen.

It was a great thing to be Queen of England, but Lady Jane was not glad. She was sad and frightened. She trembled as the duke spoke to her, then covering her face with her hands, she fell fainting to the ground.

When she came to herself again she cried bitterly for sorrow at the death of her cousin, whom she had loved dearly. She was only a very little older than he and, like him, she was fond of learning; indeed they had often had the same masters.

Lady Jane was even more clever than Edward. She could speak and write Greek and Latin, and she knew some Hebrew. This was more wonderful in those days than it would be now, for then very few people had any learning at all.

As Lady Jane wept for her cousin, the nobles tried to comfort her by reminding her how great she herself now was. But that did not comfort her. It frightened her.

"I cannot be Queen," she said. "I cannot bear so great an honour. I am not fit for it."

"It is your duty," said the duke. "You cannot put away from you the duty God gives you."

With tears running down her face, Lady Jane fell upon her knees, and clasping her hands said, "Then if it must be so, God give me strength to bear this heavy burden. God give me grace to rule for His glory and the good of the people."

The next day Lady Jane was taken in state to the Tower. But no crowds gathered to greet and cheer her as their Queen. A few people came out of idle curiosity, but they were all silent. Not one voice cried, "God save the Queen!"

But while these things were happening, the Princess Mary did not sit still. She raised an army and claimed the crown. Northumberland marched against her with another army, leaving Lady Jane in the Tower. No sooner had he gone, than many of the lords, who had joined him in helping to put Lady Jane on the throne, began to regret it. They one and all declared for Queen Mary and, marching to the Tower, demanded the keys in her name.

Lady Jane's father, who had been left to guard the Tower, was afraid to resist, and he opened the gates to Mary's friends. Then running to his daughter's room he told her that her reign was at an end.

"Dear father," she said, "these are the happiest words I have ever heard since you told me that I must be Queen. May I go home now?" she added.

But alas! it was easier to enter the Tower than to leave it, and she was kept fast prisoner.

Meanwhile Mary had been proclaimed Queen in the streets of London.

Instead of the gloomy silence which had greeted Lady Jane Grey, the people shouted with joy, "God save the Queen! God save the Queen!"

The news spread fast. The church bells rang, the people sang and shouted, bonfires were lit, everywhere there was feasting and rejoicing. Mary was Queen.

The news travelled on. It reached Northumberland and his army. The duke knew when he heard it that his cause was lost, that his hopes and his fortunes were fallen and broken. Only one thing was left to him. He, too, took off his cap and shouted with the rest, "God save the Queen!" Poor Lady Jane, the ten-days Queen, was forgotten.

But even that could not save Northumberland, and he was taken back to London a prisoner. The people hated him, and they shouted, "Traitor, traitor, death to the traitor!" as he was led through the streets, till in fear and shame he hid his face from them as he entered the Tower, out of which he never again came.

Mary was so glad and happy to have won the crown that she was at first kind to every one. She would not put Lady Jane and her husband to death—an innocent girl was not to blame, she said. But she kept them both prisoners in the Tower. It is even thought that Mary would have spared the life of Northumberland. But many of the nobles hated him. It was decided that he must die, and his head was cut off.

The new Queen's gentleness did not last long. When once she felt herself secure upon the throne, she proved to be as self-willed as her father, Henry VIII., had been.

Mary was a Roman Catholic, and she made up her mind to bring England back to that faith. At first many of the people were glad of this, for although they did not wish to come under the rule of the Pope again, they did not like the new religion. But when Mary let it be known that she meant to marry Philip of Spain, the people were very angry.

Spain was a Roman Catholic country. The English hated the Spaniards, and were afraid of them. The Spaniards they knew were cruel. They had in their country a terrible court called the Inquisition.

Inquisition means to seek out. If any one was suspected of thinking for himself in matters of religion he was brought before this court and asked searching questions, so that the truth might be sought out. Sometimes the questions were so difficult to answer that innocent people made themselves appear guilty. But whether innocent or guilty those who were brought before this court were nearly always tortured, and often condemned to be burned to death.

However much the English wished to return to the Roman Catholic religion, they did not wish this terrible Inquisition to be brought into their country. They tried to make Mary marry an Englishman. But Mary was very proud and haughty. "There is no Englishman my equal. I will not marry a subject," she said.

No one was pleased with this marriage, and the Protestants were very much afraid. Anything, they thought, would be better than to allow a Spaniard to rule in England. So a plot was formed to put Mary from the throne, and to set either her sister Elizabeth or Lady Jane Grey in her place.

But the plot failed. All the leaders were beheaded, and hundreds of their followers were hanged. Gentle Lady Jane, who had never wished to rule, was blamed for this rebellion. She was brought out of the Tower where she had been kept prisoner, and her beautiful head was cut off. Her husband, father and brother were also put to death. The Queen had begun to earn for herself her terrible name of "Bloody Mary."

CHAPTER LXVII

MARY I.—HOW THE PRINCESS ELIZABETH BECAME A PRISONER

QUEEN MARY thought that her sister, the Princess Elizabeth, had a part in the plot to put her from the throne, so, as soon as it began, she sent some gentlemen with soldiers to take her prisoner.

These gentlemen arrived late in the evening at the house where the Princess was living.

"Tell the Princess," they said to her lady-in-waiting who met them, "that we must see her at once. We come from court with a message from the Queen."

The Princess was ill and in bed, but the lady took the message to her.

"Go back to the gentlemen," said the Princess, "say to them that I welcome them, but as it is so late, I trust that they will wait to speak with me until the morning."

"No, we must see the Princess at once," replied the gentlemen when they received this answer, and without waiting for more, they followed the lady into Princess Elizabeth's bedroom.

She was very much surprised, and angry too, when she saw them. "Is there so much haste that you cannot wait until morning?" she asked.

"We are sorry to see you so ill," replied the gentlemen, somewhat ashamed of themselves.

"And I am not glad to see you here at this time of night," returned the Princess.

"There is no help for it," said the gentlemen. "We are sent by the Queen, and her message is that you must come to her at once."

"Certainly, I shall be very pleased to obey," replied Elizabeth, "but you can see for yourselves that I am not well enough to come at present."

"We are very sorry," replied the gentlemen, "but you must come. Our orders are to bring you dead or alive."

This made the Princess very sad, for she now felt sure that she had reason to be afraid of her sister, the Queen. She tried very hard to make the gentlemen go away, but they would not. At last, after a great deal of talking, she agreed to go with them next morning.

When the time came Princess Elizabeth was so ill that she fainted several times as she was being led out of the house. All her servants, crying bitterly, gathered to say good-bye to her. They loved their mistress very much, and they did not know what was going to happen.

When Elizabeth arrived at court, she was not allowed to see the Queen, but was shut up in her room, and kept a prisoner there for a fortnight.

Gentlemen of the court came and talked to her, trying to make her confess that she had helped in the rebellion against the Queen. But she said always that she knew nothing of it, and had ever been true to her sister. Then one day they told her that she was to be taken to the Tower.

The Princess became very much afraid. She knew what a dreadful place the Tower was—what fearful things happened there, and how few people who once went in ever came out alive. She begged and prayed not to be taken there.

"I am true to the Queen," she said, "in thought, word and deed. It is not right that she should shut me up in that sad place."

But the lords replied, "There is no help for it. The Queen commands and you must obey."

So a boat was brought and the Princess was rowed down the Thames to the Tower. It was a dreary morning. Sky and river were grey, and the rain fell fast. As the boat went slowly on, the Princess sat silent and sorrowful, deep in thought. At last the boat stopped. The lords stepped out, and the Princess, awakened from her sad thoughts, looked up. But when she saw that the boat had stopped at the gate of the Tower called the Traitors' Gate, she sat still.

"Lady, will you land?" said one of the lords.

"No," answered Elizabeth, "I am no traitor."

"Lady, it is raining," said another of the lords, as he tried to put his cloak round her to shelter her. But the Princess dashed it back with her hand. Then rising, she stepped on shore, saying as she did so, "Here landeth, being a prisoner, as true a subject as ever stood upon these steps."

When the Princess reached the courtyard, she would go no farther, but sat there upon a stone. Not all the entreaties of the lords could move her. Through the cold and wet of the dreary morning she sat in that grim courtyard.

"Lady, you will do well to come in out of the rain," said the Governor of the Tower. "You are but uncomfortable there."

"Better to sit here than in a worse place," relied the Princess, "for I know not where you will lead me."

Then one of her own servants, kneeling beside her, burst into tears.

"Why do you weep for me?" said Elizabeth. "You should rather comfort me and not weep." But she rose and went sadly into the Tower. Then the doors were locked and barred. The Princess was a prisoner at last.

A close prisoner Elizabeth was kept. Very few of her own servants were allowed to be with her. But one of the servants of the Tower had a little son about four years old. He used to come to see the Princess and bring her flowers, and they soon became great friends. But when Elizabeth's enemies heard of this, they thought that she would try to send messages to her friends by this little boy. So, one day, they caught him and promised to give him apples and figs if he would tell them what the Princess said to him, and what messages she sent to her friends.

But although the boy was so young, he understood that these men must be the enemies of the Princess, and he would not tell them anything, if indeed he had anything to tell. They talked for a long time, but could learn nothing from him. "Please, my lord," said the little boy at last, "will you now give me the apples and figs you promised?"

"No, indeed," replied the gentleman, "but you shall have a whipping if you talk to the Princess any more."

"I shall bring my lady more flowers," replied the little boy boldly.

But his father was told that he must now allow his son to run about the Tower any longer, and next day the Princess missed her little friend. But presently she saw him peeping through a hole in the door, and when he saw that no one was near he called to her, "Lady, I can bring you no more flowers."

Then the Princess smiled sadly but said nothing. She knew that unkind people had taken even this one little friend from her.

The Princess lived in constant fear of her life. After a time she was removed from the Tower, and was sent from prison to prison. It was no wonder that one day, hearing a milkmaid singing gayly, Elizabeth said she, too, would rather be a milkmaid and free, than a great Princess and a prisoner.

At last she was allowed to go to Hatfield, a house near St. Albans, which now belongs to the Marquis of Salisbury. There, carefully watched and guarded, she lived until Mary died.

CHAPTER LXVIII

MARY I.—HOW A CANDLE WAS LIT IN ENGLAND WHICH HAS NEVER BEEN PUT OUT

WHEN Mary had put down the rebellion which her desire to marry Philip had raised, she had her own way and married him.

He came from Spain with much pomp and splendour, and as he rode through the streets of London there was a show of rejoicing, but the people did not really like him. He brought a great deal of money with him, and gave presents to the people, but still they did not like him. Parliament took good care that he should have no share in the government, and that made him angry. No one loved him except Mary.

With Philip's help the Queen began to do what she dearly wished. That was to bring England again under the power of the Pope.

The Pope sent a messenger to England, and Philip and Mary, holding a solemn service, knelt at his feet. They confessed that Henry VIII. had done a wicked thing, when he quarrelled with the Pope. They said that the people of England were sorry for it, and humbly begged to be forgiven.

Then the Pope's messenger granted them forgiveness in his master's name, and England was once more said to be Roman Catholic.

Now began the most terrible time of Mary's reign, for it required more than a few words from King, Queen, and Pope to make England again truly Roman Catholic. The Protestants would not give up their religion. Mary was determined that they should. Those who refused were imprisoned and put to death in the most cruel way. They were burned alive.

It would make you too sad to tell stories of this terrible time. In three years nearly three hundred people were put to death by Mary's cruel orders. Yet she did no good but rather harm to her cause. For many who were at first on her side turned away with horror from her dreadful cruelties.

These men and women who suffered death so cheerfully for their religion fought for British freedom as much as Caractacus, or Harold or any of the brave men of whom you have heard. And it was much harder to die as they did, than to fall in battle fighting for their country with sword and spear. So when you hear such names as Rogers, Hooper, Ridley, Latimer, and Cranmer, honour them as heroes, and think gratefully of the many, many others, whose names we shall never know, but who suffered as bravely.

"Be of good comfort, Master Ridley, and play the man," said Latimer, as they were being led to be burned together, "We shall this day light such a candle, by God's grace, in England, as I trust shall never be put out." By this he meant that others, hearing of the brave manner in which they died, would take heart too, and fight as bravely for their faith and freedom. So instead of crushing out God's light and truth, Mary was making it shine as a light which every one might see.

Mary was not happy, She could not help knowing that her cruel behaviour did harm rather than good to the religion which she loved, yet she went on killing and torturing more fiercely than ever.

Philip grew tired of England, where he was not allowed to rule, so he went back to his own country. This was a great sorrow to Mary, for she loved her husband. Philip returned indeed once, but it was only to get money for a war with France. Very unwillingly the Parliament granted the money and help he asked, but the war ended sadly for Mary. Calais, which had belonged to the English for more that two hundred years, was lost. Mary grieved very much over this. "When I am dead," she said, "you will find 'Calais' graven on my heart." In the same year, 1558 A.D. , she died, wretched and unloved.

She was succeeded by her sister, the Princess Elizabeth, who was the daughter of Anne Boleyn, the second wife of Henry VIII.

CHAPTER LXIX

ELIZABETH—HOW THE IMPRISONED PRINCESS BECAME A QUEEN

"Then our streets were unpaved, our houses were thatched, sir,
Our windows were latticed, our doors only latched, sir,
Yet so few were the rogues that would plunder or rob, sir,
That the hangman was starved for want of a job, sir.
Oh, the golden days of good Queen Bess!

"Then our ladies with large ruffs tied under their neck fast
Would gobble up a pound of beefsteaks for their breakfast;
With a close quilled-up coif, their noddles just did fit
And were trussed up as tight as a rabbit on a spit!
Oh, the golden days of good Queen Bess!

"Then jerkin and doublet, and yellow worsted hose
With a large pair of whiskers was the dress of our beaus,
Strong beer they preferred to clarets and to hocks,
No poultry they prized like the wing of an ox.
Oh, the golden days of good Queen Bess!

"Good neighbourhood, too, there was plenty as beef,
And the poor from the rich never wanted relief,
While merry went the mill-clack, the shuttle, and the plough,
And honest men could live by the sweat of their brow.
Oh, the golden days of good Queen Bess!

"Then all great men were good and all good men were great,
And the props of the nation were the pillars of the state,
For the sovereign and the subject one interest supported,
And our powerful alliance was by all other nations courted.
Oh, the golden days of good Queen Bess!"

IN the grounds of Hatfield the oak may still be seen under which Elizabeth was sitting when messengers came to tell her that Mary was dead and that she was Queen.

The Princess listened, looking up through the bare branches to the dull November sky, then falling upon her knees, she exclaimed in Latin words, "It is the Lord's doing, and it is marvellous in our eyes!"

Afterwards Elizabeth put these words upon the gold coins which were used during her reign. Upon the silver coins she put another Latin sentence which means, "I have chosen God for my helper."

As soon as Elizabeth knew that she was chosen to be Queen, she left Hatfield and went in state to the Tower of London, for, at that time, the Tower was used as a royal palace as well as a prison. But this time she did not go as a prisoner. This time she did not enter by the Traitors' Gate. She went as a Queen, free and happy, guarded indeed, but guarded with love and honour.

As the Queen passed through the gates, she paused. "Some," she said, "have fallen from being Princes in this land to be prisoners in this place; I am raised from being prisoner in this place to be Prince in this land. That was the work of God's justice; this a work of His mercy. So must I be myself to God thankful, and to man merciful."

There were great rejoicings when Elizabeth was crowned, bonfires blazed and joy-bells rang. Yet the land and the people were in a sad and miserable state, and it needed all Elizabeth's wisdom and the wisdom of the great men who surrounded her to bring back happiness and peace to the country.

Elizabeth began her reign at a very difficult time. The quarrels between the old and new religions and the cruelties of Mary had divided the people into two parties. Each party hoped that the new Queen would favour them. But Elizabeth did not mean to make any of her subjects suffer death because of what they felt it right to believe. During her reign people were neither tortured nor killed in the name of religion.

Elizabeth was clever, but she liked to think that she was beautiful too. She loved fine clothes and she dressed in the most splendid silks and satins and jewels. Her courtiers told her that she was the most beautiful lady on earth. This was not true. Elizabeth was not really very beautiful, but she was vain and liked to hear people say that she was lovely. And her people loved her so much that very likely they really thought that she was beautiful.

Whenever it was known that the Queen would pass through the streets, the people would gather to see her. They would stand for hours waiting until she came. When she at last appeared, they would wave their hats and shout, "God save your Majesty! God save your Majesty!"

Then the Queen would stop and, looking round on them, would say, "God bless you all, my good people." The people would again cry, "God save your Majesty!" and the Queen would smile and reply, "You may well have a greater Prince, but you will never have a more loving Prince."

Then when she had gone again the people would go to their homes talking of what a splendid Queen she was, and of how they would die for Good Queen Bess, as they loved to call her.

CHAPTER LXX

ELIZABETH—THE STORY OF A MOST UNHAPPY QUEEN

AT this time in Scotland as in England there ruled a Queen. These two Queens were cousins, for Margaret, the sister of Henry VIII., had married James IV., King of Scotland, and this Mary who was now Queen of Scotland was their granddaughter and Elizabeth's cousin.

In spite of the fact that an English Princess had married a Scottish King, the two peoples continued to be enemies as they had always been, and Elizabeth of England did not love her cousin Mary of Scotland. She hated and feared her.

Mary had been brought up in France, which is a Roman Catholic country, and she had married the French King. So she was Queen of France and Scotland.

When Mary of England died, Mary of Scotland thought that she had a better right to the throne of England than Elizabeth, so she called herself Queen of Scotland, France, England and Ireland.

Many people agreed with Mary, among them the Pope, who was angry with Elizabeth because she would not be ruled by him and would no longer punish the Protestants as her sister had done. So it was little wonder that Elizabeth hated and feared her cousin. The Protestants of England hated Mary of Scotland too. They were afraid that if she became Queen of England, she would bring back the dreadful days of the English Mary.

When Mary was only nineteen, her husband, the French King, died, and she left France where she had been living and returned to Scotland. As she sat upon the deck of the ship which took her to Scotland she wept bitterly. "Adieu, France, adieu," she sobbed, "I shall never see you more."

Scotland seemed cold and dark to Mary after sunny France, and the people harsh and rough. Yet the Scots loved their Queen and were eager to show her that they did so, and Mary wanted to be loved. But Mary and her people did not understand each other. Although she was clever and beautiful she was perhaps the most unhappy and most unwise Queen who ever sat upon a throne.

In Scotland, as in England, many dreadful things happened because of the Reformation and change of religion. Mary was a Roman Catholic, while many of her people had turned to the new religion. There were other causes for quarrels, so there was sorrow and war, until at last the Scottish people imprisoned their beautiful Queen in a lonely castle, upon an island, in the middle of a loch.

But although many people hated Mary, many loved her too, and these helped her to escape. One evening, a boy called the Little Douglas, who lived in the castle where she was imprisoned, stole the keys while the Governor was at supper. In the middle of the night he unlocked the door of Mary's room. Fearfully and silently she crept with him through the dark passages till they reached the great gate. Douglas unlocked it, and Mary passed out, holding her little frightened maid by the hand. Douglas locked the gate behind them and led the way to the place where a boat was waiting for them.

They were soon out on the dark water, getting farther and farther away from the castle. Half way to the shore, Little Douglas leaned over the side of the boat and dropped the great castle keys into the water. Mary's gaolers were prisoners in the castle, and she was free.

On land some of Queen Mary's friends were waiting for her with horses, and she rode joyfully away. Soon more friends joined her, and a battle was fought near Glasgow. But Mary's soldiers were defeated, and she was obliged to flee.

She did not know where to go. It would have been safest to go to France, but no ship was ready to take her there. So she crossed the border into England, and went to ask her cousin Elizabeth to take pity on her.

Elizabeth had never seen her beautiful cousin, and she refused to see her now. She gave her a castle to live in, not as a royal guest, but as a prisoner.

Mary had had to run away from Scotland so quickly that she had brought no clothes except those she wore. She wrote to tell Elizabeth this, but although Elizabeth had hundreds of beautiful dresses, she only sent some old clothes quite unfit for a queen to wear. Poor Mary would have been badly off, but her enemies were kinder than her cousin, and sent her dresses and clothes from Scotland.

When Queen Mary found that Elizabeth meant to treat her as a prisoner and not as a friend, she begged to be allowed to go away to some other country. But Elizabeth would not set her free. She feared if she did, Mary would go to the Kings of France or Spain and ask them to make war on England. She felt it was safest to keep her great enemy in prison.

Mary was so beautiful that she had many friends, and they were very angry with Elizabeth. Plot after plot to free Mary was formed. But all plots failed. For nineteen years this poor Queen was kept in prison. She was moved from castle to castle, for it seemed as if no place was strong and safe enough to keep her from her friends. At last she was shut up in a castle called Fotheringay.

When Mary had been in prison about nineteen years, a plot to kill Elizabeth and put Mary on the throne was discovered. Then the English Parliament persuaded Elizabeth that Mary must be put to death.

Elizabeth either really felt, or pretended to feel, very unwilling to give her consent to this. But in the end she signed a paper ordering Mary's head to be cut off.

A few days later the beautiful Queen, who had been so unhappy and who had caused so much unhappiness, walked into the great hall at Fotheringay. In one hand she carried a Bible, in the other a crucifix. The hall was hung with black; at one end was a low scaffold, also covered with black.

Nineteen years before Mary had come to England, young and beautiful, and, although she was not yet old, the long years in prison had made her look like an old woman. She could only walk with difficulty, and when she laid her head upon the block, it was seen that her hair was white.

Mary's servants cried bitterly when she said good-bye to them, although she comforted them by saying that, to her, death was a happy release out of prison. Her little dog would not leave her even after she was dead, but crept close to her dress, whining sadly, as the Dean of Peterborough cried, "So perish all Elizabeth's enemies."

When Elizabeth was told that Mary was dead she was very angry. She said that although she had signed the death warrant, as the paper was called, she had not meant that Mary should be killed. It is difficult to know what Elizabeth did mean, for she was deceitful as well as clever. But whether she meant it or not, Elizabeth had no right to behead Mary.

Mary's son James, who was now the King of Scotland, was very angry with Elizabeth for the manner in which she had treated his mother, but he had neither money nor soldiers enough with which to fight against England, so he did nothing.

Although Philip had lost nearly all his ships, he did not consider that he was beaten, and the war went on until the death of Elizabeth. But the English people no longer feared the Spaniards.

CHAPTER LXXII

ELIZABETH—THE STORY OF SIR WALTER RALEIGH

THE reign of Queen Elizabeth was great, not only because she was a wise ruler, but because she was surrounded by so many wise, and great, and good men. One of these wise men, Sir Willliam Cecil, afterwards called Lord Burleigh, was her secretary of state and her chief adviser during nearly all her reign, until he died in 1598 A.D.

There were so many great men in England at this time that you could not remember all their names, and to tell stories about them all would fill a whole book. In the reign of Elizabeth it is not only the men who were soldiers that we remember as great, but the men who wrote books, the men who sailed over the sea and discovered new countries, and the men who by careful thinking and wise acts kept peace at home.

Sir Walter Raleigh was one of the great men who lived at this time. He was a soldier and a sailor, a courtier, and a writer of books. But clever though he was, until the great Queen noticed him, he remained only a simple country gentleman.

One day Elizabeth was passing along the streets, and the people as usual came crowding to see her. Among them was Sir Walter Raleigh. The Queen stepped from her coach and, followed by her ladies, was about to cross the road. But in those days the streets were very badly kept, and Elizabeth stopped before a puddle of mud. She was grandly dressed, and how to cross the muddy road, without soiling her dainty shoes and skirts, she did not know. As she paused Sir Walter sprang forward. He, too, was finely dressed and he was wearing a beautiful new cloak. This he quickly pulled off and, bowing low, threw upon the ground before the Queen.

Elizabeth was very pleased, and, as she passed on, she smiled at the handsome young man who had ruined his beautiful cloak to save her dainty shoes, and ordered him to attend her at court. Raleigh's fortune was made. He went to court, and soon became so great a favourite that at one time he even thought that he might marry the Queen.

"Fain would I climb, but that I fear to fall," he one day wrote with a diamond upon a window. And the Queen, seeing it, wrote underneath, "If thy heart fail thee, climb then not at all." So Raleigh climbed, and although he never reached the throne, he climbed high.

Elizabeth gave him money and lands till he became very rich. He wanted to sail away over the sea in search of new countries and treasure, as Drake had done. But the Queen would not let him go.

As Raleigh could not go himself, he spent a great deal of his money in buying ships and sending other men over the sea to find new lands. These men sailed to America, which was then wild and unknown. Landing there, they claimed it for England, and Raleigh named it Virginia of Elizabeth. She liked to call herself the Virgin Queen which means "the Queen who has never married." One of the United States of America is still called Virginia.

For a long time Elizabeth was very pleased with Raleigh, but at last she became angry with him and sent him to prison in the dreadful Tower. The reason for this was that Sir Walter had dared to love and marry another lady, one of the Queen's own maids of honour. Elizabeth was always very angry if any of the gentlemen in her court married. Many of them wished to marry her, but she refused them all. Still she wished them to think that she was the cleverest and most beautiful woman in all the world; she wished them all to love and admire her so much that they would never think of marrying any other lady. And when they did marry another, she was always very angry.

Sir Walter, happily, was not kept in prison for very long, and some years later he really did have his wish, and sailed away to explore America. He did not find the golden land which he had imagined, but he brought home many strange stories, and many curious and useful things.

Two of the things which Raleigh brought home with him were tobacco and potatoes. Elizabeth had given him estates in Ireland, and there he planted the potatoes, and showed the people how to grow them. Even to this day the poor people in Ireland grow many potatoes, and live on them very largely.

People were pleased with the new vegetable, but they were very much astonished when he showed them how to use tobacco. Such a thing had never been seen before, and it took people some time to grow accustomed to it.

One day, soon after Raleigh had returned home, he was sitting smoking when a servant came into the room. The man stood still in horror. Smoke filled the room and was pouring out of his master's mouth. He must be on fire, thought the servant. Without saying a word he ran away and returned as quickly as he could with a pail of water. This he threw over his master, hoping to put out the fire and so save his life.

Raleigh, you may imagine, was not very pleased at finding himself suddenly drenched with cold water, just when he was enjoying a quiet smoke, but, when he understood the mistake his servant had made, he laughed heartily.

Raleigh had many adventures. He swept the ocean in his ships, and he fought by land and sea. But he wrote books too, and one of his friends was the poet Spenser, who tells beautiful stories in his poem called *The Faerie Queen.*

The greatest writer of this time (perhaps the greatest poet of any time), was Shakespeare. His name you know, and some day you will read the stories he wrote.

Another writer, and great soldier too, was Sir Philip Sidney. He was so handsome, and brave and kind that every one loved him. Queen, statesmen and people, soldiers, courtiers and poets, all loved him. He lived well, wrote well, fought well, and died well. He fell fighting for his country. Wounded and groaning with pain, he asked for a cup of water. While it was being brought, he noticed a soldier lying beside him in great agony. "Give it to him," he said, pointing to this poor soldier. The man refused to have it. "Nay, but take it," said Sir Philip, "you need it more than I do."

Sir Philip never recovered from his wound. A fortnight later he died; still young, brave, and handsome.

CHAPTER LXXIII

ELIZABETH—THE STORY OF THE QUEEN'S FAVOURITE

ANOTHER brave and handsome man, who was a great favourite with the Queen, was the Earl of Essex. He was so handsome and graceful that the Queen liked to have him always near her, although she quarrelled with him very often.

Essex loved fighting more than attending upon the Queen, and twice when there was war he ran away without leave. Elizabeth was angry, but Essex did great deeds and helped to make the name of England famous, so she forgave him. Later she made him commander of an expedition which, however, was not very successful. Again they quarrelled.

One day the Queen and her councillors were talking about who should govern Ireland. Elizabeth wanted one man, Essex another. He grew so angry because she would not take his advice, that he turned his back upon her. This was a very rude thing to do, for one must never turn one's back to a king or queen, but must even walk out of the room backwards when leaving their presence.

Elizabeth was furious, and, springing up, she boxed the Earl's ears.

Essex had been angry before, now he was in a terrible rage. Forgetting that a man must never fight with a woman, he laid his hand upon his sword. Then a gentleman who was there threw himself between the angry Queen and Earl, trying to calm them both.

But Essex would not be calmed. "I will take a blow from no one," he cried. "I would not have endured it from her father, King Henry. I will not take it from a king in petticoats." And, swearing dreadfully, he flung himself out of the room, refusing to return.

For some time the advisers of the Queen, and the friends of the Earl, tried to make peace between them, but in vain. Essex would not apologise, the Queen would not say that she was sorry. But in the end the Queen forgave Essex, and he came back to court.

As they had quarrelled over who should be sent to govern Ireland, Elizabeth decided to send Essex himself. This was not at all what Essex wanted. It was a very difficult post, and he did not wish to accept it, but he was obliged to do so.

He went to Ireland, but he did not succeed in ruling as the Queen would have liked. She wrote bitter, angry letters to him, and he replied with letters as bitter and angry as hers.

At last Essex decided to come back to England to see the Queen, and try to make friends with her again. Elizabeth forbade him, but in spite of her orders, he came.

Early one morning he arrived in London, dusty, dirty, and untidy from his long journey. He was in such haste to see the Queen that he did not stop to make himself fit to appear at court. Dusty and untidy as he was, he rushed straight to the palace. It was so early that the Queen was not up. Hearing that, Essex ran to her room, without even waiting till some one had told her that he had arrived.

The Queen was sitting in her room with her hair hanging down, waiting for her ladies to dress her, when Essex rushed in and, flinging himself on his knees beside her, kissed her hand again and again. The Queen was so surprised to see Essex, and so sorry when she saw how miserable he looked, that she spoke gently to him and comforted him. So presently he rose from his knees, and went away feeling that he was forgiven.

But it was only surprise which had made the Queen kind to Essex. Later in the day she received him very coldly. Later still she sent him to prison.

For some time Essex was kept a prisoner, then he was set free, but he could not again win the Queen's favour. Her unkindness hurt him so much, that he grew more and more unhappy, and more and more angry. He began to say unkind things about the Queen, calling her a foolish old woman who was growing crooked in mind and body.

It was quite true that Elizabeth was growing old and, being as vain as ever, she liked to think that she was still young and pretty. She covered her grey hair with a wig and painted her face; she sang and danced although she was nearly seventy years old. But it was wrong and foolish of Essex to speak as he did, and people were not slow to carry his words to the Queen.

At last Essex grew so angry, that he tried to raise a rebellion against Elizabeth. The rebellion failed, and Essex and those who had helped him were sent to the Tower.

In spite of all their quarrels Elizabeth really loved Essex. Now she felt it very hard to condemn him to death. Still she did.

Long before this, Elizabeth had one day given Essex a ring telling him, that if ever she should be angry with him, she would forgive him, if he sent this ring back to her.

When Essex heard that he was to die he remembered this promise, and he made up his mind to send the ring to Elizabeth, hoping that she would pardon him. But he did not know how to send it. He was afraid to give it to any of the Queen's courtiers, for he knew that many of them were his enemies. They were only too glad that he should be in disgrace, and would never deliver the ring to the Queen.

At length one day, as he looked sadly from his prison window, he saw a boy passing. The boy had a pleasant, honest face, and Essex felt sure that he might be trusted. He called to him and, throwing the ring down, told him to take it to his cousin, who was a kind lady and loved him. "Tell the lady," he said, "to show this ring to the Queen, and all will be well."

The boy took the ring, promising to do as he was asked. Then Essex threw down a purse full of gold, as a reward for his kindness, and the boy went away very pleased.

But by mistake he gave the ring to the wrong lady. Instead of giving it to the cousin of Essex, who loved him, he gave it to another lady, who hated him. This lady showed the ring to her husband, and as he, too, hated Essex, they resolved to keep the ring and say nothing about it. So Elizabeth never knew that Essex had sent it.

She, too, had remembered her promise, and hoped that Essex would send the ring. She waited and waited, but day after day went past, and it never came. At last, thinking that he was too proud to ask forgiveness, she ordered his head to be cut off. So proud and foolish Essex died, believing his Queen was still angry with him.

Elizabeth was growing old; many of her friends had died and left her, and after the death of Essex she was often very sad. The people too, who had loved Essex, were angry with her for having put him to death, and that made her more sad still.

When the lady who had kept back the ring was about to die she felt very sorry for what she had done. She could not find peace until she had confessed to the Queen, and asked her forgiveness. She sent a message to the Queen, begging her to come to her. Elizabeth came, but when she heard the story, instead of forgiving the poor dying lady, she shook her fiercely, saying, "God may forgive you, I never can."

At last Elizabeth herself grew very ill, but she would not go to bed. She sat day and night upon cushions on the floor, doing nothing but staring before her, with her finger in her mouth.

Then Sir Robert Cecil, the son of the great Lord Burleigh, who had been so wise and faithful a friend to Elizabeth, said, "For the sake of your people, madam, you must go to bed."

"Must!" exclaimed the Queen, " 'must' is not a word to use to princes. Little man, little man, your father would not have dared to use that word. But you know I must die, and that makes you so bold."

But at last she allowed herself to be carried to bed. Some of her lords, knowing that she had not long to live, asked whom she wished to reign after her. "I will have no rascal's son in my seat," she said, and would say no more.

Later they asked again, "Do you desire your cousin, the King of Scotland, to have the crown?"

The Queen only moved her head, but it seemed to those around that she meant to say, "Yes." She never spoke again.

On March 24, 1603 A.D., this great queen died, having reigned forty-five years. She had loved her country and her people, and her people loved her and wept for her at her death. No ruler had ever before been so mourned.

She was the last of the Tudor sovereigns, and with her successor, James, a new race of kings, called the Stuarts, began to reign in England.

CHAPTER LXXIV

JAMES VI. OF SCOTLAND, I. OF ENGLAND—THE STORY OF GUY FAWKES

FOR hundreds of years the kings of England had tried to conquer Scotland, and make Scotland and England one kingdom under one king. Many dreadful battles had been fought, many brave people had been killed. The Scots had lost many battles, but they had never been conquered, and at last the kings of England had almost given up hope of ever being able to conquer them. But now, what they had longed for, and fought for in vain, happened quite quietly and naturally, although not at all in the way that they had expected. Instead of an English King conquering and ruling over Scotland, a Scottish King came to rule over England.

Elizabeth Tudor, Queen of England, being dead, James Stuart, King of Scotland, was the rightful heir to the throne.

James VI. of Scotland was the son of the beautiful and unhappy Mary, Queen of Scots; was descended from Margaret Tudor, the sister of Henry VIII., and was Elizabeth's nearest relative. At the Queen's death there was no man nor woman left in England who had any right to the throne, so the English sent to Scotland and asked the Scottish King to come to be their King too.

He came, and since 1603 A.D., England and Scotland have formed one kingdom with Wales and Ireland.

So now we will talk no longer of England but of Britain, for long ago the old hatred has been forgotten, and we are all Britons.

James had been King of Scotland for many years before he became King of England too. He was a very little boy when he was first made King, and Scotland had been ruled by a Regent. James had been carefully taught, but unfortunately his teachers had thought more of making him clever, than of teaching him things which would have made him a great ruler. Some people called him the "British Solomon," but because he was such a mixture of wisdom and foolishness he has also been called the "Wisest fool in Christendom."

Although his mother, Queen Mary, was a Roman Catholic, James had been brought up a Protestant. The English Roman Catholics thought however that, in memory of his mother, James would be kinder to them than Elizabeth had been. Elizabeth had not burned and tortured the Roman Catholics as her sister Mary had burned and tortured the Protestants, still they were not quite kindly treated. They had not equal rights with the Protestants, and were sometimes looked down upon.

The Roman Catholics soon found out that James had no intention of being kind to them, and they became very angry. So angry did they become that they formed a plot to kill the King and all the chief Protestants in the country. Having done this, they intended to place James's little daughter, Elizabeth, upon the throne, and make Britain a Roman Catholic country once more.

Princess Elizabeth was, of course, being brought up as a Protestant, but she was such a little girl that the Catholics knew she would only be a make-believe queen. Until she grew up, the country would really be ruled by the Catholic gentlemen, and meantime they would have time, they thought, to teach her to be a Roman Catholic.

The first thing to be done was to kill the King and all the chief Protestant gentlemen. To do this the conspirators, as the people who form a plot are called, thought of a very dreadful plan. They decided to wait until Parliament was sitting, until the King and all his wise men were gathered together in one place, and then they would blow them up with gunpowder.

Underneath the Houses of Parliament there were cellars. These cellars were let to merchants and other people who wished to store goods. It was quite easy for the conspirators to rent one of these cellars, and into it they carried thirty-six barrels of gunpowder.

Besides the gunpowder, sticks and firewood were piled into the cellars by the conspirators. This was done partly to hide the barrels, and partly, no doubt, to help to burn the Houses of Parliament when they were set on fire. Nobody paid much attention to the barrels as they were being taken in, and nobody thought of asking with what they were filled.

For a year and a half the plot went on. Very few people knew of it, and those who did were bound by an oath never to talk of it. They met secretly at night, speaking only in mysterious whispers.

At last everything was ready. Guy Fawkes, one of the most fearless of the band, was chosen for the most difficult and dangerous part. He was to set fire to the gunpowder. Having done so, he meant to try to escape, but if he could not, he was quite ready to die in what he thought was a good cause. The day was fixed for the 5th of November, when Parliament would be opened.

A gentleman, called Francis Tresham, had joined the plot. He had a friend, a Roman Catholic nobleman, who was sure to be among the lords who would attend this Parliament.

Tresham could not bear to think of his friend being killed, so he wrote a letter to him in a disguised hand, warning him not to go to this Parliament. "My lord," said the letter, "out of the love I bear to some of your friends, I have a care for your life. Therefore, I advise you, if you love your life, to make some excuse so that you need not go to this Parliament. God and man are agreed to punish the wickedness of this time. Do not think lightly of this warning, but go away into the country where you may be safe. For, although there is no sign of any stir, yet, I say, they shall receive a terrible blow this Parliament, and yet they shall not see who hurts them."

Tresham's friend was very much disturbed by this letter. He took it to Lord Salisbury, who took it to the King.

The King, who was afterwards very proud of his cleverness, said that the terrible blow which was to be given, without the person being seen, must mean "gunpowder." It was clever of the King to think of this, but some people say that Salisbury had already found out about the plot, and perhaps he put the idea of gunpowder into the King's head.

About midnight, on the 4th of Novemeber, the day before Parliament was to meet, the cellars under the Houses were searched. With hushed voices, drawn swords, and dim lanterns, the searchers moved from cellar to cellar. All seemed empty, silent and dark, till in a far corner, a faint light was seen, and near it the dark figure and pale face of Guy Fawkes.

In a moment they were upon him. He tried to defend himself, but it was useless. Stern men with drawn swords closed in upon him, and he was soon a prisoner.

He could not deny his guilt. Round him were the barrels; in his pockets were those things which he needed to set fire to the gunpowder. He knew he must die. "Oh, would I had been quicker," he said, "would I had set fire to the powder. Death would have been sweet had some of my enemies gone with me."

Guy Fawkes was taken to the Tower. In the cruel manner of those days he was tortured to make him tell the names of the others who were with him in the plot. But Guy Fawkes was very brave, although he was wrong, and he would not tell.

The others, seeing that part of their plot had failed, hoped still to succeed in gaining possession of the Princess Elizabeth. So they hastily rode to the country house where she was living.

But part of the gunpowder which they took with them was set on fire and exploded by accident. It hurt some, and frightened all of them, for they thought that it was a punishment sent upon them because of what they had intended to do to others.

The Roman Catholics in the country did not rise to hep the conspirators as they had expected, and soon all hope of success was lost. The chief of the conspirators were seized, and were put to death, along with Guy Fawkes.

After this the Protestants hated the Roman Catholics more than ever, and their lives were made very hard.

There was great rejoicing at the discovery of the plot. Bells rang, and bonfires blazed, and even now, after three hundred years, teh day is not forgotten. On the 5th of November people still have fireworks, and bonfires on which they burn a figure made of straw and old clothes, which is meant to represent Guy Fawkes.

CHAPTER LXXV

JAMES VI. OF SCOTLAND, I. OF ENGLAND— THE STORY OF THE "MAYFLOWER"

WHEN Henry VIII. broke away from the Church of Rome he did not make much change in the services or in the ruling of the Church. He merely said that the Pope had nothing to do with the Church in England, and he commanded the services to be read in English, instead of Latin. But by degrees many Protestants began to think that the Church of England was too like the Church of Rome. They wanted to have no prayer book at all. They wanted to have very simple services and very simple churches. These people were called Puritans. They were very stern and grave, but many of the best and bravest men in England joined them.

At this time men did not wear plain, dark clothes as they do now. They wore bright colors and their clothes were often made of silk and velvet, and trimmed with lace. They wore their hair long and curly, and they had feathers in their hats. But the Puritans thought this gay dress was wicked. They cut their hair short and wore dark clothes and plain linen collars, instead of lace and feathers and gay-coloured silks and satins. They even spoke in a slow and sad tone of voice, using curious and long words, and they very seldom laughed.

The Puritans felt that in England they could not worship God in what seemed to them the right way. So, although they loved their country, they resolved to leave it, and sail away over the sea to the new lands which had been discovered. There they would found a New England where they could be free.

The first of these Puritans who left England were called the Pilgrim Fathers. The ship they sailed in was called the *Mayflower.* There were only one hundred of them—men, women, and children.

Before they started there were many sad partings. All left dear friends behind; some said good-bye for ever to fathers and mothers; some left their wives and little children, hoping one day to be able to send for them, when they had made a new home, far over the sea. But sad as they were, their hearts were full of hope, and in spite of tears they sang hymns.

They started in the summer, but they had so many delays and misfortunes that it was winter before they reached America. They did not come to the part of America to which they had expected to come, but reached land much further north, where the winter was very cold—far colder than the English winter.

As the little *Mayflower* drew near, the shore of their new home looked very dark and dreary to those Pilgrim Fathers. There were no people to greet them on the beach, no houses with twinkling lights by night and cheerful smoke by day. There was nothing but the rough, rocky shore, and beyond it, a mass of bare, brown trees. There was no sound but the roar of the waves, the call of sea-birds, and the cry of wild animals.

The little band of pilgrims felt very lonely when they landed in this strange country, hundreds and hundreds of miles from any white people. Dark woods and wilderness lay in front, behind the cold grey sea separating them from all their loved ones; and round them, day and night, the fear of attack from the wild Red Indians who inhabited the land.

But in spite of dangers and hardships they did not lose heart. Soon the noise of axe and saw was heard in the forest as the Pilgrim Fathers felled trees and cut them into planks with which to build their houses. Through cold and wind and rain they worked, and a little town of wooden houses rose round the little wooden meeting-house, as they called their church.

The building went on slowly for all the Pilgrim Fathers could not work at once. Some of them had to keep watch in case of attack from the Red Indians, while the remainder built the houses and laid out the gardens.

The little band struggled bravely. They were often cold and hungry, weary and afraid, still they did not give up hope. They had very little to eat. Sometimes they did not even know at night if they would have anything for breakfast in the morning. Once an eagle was shot, and they thought it was a great treat. It tasted something like mutton. Once a sailor found a herring on the shore. As it was only enough for one, the captain had it for supper. But many of the pilgrims, unused to such hardships, died during the winter.

At last the dark days passed, and with the sunshine of the spring came brighter times. And with the spring the *Mayflower*, which had lain in the bay all winter, sailed back to England.

With sad hearts the pilgrims saw it go. It was the last link which bound them to their old home. Yet in spite of the longing in their hearts for the green fields and white cliffs of England, in spite of all the hardships they had suffered, not one pilgrim returned home with the *Mayflower*. They knelt upon the shore, watching with tear-dimmed eyes till the last glimmer of its white sails died away in the distance, then they turned back to their work. But for many days after, the bay seemed sad and empty with no little *Mayflower* riding at anchor in it.

The Pilgrim Fathers named their town Plymouth, after the town in England from which they had sailed. From these few settlers the great American nation has grown, and although America is no longer a British colony, but a separate nation, it is a nation which has grown out of the British nation.

If you look at the map of America you will see Plymouth marked in the State of Massachusetts. In that town there is a hall called Pilgrim Hall, and in front of it stands a rock which is railed round and carefully preserved.

It is the rock which the feet of the Pilgrim Fathers first touched when they landed to found New England. The people of America are proud to remember that they are descended from those stern, brave men and women, so they guard the stone as something precious, and the 22nd of December, the day on which the Pilgrim Fathers landed, is called Forefathers' Day and is kept as a holiday.

The breaking waves dashed high on a stern and rockbound coast,
And the woods against the stormy sky their giant branches tossed.

And the heavy night hung dark, the hills and water o'er;
When a band of exiles moor'd their bark on the wild New England shore.

Not as the conqueror comes, they the true-hearted came;
Not with the roll of stirring drums and the trumpet that sings of fame.

Not as the flying come, in silence and in fear;
They shook the depths of the desert gloom with their hymns of lofty cheer.

Amidst the storm they sang, and the stars heard and the sea,
And the sounding aisles of the dim wood rang to the anthem of the free.

The ocean eagle soared from his nest by the white waves' foam,
And the rocking pines of the forest roar'd, this was their welcome home.

There were men with hoary hair amidst that pilgrim band:
Why had they come to wither there, away from their childhood's land?

There was woman's fearless eye, lit by her deep love's truth,
There was manhood's brow serenely high, and the fiery heart of youth.

What sought they thus afar? bright jewels of the mine?
The wealth of seas? the spoils of war? no—'twas a faith's pure shrine.

Yes, call it holy ground, which first their brave feet trod!
They have left unstain'd what there they found, freedom to worship God!

CHAPTER LXXVI

CHARLES I.—HOW A WOMAN STRUCK A BLOW FOR FREEDOM

LIKE Queen Elizabeth, King James had favourites. But unfortunately the favourites he chose were not good and wise men who helped him to govern well, but men who although clever were bad, and who thought only of themselves. Some of these men liked money and fine clothes, and James spent so much on them that he was always poor and in debt, and this led him into quarrels with the people and Parliament.

The Tudors had been a very autocratic race of kings. Autocratic is a word made from Greek words and means that the Tudors wanted to rule quite by themselves without help or advice from any one. During the time of the Tudors, especially in the reigns of Henry VIII. and Elizabeth, the power of Parliament had been much lessened. James tried to lessen it still more.

James knew how autocratic Elizabeth had been, and he meant to be the same. But Elizabeth, although she had her own way in many things, knew when to yield and let the people have their way. James did not know how to yield. He wanted to be a despot which is another word taken from Greek and really means "master," but has come to mean "cruel master." "The King can do no wrong," said James. "What he does must be right and the people must obey and ask no questions."

King James wrote several books, and in one of them he set down his ideas about the power of a king. But the people did not agree with these ideas. They thought many of the things which the King did were wrong. As they would not do everything he wished them to do, James dismissed Parliament and ruled for many years without calling another.

When James died, in 1625 A.D., no one was very sorry. He had reigned for fifty-eight years—thirty-six years as King of Scotland and twenty-two as King of Great Britain and Ireland, and his people, English, Scots, and Irish, were discontented with his rule. Yet in spite of all he had tried to do, the people were really nearer freedom than before, for they had shown that they would not quietly submit to the rule of a despot.

James was succeeded by his son Charles. He had been taught by his father to believe that the King could do no wrong, and like his father, Charles wanted to be autocratic.

Charles, too, dismissed Parliament, because he could not have entirely his own way. He tried to make the people pay taxes and give him money without the consent of Parliament, and this made them very angry.

Like King James, King Charles had bad advisers, and one of the worst, perhaps, was his own wife, of whom he was very fond. She was a French princess called Henrietta Maria and was a Roman Catholic. She hated the Puritans, who were growing more and more important in England. Charles hated them too, and, with the advice of Archbishop Laud, who was one of his chief advisers, he treated the Puritans very hardly.

Many of the people in Scotland had become Protestant. They were called Presbyterians, and like the Puritans, they chose to have a very simple form of worship, and very simple churches. This did not please Charles. He said that the Scottish Church must use the same service as the English Church. He ordered a new Prayer Book to be made which was almost the same as the English Prayer Book. This he sent to all the Scottish ministers commanding them to begin to use it on Sunday, 23rd July 1637 A.D.

There was great excitement among the Scottish people when this order became known. On the Sunday morning many crowded to the Cathedral of St. Giles in Edinburgh, wondering what would happen.

When the Dean entered, it was seen that he was wearing a white robe instead of the black one in which the Scottish clergy usually preached.

The Dean little knew of the anger which was rising in the hearts of the stern-faced men and women round him as the words of the new prayers rang strangely through the silent church.

He began the service, using the new Prayer Book. But he had not gone far when an old woman called Jenny Geddes sprang up. "Thou false thief," she cried, "wilt thou say Mass at my ear?" and with that she threw the stool upon which she had been sitting at the Dean's head.

In a moment the whole church was in confusion. "The Mass! the Mass! popery! popery!" shouted the people. "Down with the Pope! down with him!" The women rushed at the Dean and tore his white surplice from his shoulders, and he was so hardly used that he ran the risk of being killed. The Bishop of Edinburgh went into the pulpit and tried to calm the people. But they would not listen to him. "A Pope! a Pope!" they cried, "down with him! down with him!"

At last soldiers were sent for, the church was cleared, the doors were locked and the new service was read to the few who were in favour of it. Outside the crowd yelled and hooted, breaking the windows with stones and hammering on the doors, which were locked and barred against them.

The Bishop barely escaped with his life. He was carried through the crowd surrounded by soldiers with drawn swords in their hands.

All Scotland was in arms. High and low banded together to resist the King. They drew up a paper which was signed by thousands, binding themselves to fight for the freedom of religion. This paper was called the National Covenant, and the people who signed it the Covenanters. Scotland was ready for war, and Charles was forced to recall the Prayer Book and allow the Scottish Church to be free.

Charles promised the Scottish Church freedom, but he could never keep his word. Soon he raised an army intending to force them to do as he wished. But the Scots were ready to fight and they marched into England to meet Charles. The English Puritans were on the side of the Scots and for the first time in all history a Scottish army coming into England was welcomed by the English. The fighting ended in a victory for the Scots, and once more Charles promised them freedom in religion.

If you should ever go to St. Giles Cathedral in Edinburgh you will see there a brass plate in memory of Jenny Geddes and her deed. It is set there, not because it is right or wrong to use a Prayer Book, not because it is better to worship God in one way rather than another, but because it is right that people should be free to pray to God and worship God in their own way. Neither Pope nor King has a right to say how any man or woman shall pray, and it is not because Jenny Geddes fought against a Prayer Book, but because she struck a blow for freedom, that we remember her.

CHAPTER LXXVII

CHARLES I.—THE STORY OF HOW THE KING AND THE PARLIAMENT QUARRELLED AND AT LAST FOUGHT

AS Parliament would not do exactly as King Charles wished, he ruled without one for nearly twelve years. During these years he was often in need of money and raised it in many wrong ways. But at last he could get no more money by right or by wrong ways, and he was obliged to call a Parliament.

In 1640 A.D., what is known as the Long Parliament began to sit. It was called the Long Parliament because it lasted so long. The people chose the members for this Parliament very carefully, and they were not slow to show the King how strong they were. They beheaded one of the King's advisers because they said he had been guilty of treason. To commit treason means to do anything that is hurtful to the state or government. To commit high treason is to do anything hurtful to the King. The Parliament also imprisoned Archbishop Laud, and three years later he was beheaded.

King Charles had quarrelled with every Parliament he had had during his reign. Now the quarrels grew worse and worse. At last, one day, Charles marched to the House, followed by his soldiers, meaning to seize five members, who, he thought, were his worst enemies.

Leaving his soldiers at the door of the House, Charles went in and marched up to the Speaker's chair.

"Mr. Speaker," he said, "I must borrow your seat for a time."

The Speaker rose and fell upon his knee before the King, the members standing bare-headed, while the King sat down in the Speaker's chair.

Charles looked keenly round the House, but none of the five members were to be seen. They had been warned and were not there. He called them each by name. Only silence answered.

"Mr. Speaker," said Charles at last, "where are those five members whom I have called. Are any of them in the House? Do you see them?"

"Your Majesty," said the Speaker, again falling upon his knees, "I have neither eyes to see nor tongue to speak in this place but as the House may be pleased to direct me."

"Ah!" said Charles, "I see the birds are flown." Then, after making a very angry and bitter speech, he left the House. As he passed out the silence was broken by cries of rage, for the people felt that the King was trampling on all their rights.

The quarrels grew worse and worse, and at last war broke out, war between Briton and Briton. English, Scots, and Irish, all joined in this war and it was called the Great Rebellion.

The King and the lords were on one side, and the Parliament and the people on the other. Those who followed the King were called Cavaliers or Royalists, those who followed the Parliament were called Parliamentarians or Roundheads. Cavalier comes from a word which means "horse," and the Cavaliers were so called because most of them rode upon horses. The Roundheads were so called because they wore their hair short instead of long and curling like the Cavaliers. The Roundheads were for the most part Puritans, while the Cavaliers belonged to the Church of England.

At this time there was no regular army in Britain, such as we have now, and a great many of those who fought were quite untrained. The King's army was in some ways better than the army of the Parliament, for it contained many gentlemen who were accustomed to danger and who were able to ride.

The Parliamentarians were chiefly working men who knew very little about fighting. But among them there was a brave, strong man called Oliver Cromwell. He knew how hard it would be for these working men to conquer, if they were not taught how to fight, so he drilled them and taught them quickness and obedience. So thoroughly did they learn that they became most splendid soldiers, and were called Oliver Cromwell's Ironsides.

Never were such strange soldiers seen. In those days a camp was a wild, rough place, but from the camp of Cromwell's soldiers, instead of the sound of drunkenness and laughter, came the sound of psalm singing and prayer. To many of them the war was a holy war, a battle for the freedom of religion.

"Trust in God and keep your powder dry," was Cromwell's advice to his soldiers, as one day they were crossing a river to attack the enemy.

For four years the war went on. The Royalist leaders were Lord Lindsey and the King's nephew, Prime Rupert. Prince Rupert was so fiery and eager in battle that he was called "Dashing Prince Rupert." But although he was very brave, he was not a good general and often did rash things.

The chief of the Roundhead leaders were Oliver Cromwell, Ireton and Fairfax.

Many battles were fought, sometimes one side winning, sometimes the other. But at last, at a battle called Naseby, the Cavaliers were utterly defeated. Then Charles lost all hope. He had no money left and very few friends. He felt that his cause was ruined, and thinking that the Scots would be kinder to him than the English, he gave himself up to them.

The Scots and the English were still friends and they agreed that if Charles would grant to England the same kind of religion as Scotland, they would set him on the throne again. But Charles would not promise this, so the Scots gave him up to the Parliamentarians.

But when the war was over, it was found that neither King nor Parliament ruled the land, but the army. The King being now a prisoner, the Parliament said there was no longer any need for the army, and told the soldiers to go back to their homes. But the soldiers refused to go. They knew how powerful they had become, and they resolved to become yet more powerful and get possession of the King.

One evening a man called Cornet Joyce, with about eight hundred soldiers behind him, rode to the house in which King Charles was kept prisoner. Going into the King's room he told him politely and kindly that he had come to take him away. After some talk Charles said he was willing to go, but as it was now late, Cornet Joyce must come again in the morning.

Accordingly at six o'clock next morning the King rose and, going out to the courtyard, found Joyce and all his soldiers waiting there, mounted and ready.

"I pray you, Mr. Joyce," said the King, as he looked at the company of stern men in steel armour, "deal honestly with me and show me your commission."

By a commission, the King meant a letter to say that Joyce really had orders to take him away.

"Here is my commission," said Joyce.

"Where?" said the King.

"Here," said Joyce.

"Where?" again asked the King.

"Behind me," said Joyce, pointing to the mounted soldiers. "I hope it will satisfy your Majesty."

Then Charles smiled and said, "It is as fair a commission and as well written as ever I have seen a commission in my life. It may be read without spelling. But what if I refuse to go with you? I hope you would not force me. I am your King, and you ought not to lay violent hands upon your King. I acknowledge none to be above me here but God."

"We will not hurt you, your Majesty," replied Joyce. "Nay, we will not even force you to come with us against your will."

So Charles consented to go with them, and asked, "How far do you intend to ride to-day?"

"As far as your Majesty can conveniently ride," replied Joyce.

"I can ride as far as you or as any man here," said Charles, smiling, and so they set out.

In this way the King became the prisoner of the army instead of the prisoner of the Parliament.

CHAPTER LXXVIII

CHARLES I.—THE STORY OF HOW THE KING WAS BROUGHT TO HIS DEATH

"God gives not kings the style of gods in vain,
For on the throne His sceptre do they sway;
And as their subjects ought them to obey,
So kings should fear and serve their God again.
If, then, ye would enjoy a happy reign,
Observe the statutes of our heavenly king,
And from His law make all your laws to spring.
If His lieutenant here you would remain,
Reward the just, be steadfast, true, and plain;
Repress the proud, maintaining aye the right;
Walk always so as ever in His sight,
Who guards the godly, plaguing the profane;
And so shall you in princely virtues shine,
Resembling right your mighty King divine."

THIS poetry was written by James to his son, and perhaps it would have been better both for James and Charles had they tried to rule as the poem says kings ought to rule.

After Charles became the prisoner of the army, letters and messages passed continually between him and Parliament, and between him and the leaders of the army. Both parties offered to replace the King upon the throne if he would only promise them certain things. But these things Charles would not promise, for all the time he was secretly plotting with his friends, and hoping to free himself.

The leaders of the army treated Charles very kindly, allowing him to see his friends, and to have a great deal of liberty. This made it easy for him to escape, which he did, and fled to Carisbrooke Castle in the Isle of Wight. But although he thought that he was going to friends, he found that he was again a prisoner, and more carefully guarded than before.

The struggle for power between Parliament and army still went on. But Cromwell was master of the army, and he meant to be master of Parliament too. So one day when Parliament was about to meet, a man called Colonel Pride surrounded the House with soldiers. As they arrived, each member who would not do exactly as Cromwell and the other army leaders wished, was seized and turned away. When this was done there were only about fifty members left. This was called Pride's Purge, because he purged or cleaned away all those who did not think exactly as he did. It was still the Long Parliament that was sitting, but people now called it the Rump Parliament, because it was not a real parliament, but only part of one.

Cromwell was master of King and Parliament, but the army was too strong even for him. Against his will he was driven to do a deed from which he shrank. He was driven to condemn the King to death.

Charles was accused of high treason against the nation, and was brought to London to be tried. This was a crime which had never been heard of before, as high treason means a crime against the ruler.

More than a hundred men were called as judges of the King, but scarcely half of them came. Many of them were angry with Charles, and wished him to be punished. But the punishment for treason they knew was death, and they did not wish the King to be killed.

The judges assembled at Westminster Hall, and King Charles was brought before them as a prisoner. They who had always stood bareheaded in his presence, now sat with their hats upon their heads. Seeing that, Charles too kept on his hat, but it was seen that his hair, which had been very beautiful, had grown grey, and that he looked old and worn.

Charles had been foolish, he had been wicked, but now, in the face of death, he behaved with the dignity of a king. The men who sat before him, he said, had no right to judge or condemn him. He would not plead for mercy. Three times he was brought before the court, three times he refused to plead. At last the judges, without further trial, sentenced him to death as a "tyrant, a traitor, a murderer, and a public enemy."

Calm and dignified as ever, Charles walked out of the hall after the sentence had been pronounced.

"God bless your Majesty," cried a soldier as he passed, and was struck by his officer for daring to say such words.

"Methinks," said the King, pausing and smiling at the man, "the punishment is greater than the fault."

Three days later Charles the King walked for the last time through the streets of London, from St. James's Palace to Whitehall. The way was lined with soldiers, soldiers marched in front of him and behind him; the air was filled with the noise of trampling feet and the sound of drums.

The scaffold was raised outside the Palace of Whitehall, and hundreds of people crowded to see the dreadful end of their King, some in joy, very many in grief and awe.

Charles knelt by the block amid deep silence. And when a man in a black mask held up the King's head, crying, "Behold the head of a traitor!" a groan burst from the shuddering crowd.

"He nothing common did or mean
Upon that memorable scene,
But with his keener eye
The axe's edge did try;

"Nor called the gods with vulgar spite
To vindicate his helpless right;
But bowed his comely head
Down, as upon a bed."

CHAPTER LXXIX

THE COMMONWEALTH—THE ADVENTURES OF A PRINCE

KING CHARLES was beheaded on 30th January 1649 A.D., and Parliament immediately proclaimed that kings were bad and useless, so England would have no more. The Government would be a commonwealth. Common here means "belonging to all," and wealth, although we now use it to mean money, at one time meant well-being or happiness. Commonwealth really means the well-being or happiness of all. No one was to be greater than another; all were to be equal. The House of Lords was therefore, they said, useless and dangerous, and they did away with it. They also made it a crime for any one to call Prince Charles king, although he was the eldest son of Charles I.

The people of Scotland and Ireland, however, were very angry when they heard what had happened. The Scots had never wished the King to be killed; they had hoped to force him to rule better. Now that he was dead they proclaimed his son Charles king. At the same time the Irish rebelled, and Cromwell and his Ironsides went to subdue them. Very many of the Irish were Roman Catholics, and some years before they had risen and cruelly murdered the Irish Protestants. Cromwell hated the Roman Catholics, and he intended now to punish them for their cruelty to the Protestants, as well as for rebelling against the Commonwealth, as the Government of Britain was now called.

Cromwell remained nine months in Ireland, and so cruel and pitiless was he, that for many years no Irishman could hear his name without a shudder and a curse. The country was utterly subdued. Many of the people were killed, others were sent as slaves to the West Indies, and all who could fled to far countries to escape the fury of Cromwell.

When he had finished this dreadful work, Cromwell returned to England, and then marched into Scotland. The Ironsides had never been defeated, and now they won battle after battle, and at last Charles decided to march into England and fight for his crown there.

Cromwell was very much astonished when he heard what Charles was doing, and he hurried after him as fast as he could. The English did not flock to join Charles as he had expected, and when the two armies met at Worcester, Cromwell's army was nearly twice as large as that of the Prince. A dreadful battle followed. The Scots fought gallantly for their Prince, but they were utterly defeated. Hardly any escaped, and those who were not killed were sold as slaves.

Cromwell called this battle his "crowning mercy," for with it Charles lost all hope of regaining his kingdom. It was fought on what Cromwell used to think was his "lucky day," the third of September.

Charles fled from Worcester, and had many adventures before he reached safety. Great rewards were offered to any one who would tell where he was hiding, punishment and death threatened those who helped him. Yet so many were faithful to him that he escaped.

He cut off his beautiful hair, stained his face and his white hands brown, and instead of silk and satin, he put on coarse clothes which were much patched and darned, so that he looked like a labouring man. Then with an axe over his shoulder, he went into the woods with four brothers, who really were working men, and pretended to cut wood.

All day long they stayed in the wood, and at night the four brothers guided the Prince to another place. There they found so many of Cromwell's men that it was not safe for Charles to stay in a house. That night he slept in a hay-loft. Next day, finding that even there he was not safe, he climbed into an oak-tree, and lay among the branches. As it was September, the leaves were very thick and hid him well.

Charles lay very still and quiet. His heart thumped against his ribs, and he held his breath when some of Cromwell's soldiers rode under the tree. They were so close that he could hear them talk.

"The Lord hath given the ungodly one into our hands," said one.

"Yea, he cannot be afar off."

"We will use well our eyes. Perchance the Lord may deliver the malignant even unto us."

But the kind green leaves kept close, and little did the Roundheads think that the very man for whom they were looking was close above their heads and could hear every word they said.

For a whole long day Charles lay in the oak, and at last Cromwell's men, having searched and searched in vain for him, went away. Then Charles climbed down from the tree and walked many weary miles till his feet were blistered and sore, and his bones ached.

At length he reached the house of a Royalist lady and gentleman, who were kind to him.

The lady pretended that she had to go on a journey to visit a sick friend. Charles was dressed as her servant and mounted upon a horse, and the lady got up behind him. In those days, before there were trains or even coaches, ladies very often travelled like this. They did not ride upon a horse by themselves, but mounted behind a servant or a friend.

For many miles Charles travelled as this lady's servant, having many adventures and escapes by the way. As Charles was supposed to be the servant, he had, of course, to look after the horse. One evening, as he went into the stable-yard of the inn in which they were to spend the night, he found it full of Cromwell's men. One of them looked hard at the Prince.

"My friend," he said, "I seem to know your face."

"Like enough," replied Charles, "I have travelled a good deal with my masters."

"Surely," said the man, "you were with Mr. Baxter?"

"Yes," replied the Prince calmly, "I was with him. But now make way, my man, till I see after my beast. I will talk to you later."

So Charles busied himself with his horse, and escaped from the man who took him to be a fellow-servant.

After many dangers, often being recognised in spite of his disguises, the Prince arrived at Lyme Regis, and there a little boat was found to take him over to France. But when the captain's wife heard who was going to sail in her husband's boat, she was afraid. She was afraid that Cromwell might hear of it, and perhaps kill her husband. So she told him he must not go.

"I must go," said the captain, "I have promised."

"You shall not go," said his wife, and, seeing that talking did no good, she locked him into a room and took the key away.

Charles and his friends waited in vain for the captain, and at last they left Lyme Regis in despair. After more adventures they reached Brighton, and there they really did find a boat and a captain willing to take them over to France.

The evening before starting, Charles was having supper at a little inn in Brighton, when the landlord came behind him and kissed his hand. Again he had been recognised. But the landlord was faithful, and would not betray him.

"God bless your Majesty," he said, "perhaps I may live to be a lord, and my good wife a lady." He thought that if Charles ever came back to the throne he would not forget those who had helped and served him when he was poor and in trouble.

For more than six weeks Charles had travelled in fear and danger among his bitter enemies. In spite of his disguises, many people had recognised him. Yet not one had betrayed him. Instead, they had taken a great deal of trouble and run many risks to help and save him, and now his difficulties and dangers were over.

Very early next morning, while it was still almost dark, the little party crept down to the shore. In the grey dawn Charles stepped on board the boat, the sails were set, and slowly he was carried away from his kingdom which he was not to see again for many long days.

CHAPTER LXXX

THE COMMONWEALTH—THE LORD PROTECTOR

THE British had hardly done fighting at home, when they had to fight with enemies abroad. They went to war with the Dutch, who at this time had a very famous admiral called Van Tromp. The English, too, had a famous admiral called Blake.

The Dutch and the British had several reasons for quarrelling. Each tried to spoil the trade of the other, and the Dutch would not acknowledge the new British Government. This made the Parliament very angry.

Several fierce battles were fought at sea, and when the Dutch won, Van Tromp hoisted a broom to his masthead, as a sign that he intended to sweep the British ships from the seas. Blake and the English were very angry at this. They built and manned more ships as fast as they could, and once more sailed out to fight the Dutch. When the two fleets met, the fiercest, longest battle of this sea war took place. For three days they fought, but in the end Blake was victorious and, bravely though he had fought, Van Tromp was obliged to lower his proud broom and sweep the remainder of his own fleet homeward.

It was now about four years since King Charles had been beheaded.

Cromwell was the strongest man in the country, yet no real ruler had been appointed, and the Rump Parliament was acting neither wisely nor well. Cromwell made up his mind to put an end to this.

So one day he marched to Parliament at the head of about three hundred of his soldiers. He himself went into the House, leaving some of his soldiers at the door, some in the lobby, and some on the stairs. He sat down in his usual place, and listened for some time to the talking. Then suddenly he rose up and began to speak.

He told the Parliament that the things which they did were unjust, that they were tyrants and worse. "But your hour hath come," he cried, "the Lord hath done with you," and putting on his hat, he stamped with his foot, and his soldiers rushed in.

"I will put an end to your babbling," he shouted, and at a signal from their master, the soldiers drove the members out of the hall, Cromwell calling out insulting names at them as they passed.

The Speaker refused to leave the chair, and tried to address the members, but in the noise and confusion he could not make himself heard. Then one of Cromwell's friends took him by the arm and forced him to go. In a few minutes the hall was cleared of every one except Cromwell's soldiers and followers.

On the table lay the mace. The mace is the sign of the dignity and the lawfulness of Parliament. It is carried before the Speaker as he enters and leaves the House, and lies on the table while the members talk together. It is a sign of law and order, just as the sceptre is the sign of royalty and rule. Cromwell did not like any form or ceremony. He thought it was foolish and wicked.

"Take away that bauble," he said angrily, pointing to the mace. So it was removed. Cromwell's friends then left the House, he himself coming last and locking the doors after him. This was the end of the Long Parliament. It had lasted for thirteen years.

Cromwell and his friends now set to work to form a new Parliament, and one more to their liking than the last had been. Instead of allowing the people to choose the members, Cromwell himself chose them. But this Parliament did not please him much better than the last, and in less than five months it was again dissolved.

Cromwell was now asked to become ruler. Some of his friends wished him to take the title of king, but he refused, chiefly because he knew that his greatest friends were the soldiers, and they hated the name of king. If he took that name he was sure that they would turn against him and become his worst enemies. So he became ruler under the title of Lord Protector.

Cromwell was not crowned and anointed as kings were. But there was a very solemn service held, when a beautiful purple robe was placed upon his shoulders, the sword of office buckled to his side, and the sceptre put into his hand. He was truly king in everything but name.

Cromwell was not only a king, but a very stern and autocratic one. He wanted his own way quite as much as the Stuarts had done, only he really thought of the good of the country, and the Stuarts thought only of themselves.

The troubles of the civil war now began to pass away, and under the stern rule of the Lord Protector, Britain began once more to be peaceful and prosperous at home, and famous abroad.

All the Protestants of Europe looked to Cromwell for help and protection, and so powerful was his name that he could always give help. Kings bowed and obeyed when Cromwell commanded, and Britain was famous as she had not been since the days of Elizabeth. Her soldiers were the best in the world. Her admirals won for her the name of mistress of the seas, a name which she has kept ever since.

Yet the man who had won this great place for Britain lived in terror of his life. He was a tyrant, and like all tyrants he was bitterly hated, and he knew it. Under his clothes he wore armour, he always carried weapons, and wherever he went, he was followed and surrounded by a strong bodyguard. No one ever knew where he would sleep, for he moved about from room to room in his great palace lest some one should attack him while he rested.

At last, worn out in body and brain, the great Lord Protector died on 3rd September 1658 A.D. It was his lucky day.

> *"He first put arms into Religion's hand,*
> *And tim'rous conscience unto courage mann'd;*
> *The soldier taught that inward mail to wear,*
> *And fearing God, how they should nothing fear;*
> *Those strokes, he said, will pierce through all below,*
> *Where those that strike from Heav'n fetch their blow.*
> *Astonished armies did their flight prepare,*
> *And cities strong were stormèd by his prayer;*
> *In all his wars needs must he triumph, when*
> *He conquered God still ere he fought with men."*

CHAPTER LXXXI

CHARLES II.—HOW THE KING CAME TO HIS OWN, AND HOW DEATH WALKED IN THE STREETS OF LONDON

OLIVER CROMWELL had been so strong and powerful that it seemed quite natural to the people to choose his son, Richard, as the next Protector. But Richard was a very different man from his father. He had not that in him which makes a great soldier or a great ruler. The army, the Parliament, and the people soon found this out, and troubles began. In a few months, Richard gave up his office of Protector, and went away to live quietly in his house in the country.

The people were tired of being ruled by the army. They were tired of the gloom and the sternness of the Puritans. They remembered with regret the days of Charles I., when people dressed in gay colors, when they sang and played, when it was not thought wicked to have Christmas games or village dances, and they longed for these days to come again. They forgot how cruel and bad Charles had been, they remembered that he had a son—the son whom the Scots had already crowned King.

General Monk, who had ruled Scotland under Cromwell, saw that many of the Scots had never forgotten their King. So thinking great things, but saying little, he began to march to London.

The Parliament and the army were already quarrelling and as Monk passed through England, people flocked to him from all sides begging him to try to bring peace and order into the country again. This was what Monk meant to do, how he had not settled, but letters and messages were secretly passing between him and Charles, who was at this time living in Holland.

At last Monk reached London, and one day, when Parliament was sitting, he entered the House and told the members that there was a messenger at the door with a letter from Charles.

Amid great excitement the messenger was brought in and the letter read. It promised pardon to all those who had rebelled against Charles I.; it promised freedom to all to worship God as they thought right. It seemed to bring once more the promise of happiness and peace to Britain. The people rejoiced, and shouted, "God save the King!" The Commonwealth was at an end. Britain had a King again.

A few days later Charles landed at Dover, where he was met by Monk, and, 'mid the cheers and rejoicing of the people, rode to London. Charles landed upon his birthday, 29th May 1660 A.D., and people thought it was a good sign that he should have arrived upon such a happy day.

The soldiers alone did not rejoice. They had always hated the name of king, they hated it still, and when Charles II. rode gaily into London, the army, which was drawn up on Blackheath to do him honour, stood sullen, gloomy, and silent.

For more than ten years the army had been the greatest power in the country. But Charles saw that, because the soldiers disliked him, for him it was a danger rather than a safeguard. So he disbanded the army, and sent the soldiers back to their homes.

Charles was very glad to return to his own country. From being poor and homeless he had become the ruler over one of the greatest kingdoms of the world. But, in spite of all he had suffered, he had not learned to be kind or good.

As soon as Charles was safely on the throne he forgot all the promises which he had made. Many of the people who had helped to put Charles I. to death were punished, some of them being beheaded. The old quarrels about religion began again as fiercely as ever, for the King was a Roman Catholic at heart, although he dared not own it, and pretended to belong to the Church of England. The new Parliament was called the Cavalier Parliament, because it was so full of the King's friends, and they made laws which were very hard for the Puritans and Presbyterians.

Scotland suffered much from these laws, and Charles sent a cruel man, called Lauderdale, to govern for him there. He, helped by another man called Claverhouse, tortured and put to death all those who would not worship God as the King commanded.

During the reign of Charles II. there was another war between the Dutch and the British. The Dutch had good ships, brave sailors, and brave leaders. The British, too, were brave, but their ships were badly managed. The money which should have been used to pay and feed the sailors was wasted by the King and his friends. The war, however, went fiercely on, sometimes one side, sometimes the other, having the best of it. But the Dutch grew very bold, and at last sailed up the Thames, burning and destroying many of the British ships. Then, for the only time in all history, the roar of an enemy's guns was heard in London. The people went mad with fear and shame and anger. They thought the kingdom itself was threatened, and, recalling the days of Cromwell, asked themselves if he would have suffered an enemy so to insult his country. But the danger passed, and peace was made.

While this war was going on a terrible sickness called the plague broke out in London. It began in winter time. At first no one thought much about it, for such sickness was common in those days when people were careless about keeping their houses and towns clean. But as the days became warmer, the plague became worse, and soon it was so terrible that all who could fled from the town.

It was a dreadful time. No business was done, the shops were shut, the churches were empty. The streets, which used to be so full of people hurrying to and fro, were silent, deserted, and grass-grown.

As soon as it became known that any one in a house had the plague, all who lived in that house were forbidden to leave it lest they should carry the dreadful sickness to others. Then the door was marked with a great red cross, and the words, "The Lord have mercy on us."

At night, the awful silence of the streets was broken by the sounds of heavy, rumbling carts, and the mournful cry of the men in charge of them, "Bring out your dead! bring out your dead!" For those who died of this sickness could not be buried in a peaceful green churchyard where their friends could come to put flowers upon their graves. There were far too many of them for that. Those who died during the day were carried away in a cart at night, and buried all together in a great grave which was dug for them outside the town.

The story is told of a boatman who, when his wife became ill of the plague, could no longer go near his house, but slept in his boat. He worked hard all day, and in the evening used to bring what he had earned and lay it upon a stone not far from his house. Then he would go a little distance off and call to his wife. When she heard his call, she sent one of their children out to take the money and the food which he had brought. They would speak to each other for a short time at a distance, and then the boatman would go away again, sad at heart, wondering if his wife and children would be still alive when he came again next evening. But at least he knew that his dear ones would not die of hunger, as so many of the poor people did whose friends had run away and deserted them.

This dreadful sickness was greatly caused, and made much worse, by the dirt of the streets and the houses. In those days no one thought of keeping the streets clean. People threw all the rubbish from their houses into them, and there it lay rotting and poisoning the air. The streets, too, were very narrow, and windows small, so that little air or light could come into the houses. In fact, people never thought about fresh air and light.

The doctors did not know how to cure this sickness. Make-believe doctors offered the people all kinds of medicines which could do no good, but which were eagerly bought. Many went mad with terror and horror, and at one time a thousand people died every day. But at last the dreadful summer passed, and, with the coming of the winter and the frost, the terrible sickness gradually disappeared.

CHAPTER LXXXII

CHARLES II.—THE STORY OF HOW LONDON WAS BURNED

AFTER the plague had passed away another dreadful misfortune happened to London, at least at the time it seemed like a misfortune, but really it was a good thing. This was the Great Fire which caused much of the city to be burned to the ground. Many of the dirty houses and narrow streets were destroyed, and with them the last remains of the dreadful plague were also burned away. When the houses were built again they were made better and the streets were made wider, so that the Great Fire was not altogether a misfortune.

The fire first broke out in a baker's shop. As most of the houses were built of wood, and the summer had been unusually hot and dry, the flames spread very fast. They leaped from house to house, and the people, seeing that it was useless to try to save their dwellings, tried rather to save their furniture and belongings by carrying them to other houses. But sometimes, as soon as they had done this the fire would attack these too, and the people had to fly still further away, often in the end losing all that they possessed.

For three days and nights the fire blazed and roared. A great cloud of smoke hung over the city by day, but at night there was no darkness, for the flames made it brighter than by day. The air was hot and stifling, and at last no one could go near the fire, so great was the heat. The earth seemed a blazing furnace, and the sky as if beaten out of burning copper.

To stop the fire seemed impossible. It must burn and burn until nothing more was left to destroy. So houses were pulled down in order to make a gap between the burning ones and those which were still safe. But the work went on too slowly, and before the gap was big enough, the fire had reached the workers, and they had to flee for their lives.

At last some one thought of the plan of blowing up the houses with gunpowder. This was done, and when the hungry flames reached the open spaces left by the houses which had been destroyed, they died away, for they could not overleap the ruins and attack the houses beyond.

So the roar and crackle of the flames ceased, and the great cloud of smoke rolled away, but London, from the Tower to Temple Bar, was left a smouldering, blackened ruin and two hundred thousand people were homeless.

In memory of the Great Fire a monument was raised on the spot where it first broke out, and may still be seen to this day. So fearful were people at that time about plots, and so bitter was the feeling about religion, that many thought the fire had been caused on purpose by the Roman Catholics. But there was never any real reason for believing this, and now every one thinks that it happened by accident.

About this time the King of France became very greedy, and wanted more land and power than he had a right to possess. To prevent him succeeding in his plans to get these, three other countries in Europe joined together, forming what was called the Triple Alliance. The three countries were Britain, Holland, and Sweden. Triple means "three," and alliance means "to join together," and the Triple Alliance was called so because three countries joined together.

As you know, the French and English were old enemies, and this alliance pleased the English, so that Charles was forced to join it, although he really did not care whether the French King was powerful or not.

Charles thought most of all about his own pleasure. He spent a great deal of money, and he could not always make the Commons give him more when he wanted it. Now he thought of a new way of getting money. He wrote secret letters to the King of France, offering to break with the Triple Alliance, and to help him to fight against the Dutch. This, he said, he would do, if the King of France would promise to give him a large sum of money every year.

The King of France promised, and so Charles disgraced himself and his county, not only by breaking his word, but by becoming the servant of the King of France. Openly he pretended to be a Protestant and the friend of Protestants. Secretly he was a Roman Catholic and the friend of Roman Catholics.

For a time Charles kept up the pretence of the Triple Alliance, and by telling the Parliament that he must have more sailors, in order to keep a check upon the French King, he got a large sum of money from them. He got still more money in other wicked ways and then, to the anger of the people, he made war on the Dutch.

But if France was greedy and Britain false, Holland was strong and stubborn. Bravely she fought under her great leader, William, Prince of Orange. In two years Charles came to the end of his money, and he was force to sign a peace called the Peace of Westminster, and leave France to fight alone. But he still continued to receive money from the French King.

Charles was called the Merry Monarch, because he was gay and laughter-loving. The people were glad at first to have so gay a King, for they were tired of the stern ways of Cromwell and the Puritans. But they soon found out that Charles was selfish and wicked as well as gay, and his reign proved a very unhappy one for Britain.

There was constant discontent, there were constant plots. The King plotted, Parliament plotted, Protestants plotted, and Catholics plotted. But out of all the misery and discontent and injustice of these years one good thing at least grew.

This good thing was the passing of the Habeas Corpus Act. It was indeed no new act, it was as old as the Great Charter of King John, but like much in that great charter it had been set aside by king after king. By this Act no person could be put into prison and left there as long as the King pleased, or until he was forgotten by all his friends. It commanded that every person should be brought to trial, and either punished or set free. *Habeas Corpus* is Latin for "have his body," and means that the body of the prisoner must be brought into court at a certain time to be tried, instead of being left in prison for a long, long time or perhaps sent into slavery and exile without any trial or any chance of proving himself innocent. This Act is at least one good thing to remember of the reign of Charles II., who died in 1685 A.D., having reigned for twenty-five years.

He died as he had lived, careless, witty, laughter-loving. He was clever, and it is said that he never said a foolish thing, and never did a wise one. He was lazy, selfish, and deceitful, a bad man, and a bad king. Yet Charles found both men and women to love him during his life, and to sorrow for him at his death because he was clever, good-tempered, and had pleasant manners.

CHAPTER LXXXIII

JAMES II. OF ENGLAND AND VII. OF SCOTLAND—THE FIERY CROSS

WHEN Charles II. died, he left no sons who might succeed him, so his brother James, Duke of York, came to the throne. James was a Roman Catholic. During the reign of Charles II., an Act had been passed forbidding Roman Catholics to hold any public office. Yet in spite of this law, James was made King.

James promised that he would not hurt the Protestant churches. He allowed a bishop of the Church of England to crown him, but part of the coronation service was missed—that part at which the King used to receive a Bible and be told to read and believe it.

The new King's cruel character soon began to show itself. By his orders and in the name of religion, Claverhouse continued to murder and torture the Scots in most terrible ways because they refused again to accept the teaching of the English Church. More wicked still, in England, a man called Chief-Justice Jeffreys, by his cruelties made for himself a name which has never been forgotten. He was a monster; an ogre more fierce and terrible than in any fairy tale.

But James was not allowed to take possession of the kingdom without a struggle. In Holland, numbers of Protestants who had been driven out of Britain in the reign of Charles II. were gathered together. They felt that now was the time to return and fight, for they knew that many of their fellow countrymen must hate a Catholic King.

One of these exiled Protestants, a brave Scotchman called the Earl of Argyle, agreed to raise an army in Scotland, and an English noble, called the Duke of Monmouth, agreed to raise one in England. Monmouth thought that he had a better right to the throne than James, and with the help of Argyle he hoped to be able to drive James from the throne and become King himself. The English people knew and loved Monmouth, and indeed during the life of Charles, there had been a plot to set him upon the throne.

When everything was arranged, the Earl of Argyle sailed from Holland with his little band of followers, and landed in Scotland. He was one of the most powerful of the Scottish nobles. Although, when he had fled from the country in the reign of Charles, the King had taken his land and money from him, he knew that he could trust to his clan to rise and follow him as soon as he returned.

In those days there were no telegraphs and no postmen. There were even few roads among the wild Highlands of Scotland and few people could read. So when a chief had need of his men he gathered them by means of a sign which all could understand. This sign was the Fiery Cross.

A rough cross was made from the wood of a yew-tree. The ends of this cross were set alight and afterwards the flames were put out by being dipped in the blood of a goat. The chief with his own hands then solemnly gave the cross to a swift runner. This man took it and ran as swiftly as he could to the next village. When the men of this village saw the Fiery Cross, they said, "Our chief has need of us," and they at once prepared for battle, while the Fiery Cross was put into the hands of another swift runner, who carried it over hill and glen to the next village.

On and on it went through all the countryside, the men in each village and farmhouse understanding what was needed of them and, without a word, gathering to their chief.

So it was that the Clan Campbell gathered round their chieftain Mac Callum More, as they loved to call Argyle.

But although the Earl's men were loyal to him, those who had come from Holland with him to serve as his captains would not agree and would not obey. Their foolish jealousy of their leader was so great that his army became disheartened and was scattered almost before there had been any real fighting.

The Earl was once more forced to flee. Dressed as a peasant and followed by only one faithful friend he tried to escape. But as they were crossing a little river they were seized by some of the King's soldiers. The Earl to save himself sprang into the water, but the soldiers followed him. He was armed only with pistols, and in his spring into the water the powder had been wet and they would not fire. He was struck to the ground and taken prisoner.

When Argyle saw that it was useless to struggle any more he called out, "I am the Earl of Argyle." He knew what a great name his was, and he hoped that even the King's soldiers would tremble before it and let him go.

But his name could not save him, and he was led a prisoner to Edinburgh. There the judges tried in vain to make him tell who were with him in the rebellion. He would not tell and he was condemned to death. Bravely and calmly he met his fate. One of the last things he did was to write to his wife.

"Dear Heart,—Forgive me all my faults; and now comfort thyself in Him in whom only true comfort is to be found. The Lord be with thee, bless and comfort thee, my dearest.— Adieu."

On his grave were carved some lines which he himself wrote the day before he died.

Although Argyle had refused to give the names of the other leaders of the rebellion, many were seized and beheaded. To one of them James said,

"You had better be frank with me. You know it is in my power to pardon you."

"It may be in your power, sire," replied the man, "but it is not in your nature." The man was right; James never forgave.

CHAPTER LXXXIV

JAMES II. OF ENGLAND AND VII. OF SCOTLAND—THE STORY OF KING MONMOUTH

A FEW days after Argyle reached Scotland, the Duke of Monmouth sailed from Holland and landed in England. He was received with great joy. The common people flocked to his standard, many of them armed only with scythes, and pruning-hooks fastened to poles. Nine hundred young men marched before him, twenty beautiful girls gave him a Bible splendidly bound and a banner which they had themselves embroidered. The roads wherever he went were lined with cheering crowds. "A Monmouth! A Monmouth! the Protestant religion!" they cried as he passed.

The Duke's followers begged him to take the title of king, so, on 20th June 1685 A.D., the same day on which Argyle was led captive through Edinburgh, Monmouth was proclaimed king at Taunton, a little town in the south of England. But like the real King, he was named James so, instead of calling him King James, his followers called him King Monmouth.

King Monmouth did not enjoy his title long. In the dark of the early morning of the 6th July, a battle was fought between King James's men and the followers of Monmouth, on the plain of Sedgemoor. Monmouth fought bravely, but when he saw that his men were being defeated, he turned and fled away leaving them leaderless and hopeless. This was the last real battle ever fought on English ground.

Monmouth tried to escape in disguise. He changed clothes with a poor shepherd, but the country was so full of the King's soldiers that he found it impossible to get away. For several days he lived in the fields, hiding in ditches and having nothing to eat but raw peas and beans. At last, miserable and ragged, half starving from cold and hunger, he was discovered by the soldiers and taken prisoner to London.

Bound with a cord of silk he was led before King James, and falling upon his knees he begged for mercy and forgiveness. But James never forgave. Monmouth, like so many other men, good and bad, was beheaded.

The anger and vengeance of the King did not end with the death of Monmouth. His soldiers, under a dreadful man called Kirke, tortured and murdered, in a terrible manner, the poor rebels who escaped from Sedgemoor. Judge Jeffreys followed next, and so many people did he kill, such terrible things did he do, that his journey through the country was for ever after called the Bloody Assize.

Assize means Court of Justice. At certain times in England judges make what is called a circuit or journey through the country, when they hear what wrong things people have done, and when they judge and punish. But on this dreadful journey Judge Jeffreys did not do justice. He did wrong and murder, and King James praised and rewarded him for it.

CHAPTER LXXXV

JAMES II. OF ENGLAND AND VII. OF SCOTLAND—THE STORY OF THE SEVEN BISHOPS

HAVING put down two rebellions, James made up his mind to turn Britain into a Roman Catholic country once more. It was against the law for a Roman Catholic to hold any public office but, in spite of that James began to turn away Protestants from many posts, and to put Roman Catholics in their places. The people grew more and more angry, but still James took his own way, growing bolder and bolder.

At last he issued what was called the Declaration of Indulgence. In this Declaration he said that all the laws against the Roman Catholics, and against all others who did not belong to the Church of England, and who were called Dissenters, were done away with.

James hated the Dissenters, that is the Puritans and Presbyterians, but he thought that if he made them free they would side with him and help him to free the Romish Church also. But they did not do so. They knew that James was breaking the laws of the land in issuing this Declaration, and they would not accept freedom in an unlawful manner.

The King ordered the Declaration to be read in all London churches on Sundays, 20th and 27th May, and in all country churches on Sundays, 3rd and 10th of June. But nearly every clergyman in London and in the coun-try refused to obey.

After a great deal of talking and consulting seven bishops wrote out a paper, which they all signed. In this paper the bishops told the King that they could not obey him, not because they wished people who thought differently from themselves to be cruelly and unkindly treated, but because the laws against these people had been made by Parliament. They had been passed by King, Lords, and Commons, and could only be recalled by the consent of King, Lords, and Commons. The King alone, they reminded him, had no power to recall a law, and, in ordering the clergy to read the Declaration of Indulgence in the churches, the King was ordering them to break the law. This they refused to do.

By the time that this letter was written and signed, it was late on Friday evening. There was no time to be lost, and the bishops took it at once to the King.

He received them kindly, but when he read the letter his face grew dark and angry. "This is rebellion," he said.

"Sire," said the bishops, "we are not rebels. We are true to your Majesty. We wish to keep the laws of the land."

"I tell you it is rebellion," repeated James.

Then one of the bishops, who was called Trelawney, fell upon his knees. "Sire," he cried, "do not say so hard a thing to us. No Trelawney can be a rebel. Remember that my family has fought for the crown. Remember how we served your Majesty against Monmouth."

"We are ready to die at your Majesty's feet," cried another. "We helped to put down one rebellion, why should we raise another?"

"This is rebellion! This is rebellion, I will be obeyed!" replied the King, growing more and more angry. "I will keep this paper. I will remember you who have signed it. You are rebels. Go."

The bishops went. But that very night copies of the letter which they had written to the King were printed and sold to thousands of joyful people, who in reading it knew that seven brave men were fighting for their freedom.

On Sunday morning the excitement was great. People crowded to the churches in thousands. Would the clergy read the Declaration, or would they not, was the question which everybody asked. It was soon answered. In only four of the hundred London churches was it read. In these four churches, as soon as the first words were heard the people rose and streamed out, so that when the reading was at an end the churches were silent and empty.

A week passed. The second Sunday came. Again thousands thronged to the churches. Again the Declaration was unread. Excitement grew. Another week passed. Would the country churches read the Declaration, or would they not? That question, too, was answered. The country clergy, like the London clergy, refused, and the land from end to end seemed to be filled with an outburst of joy.

Then the King ordered the seven bishops who had written the letter, and who had set the brave example, to be sent to the Tower. As soon as this became known the whole river was crowded with boats, and the banks thronged with people eager to see the bishops as they passed on their way to prison. When the bishops appeared, the people fell upon their knees begging for a blessing. All the way from Whitehall to the Tower the air was full of shouts of "God bless your Lordships!" It was like a royal procession, rather than like rebels being led to prison. As the bishops entered the Traitors' Gate, the guards knelt before them begging, too, for a blessing, and in the guard-house the rough soldiers drank to the health of the brave bishops.

All next day, to the anger of the King, great people crowded to visit the bishops, to cheer and comfort them in prison. And when ten of the chief Dissenters went to see them, his anger knew no bounds. He called these Dissenters before him to scold them, and ask what they meant by visiting their enemies. "We are all Protestants," they replied, "it is our duty to forget old quarrels, and stand by the men who are fighting for the liberties of the Protestant religion."

For a week the bishops were kept in prison, while all over the country people wondered anxiously what would happen to them. Bishop Trelawney belonged to Cornwall. The people there loved him very much, and they made a song about him of which the chorus was:—

> *"And shall Trelawney die? and shall Trelawney die?*
> *Then thirty thousand Cornish boys will know the reason why."*

After being kept in prison for a week the bishops were brought to court to be tried. The excitement was tremendous. The King and his friends did all they could to have the bishops punished. But it was in vain. The judges and the jury said that the bishops had done no wrong, and they were set free.

From street to street the joyful news spread like wildfire. Bells rang, cannon boomed, bonfires blazed, people cheered and wept and sang. Another battle had been fought for freedom, another victory won, and all England seemed mad with the joy of it.

At night, the houses were lit up; in nearly every window a row of seven candles appeared, one candle for each bishop. The streets were filled with rejoicing people, and not until day dawned, and the bells began to ring for morning service, did the weary, happy crowds go to their homes.

CHAPTER LXXXVI

JAMES II. OF ENGLAND AND VII. OF SCOTLAND—WILLIAM THE DELIVERER

ANY one could see that the people were everywhere ready for rebellion. The King alone would not see it and went on in his own way. He was angry and sullen, but very obstinate. "I will not give way," he said, "my father lost his head by giving way," and he resolved to punish the people.

But James had gone too far. The people were weary of a Popish tyrant, and they made up their minds to have a Protestant King. So they asked William, Prince of Orange, to come to rule over them, the Prince against whom Charles II. had fought in the Dutch wars. William had some claim to the throne. I will explain how.

Charles I. had a daughter called Mary. She married a Prince of Orange called William, and their son, also called William, was now Prince of Orange. He was thus the nephew of Charles II. and of James II., and besides this he had married his cousin, Mary, the eldest daughter of James II.

Although their father, James, was a Roman Catholic, Mary and her sister, Anne, were both Protestants, and except for their little brother, who was at this time a tiny baby, Mary was the next heir to the throne of Britain.

So when the British saw that James meant to rule as a tyrant and that there was no hope of any freedom or happiness for them as long as he was King, they sent messages to Holland begging William to come to take the crown.

William consented to come, and began to gather his ships and men. And one day a letter reached James telling him what the Prince of Orange was doing. As James read, he turned pale and the letter dropped from his hand. He had thought that he might ill-treat the people as he liked. Now he discovered his mistake and tried to undo the evil he had done. It was too late. His people had forsaken him.

William was ready to sail, but for some days he was prevented because of the wind which blew from the west. At last it changed, and what was known for many years after as the "Protestant East Wind" began to blow.

It blew the Prince and his great fleet to the shores of Britain. More than six hundred ships swept over the water, led by William in his vessel called the *Brill*. From the mast-head floated his standard, with the arms of Nassau and of Britain upon it, and in great shining letters the words, "I will maintain the liberties of England, and the Protestant religion." By night the dark sea glittered for miles with lights. By day the white sails glimmered in the wintry sun.

Once before in our story a great conqueror called William had sailed to these shores with mighty ships and men. This was no conqueror, but a deliverer.

On the 5th of November 1688 A.D., William landed at Torbay, in Devonshire. There the stone upon which he first placed his foot is still to be seen. Although now it is a town, then it was a little lonely village, and the Prince had to sleep the first night in a tiny thatched cottage. But over it, as proudly as over any castle, fluttered the great banner with its promise, "I will maintain the liberties of England and the Protestant religion."

Through rain and wintry weather, over roads knee-deep in mud, the Prince and his army marched northward. Worn, wet, and muddy as they were, the people crowded everywhere along the way to cheer them. The Prince rode upon a beautiful white horse, a white feather was in his hat, and armour glittered upon his breast. His face was grave and stern, his eyes keen and watchful. He looked a soldier and a King.

As he rode along an old woman pushed her way through the crowd, and afraid neither of the prancing horses nor the drawn swords of the soldiers, darted to the side of the Prince. She seized his hand, and, looking up into his face with eyes full of tears, cried, "I am happy now, I am happy now." And the grave and stern William smiled gently as he looked down upon her. The Deliverer had come.

James II., his Queen, and their little boy fled to France. No one wanted James, no one regretted him. To go to France was the best thing he could do, and the King there received him kindly and treated him as an honoured guest.

At Westminster a Parliament was called, which arranged that William and Mary should be King and Queen together. For although Mary had the better right to the throne she did not wish to reign without her husband, nor did he wish to accept a lower rank than that of his wife.

So ended the "Glorious Revolution." It had been brought about with hardly any fighting at all, and the war between the King and Parliament was at an end, for William and Mary received the throne by the will of Parliament.

CHAPTER LXXXVII

WILLIAM III. AND MARY II.—THE STORY OF BRAVE LONDONDERRY

ALTHOUGH most of the people received William and Mary joyfully, some, chiefly in Ireland and Scotland, still looked upon James as the rightful King.

In Ireland especially there were many Roman Catholics, who would not acknowledge a Protestant King. The King of France hated William, so he helped James with money and ships, which enabled him to set out for Ireland to win his kingdom again.

James landed at a town called Kinsale and the Irish people welcomed him with great joy. But he felt disheartened almost at once for there had already been much fighting, and the country through which he had to pass was desolate and deserted, and at times he and his men could find hardly enough food to keep them from starving. Most of the Protestants had fled from the land or had shut themselves up in the two towns of Enniskillen and Londonderry. The soldiers of James besieged both these towns, but it was round Londonderry that the greatest fight took place.

Londonderry is on a river called the Foyle, and the enemy not only surrounded the town on the land side, but they built a bar across the river so that no ships could come to the town with food or help.

The walls were weak and the cannon few, and the Irish thought that the town could not hold out for long. The Governor, too, was a cowardly man, and did his best to dishearten the people, until it was suspected that he was a traitor. Indeed, he would have given in, but a brave old clergyman, called Walker, marched into his pulpit one morning with a sword in one hand and a Bible in the other, and preached such a rousing sermon that the people took heart and never lost it again through all the long weeks of hunger and suffering which they had to endure.

It was a dreadful time. The people had hardly anything to eat, but they held bravely on, hoping against hope that help would come to them from England. But day after day passed and no help came. Rats, mice, dogs, and horses, all were eaten, only tallow and skins remained. Still they held on. The soldiers were so weak at last from want of food that they could hardly stand, far less fight. They resolved to hold out for two days longer. Then the end must come.

But just as the sun was setting on the 28th of July, the day before they were going to give in, the eager watchers on the walls saw the gleam of sails far down the river. Help! Help at last! How their hearts beat, how they shouted with all the little strength they had, as nearer and nearer sailed the ships.

There were three of them. On they came with all sail set. But how could they pass the dreadful bar which lay right across the river? On they came. One ship called the *Mountjoy* took the lead and, sailing with all its force, it crashed against the boom, as the bar was called.

With a tremendous noise the boom shivered and cracked, but the *Mountjoy* was not strong enough to break it through. The shock was so fierce that the ship was thrown backward and stuck in the mud, for the river was shallow.

A groan rose from the people on the walls, and their hearts grew sick with disappointment and fear, while the Irish soldiers on the bank cheered with triumph. But as the *Mountjoy* was thrown back, the second ship followed and dashed at the spot which the *Mountjoy* had hit. The boom, which was already cracked, gave way and, amid the noise of joyful cheers and of tearing, splintering wood, she sailed gaily over. Londonderry was saved.

That same night, eager hands unloaded the ships and, for the first time for three months, the people had enough to eat. A day or two later the army of James burned the tents and cabins in which they had lived while besieging the town, and went away.

But the struggle was not over. It lasted until the following year, when William himself came to Ireland. Then there was a great battle between the soldiers of James and the soldiers of William. It was called the Battle of the Boyne, because it was fought near a river of that name. James was beaten, and fled again to France, and William, with the crown upon his head, entered Dublin, the acknowledged King of Ireland.

CHAPTER LXXXVIII

WILLIAM III. AND MARY II.—THE STORY OF A SAD DAY IN A HIGHLAND GLEN

THE friends of James were called Jacobites, from *Jacobus* which is Latin for James. There were many Jacobites in the north of Scotland. They rose under Claverhouse, the man who had treated the Covenanters so badly, and a battle was fought at Killiecrankie Pass. The Jacobites won the day, but their leader was killed, so, although many of the clans continued to be discontented, they were without a leader and could do little.

The discontent and rebellion went on for a year or two, and at last William determined to put an end to it. He proclaimed that he would forgive all those who had rebelled, if they would take an oath, before 1st January 1692 A.D., acknowledging him as King, and promising to live quietly and peacefully under his rule. Those who did not take the oath would be punished.

All the Highland chieftains, except the chief of the Macdonalds of Glencoe, took the oath. This chief was very unwilling to own William as King, and he could not bring himself to do so until the very last day. Then he started off from his lonely glen and went to the nearest town, where he expected to find one of the King's officers to whom he could swear the oath. But to his dismay he found that he had come to the wrong town, and that there was no one there who could receive his oath.

He started off again, as quickly as he could, to go to the right town. But it was deep winter, and traveling was very slow in those days, and he was six days late when he arrived. However, his oath was accepted, and he went home feeling safe and happy.

But a man called the Master of Stair, who was governing Scotland for William and Mary, hated all Highlanders, and the Campbells, another clan, hated the Macdonalds. So the Campbells and the Master of Stair decided that, as the chief had been a few days late in swearing to obey William, they had a good excuse for killing all the Macdonalds.

William was not told that Macdonald had sworn. He was made to believe that he had not done so, and that the whole clan was a set of robbers, and he signed an order for them to be destroyed. Although it is said that William did not know what he was doing when he signed this order, he ought to have known, and the Massacre of Glencoe, as it is called, is the darkest spot on his reign.

The Master of Stair had the King's order, but he did not do his work openly. He sent Campbell and his men to live in Glencoe for nearly a fortnight, so that Macdonald should suspect nothing. The old chief received the men kindly, and treated as his guests those who were ready to betray and murder him.

At five o'clock one dark winter's morning, the Campbells crept silently out of the houses and along the snow-covered paths to the scattered cottages. A few minutes later the glen was awake with the sounds of shots and screams. Campbell and his soldiers were at their work. Without mercy men were killed almost in their sleep. Those, who were able, fled through the darkness and the snow with their wives and children, many of them only to die of cold and hunger among the lonely mountains and glens. The soldiers murdered all they could, then they set fire to the empty houses and marched away, driving before them the cattle and horses belonging to the Macdonalds. And when the sun rose high over the valley of Glencoe, it shone only on blood-stained snow and blackened, smoking ruins, where peaceful homes had been but a few hours before.

For some time Britain and France had been at war, for the French King hated William, and would not acknowledge him as King of Britain. William spent a part of every year abroad directing this war and ruling Holland. While he was gone, Mary ruled in England. She governed so well, and was so sweet and gentle, that the people loved her dearly. They loved her far more than they loved William, who was so quiet and stern as to seem almost sullen.

But in 1694 A.D., Mary became ill of a very dreadful disease called smallpox, and died in a few days. William had loved her very much, and he was very sad when she died. "I was the happiest man on earth," he said to one of his friends, "now I am the most miserable. She had no fault, none; you knew her well, but you could not know, nobody but myself could know, her goodness." And if the King sorrowed, the whole country sorrowed with him.

After the death of Mary, William ruled alone.

At last the King of France made peace with William, perhaps because he was tired of fighting, perhaps because he was a little tired of helping James, who was really very dull and stupid. By this peace the French King consented to acknowledge William as the rightful King of Britain, and to give back the lands he had wrongfully taken from Germany and the other countries he had been fighting against.

A few years later James died, and Louis XIV., the French King, forgot the promise he had made to William. He proclaimed the son of James to be King of Britain under the title of James III. This made the British very angry, although it really did not matter much. A French King might call James King of Britain, but that could not make him so truly. However, William wanted to go to war with France again for another reason, and this act of the French King decided the people to do so. This other reason was that the King of Spain had died, and Louis wanted to make his own grandson King of Spain, so that France and Spain should in time come to be one kingdom. But some of the Kings in Europe thought that it would be most dangerous to allow this, as then the King of France might become too powerful, and want more than ever to take lands which did not belong to him. So William and the other Kings of Europe formed what was called the Grand Alliance, and the war which now began was called the War of the Spanish Succession, because the quarrel was about who should succeed to the throne of Spain.

But before war was declared, William died. He had always been rather ill although, in spite of that, he had both thought and worked hard, and for some time now he had been very unwell. One day when he was out riding he was thrown from his horse, and broke his collar-bone. This might not have hurt a strong man, but William was not strong, and a few days later, 8th March 1702 A.D., he died.

William was a great and brave man. He did much for Britain, yet he was never loved by the people. They felt that he was a Dutchman, and that he cared more for Holland than for his kingdom of Britain, and that made it difficult for them to love him.

CHAPTER LXXXIX

ANNE—HOW THE UNION JACK WAS MADE

WILLIAM and Mary had no children, so Mary's sister, Anne, the younger daughter of James II., succeeded to the throne. From the very beginning of her reign Britain was at war with France, and indeed not only Britain, but all Europe was fighting on one side or the other. The British troops were led by a famous soldier called Marlborough. He won many battles, the chief of which were called Blenheim and Ramillies. This War of the Spanish Succession went on for more than ten years, till all Europe was weary of fighting, and many places, where there had been houses and gardens and green fields, were nothing but deserted wildernesses.

At last a peace was made called the Peace of Utrecht. By this treaty Louis acknowledged Anne as the rightful Queen of Britain, and also promised to send James the Pretender, as the son of James VII. was called, out of his kingdom, and not to help him any more. Once before, Louis had promised something very like this to William, and he did not keep his promise. There were other agreements in this treaty, one of them being that Britain should keep the strong fortress of Gibraltar in Spain, which has belonged to the British ever since.

Marlborough was a famous soldier, but he was also a great statesman, and indeed he and his wife, the Duchess of Marlborough, ruled the Queen for many years. He was brave and clever, but he was greedy and not quite honest. He made many enemies, who succeeded at last in having him disgraced, and both he and his wife were sent away from court.

The Duchess had a very bad temper, and she was so angry when she had to leave court that she smashed all the furniture in her rooms, and threw the Queen's keys at the Duke's head, when he was sent to ask for them. It was no wonder that the Queen, who was gentle and kind, had been afraid of the Duchess, and had been ruled by her.

Other clever men succeeded Marlborough, and another clever woman succeeded the Duchess, for Queen Anne was not a strong-minded woman, and she allowed herself to be ruled and led by favourites and statesmen. Like Queen Elizabeth she had many great men around her, and although they thought more perhaps of making themselves famous and powerful than of what was best for the country, still the country prospered.

The greatest thing that happened in the reign of Anne was the union of the Parliaments of England and Scotland.

Since 1603 A.D., when James VI. of Scotland became King of England, there had been very little real union between the two countries. For union means "oneness," and although there had been only one King there had been two Parliaments, one in England, and one in Scotland, each making laws. Sometimes the Scottish Parliament would make laws which the English Parliament thought were dangerous; sometimes the English Parliament would make laws which the Scottish Parliament did not like. It almost seemed at times as if the union of the crowns had done no good at all, and the two countries were ready to quarrel and separate.

Wise men saw that there could be no real union until there was only one Parliament, until English and Scots met and discussed the laws together. Cromwell indeed had called English, Scottish, and Irish members to his Parliament, but it had been for so short a time, and in such troubled days that people had almost forgotten about it.

Even now it was not an easy thing to do, but at last all difficulties were smoothed away. It was agreed among other things that each country should keep its own law courts and its own religion, but that they should have the same King, the same Parliament, the same money, and the same flag, and that the country should be called Great Britain.

The English flag was a red St. George's cross on a white ground. The Scottish flag was a white St. Andrew's cross on a blue ground. So to make one flag, the two crosses were placed one on the top of the other, and they made something very like the Union Jack; but not quite. The Union Jack was not complete until the Irish cross of St. Patrick (which is the same as a St. Andrew's cross, but was red on a white ground) was added to the other two. Then the flag we love was complete.

The reason we call our flag the Union Jack is because James VI. used to sign his name in French—Jacques—which sounds very like Jack. His two flags, the English and the Scottish, came to be called the Jacks, and when the two were made one the flag was called the "union" Jack.

When the Queen gave her consent to the act of union, as it was named, she called both Lords and Commons together, and made a speech to them. "I desire and expect from all my subjects of both nations, that from henceforth they act with all possible respect and kindness to one another, that so it may appear to all the world they have hearts disposed to become one people. This will give me great pleasure." Then the last English Parliament rose, and, on 23rd October 1707 A.D., the first British Parliament met.

It was a great state ceremony. Each Scottish lord was led to his place by two English lords. The Queen in her royal robes made a speech from the throne in which she heartily welcomed the new members, and ever since that day, in spite of difficulties and troubles, England and Scotland have really been one country.

Queen Anne died on 1st August 1714 A.D. She was not a great Queen, yet her reign will always be remembered as great. Like Elizabeth, she had clever men as her soldiers and advisers; and, as in the time of Elizabeth too, there were many writers whose books are still remembered and read.

CHAPTER XC

GEORGE I.—THE STORY OF THE EARL OF MAR'S HUNTING-PARTY

QUEEN ANNE was the last of the Stuarts, and her husband and all her children died before she did. She had no near relatives except her brother, who was called the Pretender. He was a Roman Catholic and, therefore, could not succeed to the throne; for, in the time of William and Mary, a law had been made that no Roman Catholic should ever again wear the crown. The people had foreseen that after Queen Anne died, there might be quarrels as to who should reign next, so that, too, had been settled by law in the time of William and Mary.

James I. of England had a daughter called Elizabeth, who married the King of Bohemia, and her grandson, George, Elector, or King of Hanover, was the nearest Protestant heir to the throne. He was the great-grandson of James VI.

So, as soon as Queen Anne died, George was proclaimed King in England, Scotland, and Ireland, without any fighting or quarrelling. But although his grandmother had been Bristish, George himself was as German as could be, and he could not even speak a word of English. He was fifty-five years old when he came to the throne, and was too old ever to learn the English language or English ways and manners.

The Jacobites had never lost hope of having once more a Stuart King. Now they felt was the time to try. The new King was a German, and the people, they thought, would surely rather have a man of their own country than an old German to reign over them.

The Earl of Mar, making believe that he was going to have a great hunting-party, ask a number of the Highland lords to his house. They came, but soon it was seen that it was not deer they meant to hunt, and a large army gathered round Lord Mar and the standard of James VIII., which was the title the Pretender took. In their caps they wore his badge of white cockade or rosette.

The Pretender's standard was of blue silk, having on one side the arms of Scotland worked in gold, and on the other the Scottish thistle, with the motto, *Nemo me impune lacessit*, which means, "those who touch me will suffer for it." It had also two streamers of white ribbon, on one of which were the words, "For our wronged King and oppressed country," and on the other, "For our lives and liberties." There was great rejoicing when the standard was unfurled, but scarely had it been done when the golden ball fell from the top of the staff. That made the Highlanders very sad, for they were superstitious and thought it meant bad luck.

"But when our standard was set up,
so fierce the wind did blow, Willie,
The golden knop down from the top
Unto the ground did fa', Willie.
Then second-sighted Sandy said,
We'll dae nae gude at a', Willie;
While pipers played frae right to left
Fy, furich Whigs awa', Willie."

In the north of England, Lord Derwentwater and another gentleman gathered an army of Jacobites and proclaimed James King. But neither Lord Mar nor Lord Derwentwater were good generals. Having got their soliders together, they did not seem to know what to do with them. So when King George's army met Lord Derwentwater's army, the Jacobites yeilded almost without a struggle.

In Scotland, the Jacobites under Lord Mar, and the King's soldiers, under the Duke of Argyle, met at a place called Sheriffmuir, near Dunblane. Lord Mar called a council of war and asked his captains, "Shall we fight or shall we go back?"

And all the captains called out, "Fight! fight!"

Lord Mar agreed, and they all went to their places. No sooner did the Highlanders know they were to fight than a great cheer went through the army, every man tossing his cap in the air. Every Scotchman there was glad at the opportunity of fighting his old enemies the English.

With broadswords drawn, colours flying, and bagpipes playing, they rushed to battle. But brave and fierce though the Highlanders were, they lacked a clever leader. So it happened that one half of Mar's soliders beat one half of Argyle's, but the other half of Argyle's beat the other half of Mar's, so each side claimed the victory.

"There's some say that we wan,
Some say that they wan,
Some say that nane wan at a', man;
But one thing I'm sure,
That at Sheriffmuir
A battle there was, which I saw, man;
And we ran, and they ran, and they ran, and we ran,
And we ran and they ran awa', man."

"If we have not gained a victory," said one Jacobite general, "we ought to fight Argyle once a week until we make it one." But Mar did nothing, and James, who had promised to come from France, did not arrive. So, disappointed and discontented, many of the chieftains and their followers went home again.

But at last James landed. He was greeted with great joy, and rode into Dundee with three hundred gentlemen behind him. "Now," thought the Jacobites, "we have a King. Now we will be led to battle and victory."

But they were again disappointed. James was no soldier. He was pale, grave, and quiet; he never smiled and he hardly ever spoke. The men soon began to despise him, and to ask if he could fight or even speak.

Day after day passed and nothing happened.

"What did you call us to arms for?" asked the angry Highlanders, "was it to run away?"

"What did the King come for? Was it to see his people butchered by hangman, and not strike one blow for their lives?"

"Let us die like men, and not like dogs."

"If our King is willing to die like a King, there are ten thousand gentlemen who are not afraid to die with him."

But it was of no use. Nothing was done. The Pretender, taking the Earl of Mar with him, slunk back to France, a beaten man for want of courage to strike a blow. And, sad and angry, the Jacobite army melted away. Some of the leaders escaped to foreign lands, others were taken prisoner to the Tower and afterwards beheaded. Among those was Lord Derwentwater.

This rebellion is known as "The Fifteen" because it took place in 1715 A.D.

"O far frae my hame full soon will I be,
It's far, far frae hame, in a strange countrie,
Where I'll tarry a while, return, and with you be,
And bring many jolly boys to our ain countrie.

"I wish you all success till I again you see,
May the lusty Highland lads fight on and never flee.
When the King sets foot aground, and returns from the sea,
Then you'll welcome him hame to his ain countrie.

"God bless our royal King, from danger keep him free,
When he conquers all the foes that oppose his Majesty,
God bless the Duke of Mar and all his calvalry,
Who first began the war for our King and our countrie.

"Let the traitor King make haste and out of England flee,
With all his spurious race come far beyond the sea;
Then we will crown our royal King with mirth and jollity,
And end our days is peace in our ain countrie."

CHAPTER XCI

GEORGE II.—THE STORY OF BONNIE PRINCE CHARLIE

GEORGE I. died in 1727 A.D., and was succeeded by his son, George II. Like his father he was very German, but he could speak a little English. He had a very clever wife called Queen Caroline, and she helped him to rule. He had also a very clever Prime Minister called Walpole.

Walpole had begun to be powerful under George I., and although George II. did not like him, he still remained in power. He was the first "peace minister" Britain ever had. Instead of urging the King and people to fight, he tried in every way he could to keep the peace.

He saw that the best thing for the country was to be at peace. He saw that it was best for the people to have time to sow and reap, to build ships, to make goods, and to trade with other countries, and that they could neither have time nor money to do this if they were always fighting. So he would not fight, and Britain grew prosperous.

But the people did not all think as Walpole did. A quarrel with Spain arose and, try how he might, Walpole could not keep the peace, and war was declared. Strange to say, the people rejoiced at the news. They decorated their houses, lit bonfires, and rang bells as if some great good fortune had befallen the country. "They may ring their bells now," said Walpole sadly, "but they will soon be wringing their hands." The peace which had lasted twenty years was broken, and Walpole was quite right when he said that the people would soon be wringing their hands, for the war with Spain was a miserable failure and brought much trouble and sorrow upon them.

This war was followed by another called the War of the Austrian Succession. The Emperor of Austria died leaving his kingdom to his daughter, Maria Theresa. But some of the kings of Europe thought that they would take her lands from her and make their own kingdoms greater. To prevent this the British fought for Maria Theresa against France and Spain, and George II. and his soldiers defeated the French in a battle called Dettingen. This is the last battle in which a British King led his soldiers himself. People began to see that kings could serve their countries in better ways than by fighting.

While this war was going on the Jacobites tried again to set James Stuart upon the throne. This time it was not James but his son Charles who landed in Scotland. He came with only seven followers, and at first the people were afraid and unwilling to follow him.

But Charles was very different from his father. He was gallant and brave, and handsome. He talked and smiled and won his way to the brave Highland hearts till he was at the head of fifteen hundred men, all willing and ready to die for their King and Prince.

"Go home," said one old chieftain to him, when he first landed, "there is no safety for you here."

"I have come home," replied Prince Charlie.

"Charles Stuart," he said to another chief, called Cameron of Lochiel, "has come to claim his own and win the crown of his ancestors, or die in the attempt. Lochiel, if he chooses, may stay at home and learn the fate of his Prince from the newspapers."

"No," replied Lochiel, "no, I will share the fate of my Prince, and so shall every man over whom I have power."

So in a dark Highland glen the standard of the Prince was raised. It was red silk, and on it were the proud words, *Tandem Triumphans*, which means "Triumphant at last." And as the red silk folds fluttered out on the mountain breeze it was greeted by the sounds of bagpipes and the shouts of the people.

"Then raise the banner, raise it high,
For Charles we'll conquer or we'll die:
The clans a' leal and true men be,
And show me who will daunton thee.
Our good King James will soon come hame,
And traitors a' be put to shame;
Auld Scotland shall again be free;
There's nane on earth can daunton thee."

After the raising of his standard Charles marched south till he reached Edinburgh, his army growing as he went. Lochiel and his followers marched into Edinburgh, and there, at the Market Cross, amid the cheering of some of the people and the sullen silence of others, James VIII. was once more proclaimed King of Scotland. A beautiful lady on horseback, with a drawn sword in her hand, gave the white cockade to those who crushed round her, impatient to enter the service of the Prince.

Later in the day, Charles himself rode into the town and the people crowded to meet him, cheering and weeping, eager to kiss his hand or touch his clothes, covering even his boots with tears and kisses.

The castle of Edinburgh was held by the soldiers of King George, and as the Prince reached Holyrood, the old palace of the Stuarts, a cannon from the castle thundered out, and a shot struck the wall of the palace not far from where Charles stood. But he was neither startled nor afraid and, turning, walked quietly into the palace.

That night the Prince gave a ball. The old palace, which had stood so long empty and silent, was gay with lights and flowers. The sounds of laughter and music were heard there, perhaps for the first time since the days of the beautiful Mary, Queen of Scots.

Lovely ladies and brave men crowded to see and do honour to their Bonnie Prince Charlie, and they went away happy if they had touched his hand or heard his voice.

But there were other things to do besides dancing. The army of King George, under Sir John Cope, had landed at Dunbar and was marching to Edinburgh. Charles decided to march out to meet him.

Early on the morning of the 20th September, the Highlanders rose and made ready for battle. Prince Charlie placed himself at their head and, drawing his sword, cried, "Gentlemen, I have thrown away the scabbard." By that he meant that there was no turning back, and that his sword would never again be sheathed until he conquered or died, and the men, hearing the words, shouted and cheered as they followed him.

Next day a battle was fought at Prestonpans, near Edinburgh. Prince Charlie and his men were up so early that they were ready to attack before Sir John Cope and his soldiers were prepared. The Highlanders gave them no time to prepare, but charged so fiercely and quickly that in about five minutes the battle was over. The soldiers of King George ran away and Charles won a complete victory. Sir John ran away too, and was the first to bring the news of his own defeat to Berwick.

"Cope sent a challenge frae Dunbar,
'Charlie, meet me an ye daur,
And I'll learn ye the art of war,
If ye'll meet me in the morning."

"Hey! Johnnie Cope, are ye waking yet?
And are your drums a-beating yet?
Oh, haste ye up, for the drums do beat,
Oh fye, Cope, rise up in the morning.

"When Charlie looked the letter upon,
He drew his sword the scabbard from,
'Come , follow me, my merry merry men,
And we'll meet Johnnie Cope in the morning."

"When Johnnie Cope to Berwick came
They speired at him, 'Where's a' your men?'
'In faith," say he, 'I dinna ken,
I left them a' this morning.'

"Now Johnnie, troth ye were na blate,
To come wi' the news o' your ain defeat,
And leave your men in sic a strait
So early in the morning."

A few hours after the battle the Highlanders were back in Edinburgh marching up and down the streets playing, "The King shall enjoy his own again," on the bagpipes. All the Jacobites rejoiced and thought that they had really triumphed at last.

CHAPTER XCII

GEORGE II.—THE STORY OF FLORA MACDONALD

"To your arms! to your arms! Charlie yet shall be your King.
To your arms! all ye lads that are loyal and true.
To your arms! to your arms! his valour nane can ding,
And he's on to the south wi' a jovial crew.

"For master Johnnie Cope, being destitute of hope,
Took horse for his life and left his men;
In their arms he put no trust, for he knew it was just
That the King should enjoy his own again.

"To your arms! to your arms! my bonny highland lads.
We winna brook the rule o' a German thing.
To your arms! to your arms! wi' your bonnets and your plaids,
And hey for Charlie and our ain true King."

AFTER the battle of Prestonpans, Charles returned to Edinburgh and remained there for some days gathering men and money. It was a gay time. There were constant balls and parties, and Bonnie Prince Charlie was loved more and more each day. The Bonnie Prince, who "could eat a dry crust, sleep on peas-straw, take his dinner in four minutes, and win a battle in five," was toasted everywhere.

At last Charles and his army were ready and marched into England. But although no one resisted him, although he took several towns without a blow being struck, hardly any of the English joined him. The Highlanders grew weary of marching through strange country, and home-sick for their mountains, and many of them deserted and went home. By the time Charles reached Derby, the leaders were so disheartened that they persuaded him to turn back to Scotland. Yet the people in London were awaiting his coming in terror, and King George was ready to run away.

It is difficult to guess what might have happened had the Prince gone on. But he did not. He turned again towards Scotland, and began the long, sad march homeward.

The wearied army reached Glasgow at last, having marched six hundred miles through snow and rain and wintry weather in less than two months.

Charles now decided to take Stirling Castle. He met the King's army at Falkirk and defeated them, but after that, instead of trying to take Stirling, as he had intended, he listened to the advice of some of the Highland chiefs and marched northward.

As Charles had defeated two generals, King George now sent his own son, the Duke of Cumberland to command his army. At Culloden, near Inverness, the last Jacobite battle was fought. The royal army was much larger than the Jacobite one, and although the Highlanders fought with all their usual fierce courage, they were utterly defeated. Charles would have been glad to die with his brave followers, but two of his officers seized the bridle of his horse and forced him against his will to leave the field. The battle was turned into a terrible slaughter, for the Duke of Cumberland behaved so cruelly to the beaten rebels that ever after he was called the Butcher.

The Stuart cause was lost, and Bonnie Prince Charlie was a hunted man. The King offered £30,000 to any one who would take him prisoner. But although the money would have made many a poor Highlander richer than he had ever imagined it possible for any one to be, not one of them tried to earn it. Instead, they hid their Prince, fed him, clothed him, and worked for him. At last, after months of hardships and adventures, he escaped to France.

Many people helped Prince Charles, but it was a beautiful lady, called Flora Macdonald, who perhaps helped him most. She served him when he was most miserable and in greatest danger. The whole country round was filled with soldiers searching for him. He scarcely dared to leave his hiding-place, and was almost dying of hunger. No house was safe for him, and he had to hide among the rocks of the seashore, shivering with cold and drenched with rain.

With great difficulty and danger to herself, Flora Macdonald reached the place where the Prince was hiding, bringing with her a dress for him to wear. The Prince put it on, and together they went to the house of a friend, where Flora asked if she and her maid "Betty" might stay that night. This friend was very fond of Flora, and very glad to see her. She was a Jacobite, and when she was told who "Betty" was she made ready her best room for the Prince. A little girl belonging to the house came into the hall while Betty was standing there, and ran away frightened at the great tall woman, but no one suspected who she was.

Disguised as Flora Macdonald's maid, Prince Charlie travelled for many days, escaping dangers in a wonderful way. For the Prince made a very funny-looking woman. He took great strides, and managed his skirts so badly that, in spite of the danger, his friends could not help laughing. "They do call your Highness a Pretender," said one. "All I can say is that you are the worst of your trade the world has ever seen."

When there was no need for Flora to go further with the Prince, they took a sad farewell of each other. "I hope, madam," said he, bending over her hand and kissing it, "we shall yet meet at St. James's." By that he meant that he still hoped to be King some day, and welcome her in his palace of St. James's in London. Then he stepped into the boat which was waiting for him, and Flora sat sadly by the shore, watching it as it sailed farther and farther away.

"Far over yon hills of the heather so green,
And down by the corrie that sings to the sea,
The bonnie young Flora sat sighing her lane,
The dew on her plaid and the tear in her e'e.
She looked at a boat which the breezes had swung,
Away on the wave like a bird on the main;
And aye as it lessened, she sighed and she sang,
Farewell to the lad I shall ne'er see again;
Farewell to my hero, the gallant and young,
Farewell to the lad I shall ne'er see again.

"The target is torn from the arm of the just,
The helmet is cleft on the brow of the brave,
The claymore for ever in darkness must rust,
But red is the sword of the stranger and slave;
The hoof of the horse and the foot of the proud
Have trod o'er the plumes in the bonnet of blue.
Why slept the red bolt in the heart of the cloud
When tyranny revell'd in blood of the true?
Farewell, my young hero, the gallant and good!
The crown of thy fathers is torn from thy brow."

This rebellion is called "The Forty-five" because it took place in 1745 A.D.

Prince Charlie reached France safely, but the rest of his life was sad. He was a broken, ruined man, and he lived a wanderer in many lands. At last, he died in Rome, on 30th January 1788 A.D., the anniversary of the day on which Charles I. had been beheaded.

In St. Peter's at Rome there is a monument, placed there, it is said, by King George IV., upon which are the names, in Latin, of James III., Charles III., and Henry IX., kings of England. They were kings who never ruled, and are known in history as the Old Pretender, the Younger Pretender, and Henry, Cardinal of York, brother of the Young Pretender.

CHAPTER XCIII

GEORGE II.—THE STORY OF THE BLACK HOLE OF CALCUTTA

BESIDES the civil war, Britain had other wars to fight. France, England's old enemy was still the enemy of Britain. Once again there was war between them, and this time the fighting was not in France, nor in England, nor on the seas, but in far-off lands.

Long ago in the days of Elizabeth, you remember that Englishmen sailed over the seas to the newly-discovered country of America, and made their home there. You remember how Raleigh claimed Virginia for England, and how later the stern Puritans sailed away in the *Mayflower*, and founded a new Plymouth and a New England over the sea. Little by little these colonies (as such new countries which are peopled by an old country are called) grew. Towns sprang up, harbours were built, and the colonies became a rich and powerful part of Great Britain.

In another country, called India, Britain had also possessions, and trade with India had become of great importance, and was carried on chiefly by a company called the East India Company.

But France, too had colonies in India and in America, and the French and the British became so jealous of each other that war broke out in both countries. The French were much stronger in India at this time than the British, and they made up their minds to drive the British away altogether. They might have succeeded too, but for the cleverness of a young man called Robert Clive. He was a clerk in the East India Company's office, and not a particularly good clerk either, because the work he had to do was not at all the kind of work for which he was fitted.

When war broke out Robert Clive gave up being a clerk and became a soldier, and he soon showed that he was a clever one. Some of the native Indians fought for the French and some for the British. But Clive and his sepoys, as the native soliders were called, won, and the French governor was obliged to leave the country.

A few years later, one of the native princes who had fought for the French, attacked the British who were living in Calcutta. He killed many of them, destroyed their houses and factories, and those who were left alive he shut up in a horrible prison called the Black Hole.

There were one hundred and forty-six prisoners, and the Black Hole was so small that there was hardly room in it for them to stand. The windows were so tiny that hardly any air could come through them. When the prisoners were told that they were all to go into this dreadful place they could not believe it. They thought at first that the Prince meant it as a jest. But they soon found out that it was no jest, but horrible, sinful earnest. In spite of their cries and entreaties, they were all driven in and the door fastened.

It was a hot summer night. What little air came through the tiny windows was soon poisoned by being breathed over and over again. People fainted, went mad, died. The cruel Indians held torches to the windows and, looking in, laughed at the terrible sufferings of the poor prisoners, who cried for mercy as they beat upon the door trying vainly in their agony to break it down. In the morning only twenty-three came out from the dreadful Hole alive.

When Clive heard of this horrible deed, he marched against the native Prince, and utterly defeated him in a battle called Plassey. He drove him from his throne, and placed another Prince, who was friendly to the British, upon it; he drove the French from their fortress there, and ever since then the power of Britain has grown and grown in India, until to-day our King, the King of Great Britain and Ireland, is also the Emperor of India.

CHAPTER XCIV

GEORGE II.—THE STORY OF HOW CANADA WAS WON

WHILE these things were happening in India, the French and British were fighting in America also.

The French colonies there were called Canada and Louisiana. Canada lay north of the British colonies, beyond the St. Lawrence river. Louisiana lay west of the British colonies, beyond the Mississippi river. If you look on the map, you will see that in this way the British colonies were quite shut in by the sea and by the French on all sides.

This did not please the British. They wanted to be able to enlarge their colonies and to stretch out to the west, to the great forests and unknown land beyond Louisiana. The French, on the other hand, hoped to drive the British away from America altogether, and they built forts along the rivers and lakes to keep them as far as possible from the west. There were many quarrels, which grew more and more bitter, till at last war broke out.

At first the British were not successful. But just as Walpole had been a great peace minister, so William Pitt, who was now in power, was a great war minister. He was quick to see what needed to be done, and just as quick in choosing the best men to do it. He did not ask whether a man was rich or powerful, or whether he had great relations. He asked, "Is this the best man I can find to do this piece of work?" So it came about that at this time the British all over the world were successful.

Among the men whom Pitt sent to fight in America was a young man called James Wolfe. Wolfe was sent from England with eight thousand soldiers, and was told that he must take Quebec, the capital of Canada. He reached Canada and sailed up the St. Lawrence, greatly to the surprise of the French, for it was a very difficult passage, full of rocks and banks of sand. Yet Wolfe took his great war-ships where the French would have feared to venture with their little trading vessels. He anchored opposite Quebec, and landed his soliders on the island of Orleans.

Quebec was a very strong town. It was built upon rocks high above the river, and was defended by the great French general, Montcalm.

For a long time Wolfe tried in vain to take the town. Montcalm was too clever and watchful. Day by day passed, and Wolfe grew ill with care and weariness. Many of his soliders were killed, and the fresh troops which he expected did not arrive. At last he decided upon a bold and daring plan.

There was one place which the French did not guard very strongly, because they thought it was quite impossible for the British to attack them there. This was a steep cliff. But Wolfe noticed that there was a narrow pathway up this cliff, and he decided to take his soliders by that path. He felt so doubtful of success, however, that he wrote a sad letter home before he made the attempt. "I have done little for my country," he said, "I have little hope of doing anything, but I have done my best."

One dark night the British soldiers were rowed over the river. No one spoke, every one moved as quietly as possible. The oars even were muffled, so that the sound of rowing might not be heard by the French. Only Wolfe, as his boat went silently down the river, repeated a poem to his officers in a low voice. The poem was called "An Elegy in a Country Churchyard" and it had been written a few years before by an English poet called Gray.

"The curfew tolls the knell of parting day,
The lowing herd winds slowly o'er the lea,
The plowman homeward plods his weary way,
And leaves the world to darkness and to me.

"Now fades the glimmering landscape on the sight,
And all the air a solemn stillness holds,
Save where the beetle wheels his droning flight,
And drowsy tinklings lull the distant folds."

That is how the poem begins. It is a long poem, and very beautiful, and, when Wolfe had finished repeating it, he turned to his officers and said, "Now, gentlemen, I would rather be the author of that poem than take Quebec."

The boat reached the Quebec side of the river, and Wolfe was among the first to spring ashore. Silently, quickly, with beating hearts and held breath, the men followed. Then as silently and quickly the boats put off again, for there had been room in them only for half the soliders, and they returned to bring the rest.

The climb up the narrow pathway began. It was so narrow in places that only one could go at a time. But every man was full of courage and hope. They struggled up as best they could, clinging on to bushes, rocks, roots of trees, anything that would give them the least grip for hand or rest for foot. A regiment of Highlanders were among the first to lead the way, for they were used to scrambling and climbing among the rocks of their homeland.

Nearer and nearer to the top they came, unseen and unheard by the French sentinels above. But at last the rustling among the bushes and leaves down the slope caught their ear. "What was that?" they asked, and fired at randow down into the darkness. But it was too late, the first soldiers had reached the height, others followed after them and, terrified at the sudden appearance of men where they had thought no men could be, the French sentinels ran away.

As soon as the British reached the top, they fell into fighting order, and when day broke, the sun shone on their red coats as they stood drawn up in line upon the heights of Abraham, as the place was called.

At first the French leader, Montcalm, could hardly believe that he saw aright. Then he said quietly, "I see them where they ought not to be. We must fight them, and I am going to crush them."

A fierce battle followed. Wolfe was struck in the wrist, but he tied his handkershief round it and went on fighting and giving orders, as if nothing had happened. A second time he was hit. Still he went on. A third shot struck him in the breast. Then he sank to the ground with a groan.

Wolfe was quickly carried out of the fight, but nothing could be done for him. He was dying. His officers stood sadly round him, when suddenly one of them cried, "See, they run, they run."

"Who run?" asked Wolfe, opening his eyes and trying to raise himself.

"The enemy, sir," replied the officer, "they are running everywhere."

"Thank God," said Wolfe, "I die happy." Then he fell back and never spoke again.

The brave French leader, Montcalm, was also killed in this battle. "So much the better," he said, when he was told that he was dying. "I shall not live to see Quebec surrender."

Quebec did surrender, and Canada was won, and ever since then it has belonged to Britain, and to-day it is one of the greatest of her colonies.

A few days after Wolfe's sad letter reached hone, another both sad and joyful followed. It told of the taking of Quebec; it told, too, of the death of the brave young leader.

"Not once or twice in our fair island story,
The path of duty was the way to glory:
He, that ever following her commands,
On with toil of heart and knees and hands,
Thro' the long gorge to the far light has won
His path upward, and prevail'd,
Shall find the toppling crags of Duty scaled
Are close upon the shining table-lands
To which our God Himself is moon and sun.
Such was he: his work is done.
But while the races of mankind endure,
Let his great example stand
Colossal, seen of every land,
And keep the soldier firm, the stateman pure:
Till in all lands and thro' all human story,
The path of duty be the way to glory."

CHAPTER XCV

GEORGE III.—THE STORY OF HOW AMERICA WAS LOST

GEORGE II. died in October 1759 A.D., and was succeeded by his grandson George III., whose father, the Prince of Wales, had died some years before.

George III. had been born in England, and seemed more of an Englishman than either George I. or George II. For that reason, and because he was young and handsome, the people were glad when he came to the throne. But he proved himself to be an unwise King, and it was during his reign that Britain suffered a great loss—the loss of all the American colonies except Canada.

The wars which Britain had been fighting all over the world had cost a great deal of money. When Pitt saw a thing needed to be done he did not stop to ask how much it would cost—he did it, and afterwards the country had to find ways and means of paying. War always costs a great deal, and the country had been fighting so much that it was now deeply in debt. The King's ministers, therefore, had to find some new way of raising money. It seemed to them that, as the war in America had been for the benefit of the colonies, the colonists ought to pay some of the cost. This being so, King George decided to tax the Americans.

You know what a tax means. If a certain thing costs one shilling a pound, and the Government said, "We will put a tax of twopence a pound on this thing," then it would cost one shilling and twopence, and the extra twopence would go to Government to help to pay the expenses of the country. For it requires money to keep up a country just as mush as to keep up a house.

You also know that the King could not make the people pay taxes without the consent of Parliament. That was a right for which the people and Parliament had fought over and over again, and which they had won at last. And if Parliament consented to a tax, it was really the people who consented, as the members of Parliament were chosen by the people.

Now the people of America sent no members to the British Parliament. When King George tried to make them pay taxes, they at once said, "No, that is not just. It is against the laws of Britain. If we are to pay taxes we must be allowed to send members to Parliament as England and Scotland do. If we are to pay taxes we must have a share in making the laws and saying how the money is to be spent."

This was quite reasonable, but King George was not reasonable. He said, "No."

The Americans were very angry at this, and they made up their minds to do without the things which the King wanted to tax. This was very hard for them, especially as one of the things taxed was tea. You can imagine how difficult it would be to do without tea.

While these things were happening, the great Pitt had been ill. When he was well again, and heard what George III. and his foolish ministers had been doing, he was very angry. He said the Americans were quite right, and he talked so fiercely that all the taxes were taken off again, except the one on tea. George insisted on keeping that on. He was very angry with both Pitt and the Americans. He called them rebels, and Pitt the "trumpet of rebellion."

But the Americans would not yield even to one tax. There were meetings all over the States and the young men banded together under the name of "The Sons of Liberty." They swore to do anything rather than use taxed tea.

At last ships arrived in Boston harbour laden with tea. The Americans knew that if once that tea got ashore it would be very difficult to keep the people from buying it. They determined that it should not be landed.

While some of the wise people were talking and advising each other as to what should be done, about twenty young men dressed themselves as Red Indians. They painted their faces brown, stuck feathers in their hair, and put on clothes such as Red Indians wore.

Red Indians are the natives of America and, although they have nearly died out now, in those days it was quite common to see them even in the towns.

With wild war-whoops these make-believe Red Indians ran to the harbour. They sprang on board the tea ships, they seized the chests, opened them with their hatchets, and poured the tea into the water. Chest after chest, chest after chest was burst open, and the tea poured over the ship's side, till three hundred and forty-two chests had been emptied, and the harbour was black with tea leaves.

Many an honest merchant looked sadly on, many a thrifty housewife sighed to see the waste, but no one stopped the work. It was the greatest tea-making that had ever been seen, and for long after it was called the "Boston Tea-Party."

When King George heard about this tea-party he was very angry. To punish the people of Boston he forbade any ships to go there at all, so that the trade of the town was ruined, and the people became quite poor. He sent soldiers to frighten them into obedience, and did many other things in order to punish the rebels.

But the Americans would not bear such treatment, and they talked of war. King George seemed to be quite pleased at the idea of fighting the Americans. "We will soon bring them to their senses," he said; "they will only behave like lions as long as we behave like lambs. I will show them that I mean to be firm, and they will soon be meek enough." But the Americans were not meek at all. They made ready to fight.

Soon twenty thousand colonists were in arms, and George Washington, a young soldier, who had already shown his bravery and skill in fighting against the French, was their leader. The war began in the year 1775 A.D., and it was quite as dreadful as a civil war. The colonists looked upon Britain as their mother-country, they talked of it as "home," and now for want of a little kindly feeling and understanding between them, mother and children were fighting bitterly.

As time went on, the Americans became more and more determined not to give in. On the 4th of July 1776 A.D., they very solemnly made their Declaration of Independence. "We, the representatives of the United States of America in Congress assembled, appealing to the Supreme Judge of the world for the rectitude of our intentions, solemnly publish and declare that these United States are, and of right ought to be, Free and Independent States." This means that the Americans felt that they were doing right and not wrong in fighting against the mother-country. They felt that they ought to be free, and they declared that they were free and independent. Independent means standing alone.

While the war was being carried on in the States, at home Pitt, the great war minister, who was now called Lord Chatham, was struggling for peace. He had worked very hard to make Britain great, and to make the colonies great. Now, he saw that all his work was to be ruined by civil war, and he tried to stop it. "You cannot conquer America," he said. "They are of our own blood. If I were an American, as I am an Englishman, I would never lay down my arms—never, never, never."

But the King and his friends would not listen to Pitt, and the war went on. Then a worse thing happened. France joined America against Britain. Britain, by driving the French out of America, had given the Americans peace. Now, Britain's old enemy had joined with her own people against her. That was the worst blow of all. It frightened the Parliament, and some members wanted to acknowledge the freedom of America.

Old and ill although he was when Pitt heard of it, he rose from his bed, and once more went to speak in the House. His voice was weak and feeble as he spoke. "I am glad," he said, "that I am still alive and able to lift up my voice against breaking up the empire."

Pitt had wanted to give the Americans what they asked for, but now he wanted to fight with France. France, he felt, had no right in the quarrel. He would not yield to French threats what had been refused to America alone.

But Pitt was old and feeble, the excitement of speaking was too much for the great statesman. He fell senseless to the ground, and was carried home to die.

Then not only France but Spain joined with America, and at last the bitter end came. Britain was obliged to give way, and, in 1782 A.D., after a war which had lasted nearly eight years, the United States were acknowledged to be a free and independent country, and Britain lost all her possessions in North America except Canada.

CHAPTER XCVI

GEORGE III.—A STORY OF THE SPINNING-WHEEL

WHILE Britain was fighting and losing a great colony, another battle was being fought and won. This was a peaceful battle—the battle of industries and inventions. To invent really means to find out, and people were now finding out all kinds of things which made living much more easy and comfortable.

The two chief things which were found out about this time were, first, how to spin cotton, wool, and linen by machinery instead of by hand; second, how to use steam to make this machinery work, and how to make it draw trains along lines and carry ships over the sea.

Before spinning-frames were invented, women used to spin with wheels in their own homes. But that was such slow work that the weavers could not get enough yarn to keep their looms going, and because of that they could not make as much cloth as they might otherwise have done. They grumbled so much about this that clever people began to wonder if it would be possible to spin in some quicker way. Among these clever people was a man called Richard Arkwright.

Richard Arkwright's father and mother were very poor and they had a great many children—thirteen in all, and of those thirteen Richard was the youngest. As Richard's father and mother were so poor and had so many children they had no money to spend in sending them to school, and in those days there were no free schools. So Richard hardly knew how to read or write. What he did know he taught himself with the help of an uncle who was very kind to him.

When Richard grew up he became a barber. He rented a little cellar and there he stuck up his red and white pole which is the sign of a barber's shop. Then he waited for people to come to have their hair cut and to be shaved.

But for some reason or other very few people came. Perhaps it was because Richard's shop was little and dark and down stairs. Perhaps it was because he was always thinking of other things and so did not make a very good barber. Whatever the reason was, few people came and Richard became poorer and poorer.

At last he had a great idea. If people would not come to be shaved for two pence, which was the usual price, why then he would shave them for one penny, and in this way cut out all the other barbers. So he wrote a big sign and pasted it over his doorway. "Come to the Subterraneous Barber. He shaves for a penny!!" Subterraneous means underground. It was not long before some people saw this sign. "Hullo!" they said "what is this? Shave for a penny? Well, there is no harm in trying."

So they tried, and Richard's shop became the fashion. It was crowded, while those of other barbers were empty.

The other barbers were very angry. But what was to be done? People were not likely to pay two pence, when they could be shaved for one penny.

But at last the barbers all agreed that they, too, should put up signs saying that they shaved for one penny. Richard, however, did not want to lose all the trade which he had gained. He wrote out a new sign, "Come to the Subterraneous Barber. He shaves for a halfpenny!!" So he was still the cheapest barber in the town. But shaving for a halfpenny did not pay very well.

At this time nearly every one wore wigs. Even people who had hair enough of their own cut it short and wore wigs of long hair, tied behind with ribbon, as you can see in the picture.

Arkwight found out how to dye hair different colours, so he left off shaving, and travelled about the country buying hair from people who were willing to sell it. Then he dyed it to the fashionable colour, and made it into wigs for fine gentlemen. This paid very much better than shaving people for a halfpenny, and soon Arkwright's hair was known to be the best in the country. He got on so well that he gave up his little shop in the cellar and took a better one.

But Richard was not really interested in making wigs. What he really liked was machinery, and he spent all his spare time making models of a spinning-frame. He got a man called Kay, who was a watchmaker, to help him, and Richard soon became so interested in his machinery that he neglected his business and became quite poor again.

Richard's wife, finding that they were growing poorer and poorer, thought that this was all the fault of the models, so one day she smashed them, hoping her husband would go back to his wig-making. Richard was very grieved when he found his beautiful models broken, but far from giving up, he became even more determined to go on making models. He was so poor by this time, and his clothes were in such rags that he could not go out in the streets.

Richard got leave to set up his machine in a school house. The house was in a quiet place surounded by a garden, so that Arkwright and Kay could work in peace. This was very necessary, for Richard Arkwright's wife was not the only person who wished to smash models or even machinery itself. The work-people were very ignorant, and they hated these new inventions which they thought were going to take away their work. They hated them so much that, when the new inventions came into use, the work-people often broke into the factories and wrecked the machines.

But even in his quiet garden, Richard was not quite safe, for two old women who lived not far off could hear the whirring and humming of the machinery. They were very frightened at these new strange noises which they thought must be made by evil spirits. They told people that the sound was as if the wicked one was tuning his bagpipes while Arkwright and Kay danced a jig. The people would have broken into the house to see what really was there, but they were too much afraid of the evil spirits.

At last Arkwright conquered all his difficulties. His spinning-frame was a success and although his troubles did not end for a long time, he at length made a great fortune and died Sir Richard Arkwright. He not only made a great fortune for himself, but he helped to make Britain wealthy. After Arkwright's invention came into use, the looms could make so much cloth that the merchants had enough not only to supply Britain, but to sell to other countries. Britain began to be called the workshop of the world, and a few years later, a great Frenchman called us "a nation of shopkeepers," a name of which we have no reason to be ashamed.

Other men besides Arkwright invented spinning-frames, but I have told you about Arkwright because his was the first really successful frame, and the machines which are used to-day are almost the same as those he invented.

Arkwright built mills and taught his work-people how to use the machines, and from his time the great factories began to grow up which now give work to so many people, and which have made so many towns rich and famous. Arkwright's frames were first worked by water, so that a factory could only be built near a stream. But later, when Watt and Stephenson discovered the power of steam, they were worked by steam.

When Watt and Stephenson made their engines and built railways, when British steamships carrying British goods sailed proudly over the seas, Britain was more than ever mistress of the waves, and she was also the workshop and the market of the world.

CHAPTER XCVII

GEORGE III.—ENGLAND EXPECTS THAT EVERY MAN WILL DO HIS DUTY

"This island loves thee well, thou famous man,
The greatest sailor since our world began."

IN 1789 A.D. a revolution broke out in France. The French people rose against their King and Queen and killed them and many of the nobles as well. Then they declared the country to be a Commonwealth or Republic as the English had done in the time of Cromwell.

At this time William Pitt the younger, son of the great William Pitt, Lord Chatham, was Prime Minister. He, unlike his father, was a peace minister. Britain with her new factories and new trade was growing wealthy, and Pitt tried hard to keep the country at peace. But he tried in vain, for France declared war. Once more, for nearly twenty years, Britain was fighting by land and by sea.

The French were led by Napoleon Bonaparte. He was one of the most wonderful men who have ever lived. Beginning life as a poor unknown soldier, he soon rose to be leader of the French army. He rose and rose until the people made him Emperor of France. His one desire was to be great and powerful, and he did not care how others suffered or how many people were killed so long as he had what he wanted. He made war all over Europe. He conquered kings and gave away their thrones and crowns to his own friends and relatives, and only the British were strong enough to stand against him.

Napoleon made up his mind to conquer Britain. He raised an army which he called the Army of England, and he made a medal in honour of the conquest of Britain which never took place, and engraved upon the medal, "Struck at London," although he never reached there. It was like Caligula and his army gathering shells on the shore, for Napoleon and his men came no nearer conquering Britian than those old Romans did.

Many of the Irish hated the English and would have been glad to help the French. Napoleon knew this, and he decided that Ireland was the best place at which to begin the attack. He fitted out a great fleet with the intention of landing in Ireland. But his ships were shattered by the winds as the ships of the Armada had been, and nothing came of this invasion. A little later the French really did land in Ireland, but the King's army was ready for them and they were forced to go away again.

Up till this time Ireland had still a separate Parliament, just as Scotland had before 1707 A.D. Ireland made laws for itself, and in fact, except that it had the same King as Britain, there was no union between the countries. Pitt and other wise men felt that this was not right. They saw how much more difficult it would be for Napoleon to conquer Ireland if it was really united to England and Scotland. So they worked hard till at last it was arranged that the Irish Parliment should join the British.

In January 1801 A.D., the first Imperial Parliament was called, and since then, English, Irish and Scottish members have sat together in the same House and have made the laws for the whole land.

On the 1st of January, King George made a proclamation saying that his title should now be, "George III., by the grace of God, of the United Kingdom of Great Britain and Ireland, King, Defender of the Faith." For the first time since the days of Henry V. the King of Britain no longer called himself King of France too. For in spite of the fact that the Kings of Britain had never really been Kings of France, they had always claimed the crown of France as a right. The great seal was also changed, and the royal standard, instead of bearing the arms of England and the *fleur de lis* of France, now bore the arms of England, Scotland and Ireland.

Meanwhile British ships under the great sailor Nelson were victorious by sea, and on land British soldiers hindered and spoiled Napoleon's plans. At last, as every one was tired of the war, peace was signed.

But peace did not last long. The following year war broke out again and Napoleon threatened once more to invade Britain. But the British built watch-towers and beacons along the coast so that warning could be sent from town to town if the dreaded tyrant should come. The young men drilled as volunteers to guard their homes. Every one was ready for the ogre Napoleon who never came.

While these preparations were being made at home, Nelson swept the seas searching for the French and Spanish navies, and at last they met in Trafalgar Bay, off the coast of Spain.

A few days before they met, Nelson wrote to a friend, "Here I am watching for the French and the Spaniards like a cat after the mice. If they come out, I know I shall catch them; but I am also almost sure that I shall be killed in doing it."

On the 21st October 1805 A.D., the battle began. Every captain in the fleet had received his orders and knew exactly what to do. But Nelson felt there was still something wanting, and, from the top-gallant mast of his own ship the *Victory*, a message was signalled through all the fleet, "England expects that every man will do his duty." The message was greeted with cheer upon cheer from every ship along the line, and every sailor felt his courage rise.

The battle soon became fierce—shot and shell flew thick and fast. Once as Nelson and Hardy, the captain of the *Victory*, stood on deck together, a shot fell between them tearing off one of Captain Hardy's shoe buckles.

Each looked at the other fearing he was wounded. Then seeing neither of them were hurt, Nelson smiled and said calmly, "This is too warm work, Hardy, to last long."

Everything went well with the British. Already it seemed as if the victory was sure, when a chance shot struck Nelson and he fell forward on the deck.

"They have done for me at last, Hardy," he said, as some sailors, seeing their dear admiral fall, ran forward to carry him to a safe place. As Nelson was being carried past those who were fighting, he covered his face and the stars and medals on his coat in case they should see that he was wounded and feel discouraged, for his sailors loved him dearly.

The great admiral was dying fast, but before he died Hardy was able to bring him the news that victory was theirs and that fourteen or fifteen of the enemies' ships had surrendered.

"I hope," said Nelson, "that none of *our* ships have struck their colours."

"No my Lord, there is no fear of that."

"That's well! that's well!" he answered.

"Kiss me, Hardy," he said, a little later. Hardy knelt and kissed him. "I am satisfied now," he said. "Thank God I have done my duty." These were his last words.

With the battle of Trafalgar, which was fought on 21st October 1805 A.D., Napoleon's power by sea was utterly shattered and Britain was saved from all fear of invasion. The little ribbon of water between France and England was enough to keep her safe from the threats of the master of half Europe.

"'Twas in Trafalgar's Bay
We saw the Frenchmen lay,
Each heart was bounding then;
We scorned the foreign yoke,
Our ships were British oak,
And hearts of oak our men.
Our Nelson marked them on the wave,
Three cheers our gallant seamen gave,
Nor thought of home or beauty.
Along the line the signal ran—
England expects that every man
This day will do his duty.

"And now the cannons roar
Along the affrighted shore;
Our Nelson led the way,
His ship the Vict'ry named;

Long be that Vict'ry famed,
For vict'ry crowned the day.
But dearly was that conquest bought,
Too well the gallant hero fought,
For England, home, and beauty.
He cried, as midst the fire he ran,
England expects that every man
This day will do his duty.

"At last the fatal wound,
Which spread dismay around,
The hero's breast received;
Heav'n fights on our side,
The day's our own, he cried,
Now long enough I've lived;
In honour's cause my life was past,
In honour's cause I fall at last,
For England, home, and beauty.
Thus ending life as he began,
England confessed that every man
That day had done his duty."

CHAPTER XCVIII

GEORGE III.—THE BATTLE OF WATERLOO

NAPOLEON hated Britain so much that besides fighting against her with soldiers he tried to fight in another way. He tried to ruin British trade. Napoleon forbade other countries to trade with Britain. But it was of little use, and so ill did he succeed that his very own soldiers were dressed in British-made cloth and wore British-made boots.

As Portugal still traded with Britain, Napoleon made that an excuse for invading Portugal. At the same time he seized the King of Spain and his son, and forced then to sign a paper saying that they gave up the throne of Spain. Napoleon then made his own brother, Joseph Bonaparte, King. But although the King and Prince had been forced to sign away the throne, the people of Spain had something to say about it. They refused to have Joseph Bonaparte as their King. They rose to a man and rebelled against him, and they asked the British to help them. So two years after Trafalgar the Peninsular war began. It is called the Peninsular war because it was fought in and for the Peninsula formed by Spain and Portugal.

At first the war was not very successful, but when Arthur Wellesley, afterwards Lord Wellington, took command, things went better. Gradually the French were driven back to France, and the war ended with the battle of Toulouse, on 14th April 1814 A.D.

While this war was going on, Napoleon had also been fighting with Russia. There he was utterly crushed. Everywhere the peoples he had conquered revolted against him, and, a few days before the battle of Toulouse, he had been made to give up the throne of France, and was banished to the island of Elba.

Of the many kingdoms which Napoleon had conquered, this little island in the Mediterranean Sea was all that he was allowed to keep. But he soon grew tired of playing at being Emperor there. The following year, while the Kings and Princes of Europe were gathered at Vienna, trying to bring order and peace to the lands which Napoleon had upset with his wars and conquests, he left Elba and made straight for Paris. Cruel and selfish though he was, his soldiers loved him, for he had so often led them to victory. When he suddenly appeared among them, they flocked to him, and the people cheered and welcomed him.

Once more Napoleon was Emperor of the French, but this time his rule only lasted one hundred days.

The Kings and Princes at Vienna had not been able to agree about settling the affairs of Europe, but, when they heard that Napoleon was once more in Paris, fear of him made them all unite. They gathered their armies for a great struggle against the terrible Emperor.

Wellington had command of eighty thousand men, but only about half of these were British. The rest were Dutch, Belgian, and German. Blücher, the great German general, had another army of one hundred and fifty thousand men, and there was yet a third army of Russians and Austrians, and all these armies marched towards France.

But Napoleon did not wait for them to come. He marched out to meet them, and a great battle took place on 18th June 1815 A.D. at Waterloo, not far from Brussels.

"Ah," said Napoleon, "at last I shall measure swords with this Vilainton." For although the French and British troops had often met, Napoleon had always been fighting elsewhere, and had never met Wellington in battle.

The fight was fierce and long, and as Wellington watched and directed, he anxiously looked for Blücher and his Prussians, who had promised to join and help him.

"Night or Blücher," said Wellington, "night or Blücher," for he knew that the coming of either would put an end to the dreadful fight. At last, about seven in the evening, Blücher and his Prussians came.

Then Napoleon made one more desperate struggle for victory. The soldiers of his Old Guard, who had been kept in reserve, were ordered forward, but they broke and fled before the British charge. Napoleon, as he watched, became deadly pale. "All is lost," he said, turning to his officers, who surrounded him, "we must save ourselves." And he rode from the field.

Not till after the battle did Blücher and Wellington meet. In German fashion, the old Prussian general threw his arms round Wellington, and kissed him. It was a great victory, and by it Europe was saved from tyranny, yet Wellington was sad as he looked round on the dead and the dying.

The British troops were worn out with the long day's fighting, but the Prussians were still fresh, and Blücher started off to chase the flying Frenchmen, who ran as fast as they were able. They hid in the woods and ditches, and threw away their arms, knapsacks, and every thing they could, so that they might run the faster and escape from the pursuing Prussians. They fled till they passed the borders of France, where they scattered to their homes, a broken, beaten army, never to be gathered together again.

Napoleon gave himself up to the British. He was taken to England on board a British man-of-war called the *Bellerophon,* but he was not allowed to land.

He was kept on board the *Bellerophon* until the Kings of Europe decided to send him to St. Helena, a lonely island in the Atlantic ocean. There he could do no harm, and there he stayed until he died, six years later.

CHAPTER XCIX

GEORGE IV.—THE FIRST GENTLEMAN IN EUROPE

GEORGE III. died in January 1820 A.D., and was succeeded by his son George IV. George IV. had already been reigning as Regent for ten years, for, during that time, his father had been mad and so unable to rule, and towards the end of his life he had become blind, and deaf as well.

George III. was called Farmer George, because he liked a peaceful country life, and would have been a very good farmer, although he was not a very wise King. He had reigned sixty years, including the last ten, during which he really did not rule.

George IV. was called "the first gentleman in Europe," because he was handsome, and had fine manners, very different from those of his homely father. He tried to make friends with all his people through his fine manners. Soon after he became King he went to Ireland, where the people received him with great joy. He made speeches to them, and laughed and cried with them. He wore the order of St. Patrick on his breast, and great bunches of shamrock in his cap. He told them that he loved his Irish people, and that he was Irish at heart, and altogether acted his part very well. But it was merely acting, for George IV. only cared for himself, and was not in the least a good king. The warm-hearted Irish people, however, believed in him and, when he sailed away again, some of them were so eager to catch a last glimpse of their King, that they fell into the sea, and were nearly drowned.

George next went to Hanover, for he was King of Hanover, as well as king of Britain. There he talked German, and wore a Hanoverian Order, sang German national songs, and told the people with tears in his eyes that he was truly German at heart; and perhaps the German people believed him too.

Next he went to Scotland. Since the time of Charles I. no king had visited Scotland, and the people crowded to welcome him. The road from Leith to Edinburgh was lined with gentlemen to do him honour, and as King George drove along through the lines of cheering people, it was seen that he was dressed in Stuart tartan, and that he wore the Order of the Thistle.

George had wept and laughed with his Irish subjects, yet when a chance came for him to prove that he loved them as he had said he did, he did not willingly take it.

In the fierce old days the Roman Catholics had killed and tortured the Protestants whenever they had the power and, in dread of them, an act had been passed forbidding Roman Catholics to hold any public office. Those days were long passed. No one was now killed or tortured because of his religion, yet the laws against the Roman Catholics still remained. No Catholic might be an officer in the army or navy, no Catholic might sit in Parliament, or serve his country in any way.

Yet nearly all the Irish people were Roman Catholics, and generous men for many years had felt these laws to be unjust. The younger Pitt had tried in vain to make George III. do away with them. Now wise men tried to make George IV. repeal them. But the King, who said he was Irish at heart, refused. "My father," he said, "would have laid his head on the block rather than yield, and I am equally ready to lay my head there for the same cause."

The great Duke of Wellington was Prime Minister at this time, and as he had conquered Napoleon in war, so now he conquered George IV. in peace. He stood firm, and at last the King was forced to give way. A bill called the Catholic Emancipation Act, which means "freeing" Act, was passed by Parliament. Since then Roman Catholics have been allowed to sit in Parliament, to be officers, or to hold any other post which is open to Protestants, although no king may rule in Britain unless he is a Protestant.

George IV. died in June 1830 A.D., having reigned ten years. He was an utterly selfish man, and a bad King. Yet the British nation had grown so strong that even a bad King could not do much harm, while there were great men around him to work for their country.

CHAPTER C

WILLIAM IV.—THE STORY OF TWO PEACEFUL VICTORIES

GEORGE IV. had only one child, a daughter, and she died some time before her father, so he was succeeded by his brother William, who was sixty-five years old when he came to the throne.

William was called the Sailor King because he had served in the navy. He was bluff and rough and good-natured, not at all like a King. He used to be fond of strolling about London with a walking-stick or an umbrella just like an ordinary man. But British people have always loved a sailor, so they were glad when William became King, and hoped that he would prove a better one than George IV.

That some of his people had not much reverence for him, is shown by one man who wrote of him, "He seems a kind-hearted, well-meaning, not stupid, bustling old fellow, and if he doesn't go mad, may make a very decent King." Later the same man called him, "One of the silliest old gentlemen in his dominions." If he had been left to himself, the "Well-meaning old fellow" would have been quite pleased to jog along without troubling about his kingdom or his duties. But that was not to be. The days of the clatter and jangle of steel armour were over, the roar and crackle of musket and cannon were silent for the time, but in the peace and silence men were thinking and planning and working for the good of the nation.

For hundreds of years the people of Britain had had the right of choosing men to send to Parliament to tell their troubles and their wrongs, and to help to make just laws for the ruling of the country. The whole nation, of course, cannot go to Westminster, for no building would be large enough to contain them all, and the talking would never be finished, and no laws would ever be made. So each country and each big town chooses a man who goes to Parliament to speak and vote in the name of those who send him.

That is what is intended, but at this time the reality was something quite different.

During the hundreds of years which had passed since it had been first arranged which towns should send members to Parliament, there had been many changes. Places which had once been large towns had for some reason or another become deserted. Where there had been houses, churches, shops, and crowded, busy streets, there was now perhaps only one lonely house, or perhaps only a deserted hillside. Yet that lonely house or deserted hill-side continued to send a member to Parliament. On the other hand since factories had been built, great towns had sprung up, where a hundred years before there had been perhaps only a single cottage. But these great towns with all their hard-working people had no right to send a member to Parliament, and could have no voice in making the laws.

This seems very absurd. Nowadays, we think it would be quite easy for any sensible man to see that this state of affairs was wrong. But a hundred years ago many sensible people did not see it. They were pleased with things as they were, and very angry with those who tried to alter them.

But some people were quite determined they should be altered, and two men called Lord Grey and Lord John Russell, brought into Parliament what is called the Reform Bill. This Bill took the right of sending any one to Parliament away from the bare and lonely hillsides, and gave the right to the new and busy towns, so that the people should really be represented, that is, should have some one in Parliament to act and speak for them.

There was a long and fierce struggle before this Bill became law. You know that there are two Houses of Parliament, the House of Commons and the House of Lords. A bill to become law must be read in both Houses, and must be voted for by the greater number of the members in each. That is, more than half the members must vote for it. For instance, if there were only one hundred members, at least fifty-one must vote for a bill before it is said to have passed. Having passed both Houses, it must receive the consent of the King, before it can become law.

After a great deal of difficulty the Commons were made to consent to the Reform Bill, but the Lords did not want it, neither did the King, and again and again they refused consent.

The country, however, had become so determined about it that there were riots everywhere when it became known that the Lords would not pass the Bill. The people who had been quite ready to love their King began to hate him, and instead of cheering when he appeared, they hissed and groaned.

So bitter did the feeling become that the friends of the Bill feared there would be another revolution, and at last they forced the King to give his consent. The Lords followed, and the Bill became law.

One more step toward liberty had been taken.

Another great thing which happened during the reign of William IV. was the freeing of slaves.

For many years people had been in the habit of stealing black people from their homes in Africa, and selling them as slaves in the colonies. People had grown so used to it that they did not see how wicked and cruel this was. These poor black people were taken to market and sold like cattle, they were branded like cattle, and beaten like cattle. They had to work very hard, were paid no wages, and were often very cruelly treated. All masters, of course, were not cruel, some of them were even kind to their poor slaves, but still they had very unhappy lives. They had no rights whatever, their children might be taken from them and sold, sometimes even husbands and wives were sold to different masters, and never saw each other again. A master might treat his slaves as badly as he chose, and no one could punish him.

In the old, rough, wild days no one cared about the sufferings of these poor black people. They were only niggers, and made for work and suffering, and nothing was thought about it.

But, as time went on, people became less rough and more kind-hearted, and good men began to try to make people see the wickedness of slavery. For some years, a man called Wilberforce had been doing his best, and now he was joined by others, among whom was Macaulay, the father of the great writer. Mr. Macaulay had himself been a manager of a sugar plantation in the West Indies where slaves worked. But he gave up his post because he could not bear to see the misery and unhappiness of the slaves, and came home to try to do something for them.

It was not a very easy thing to do, because all the work on the sugar and coffee plantations in the West Indies was done by slaves. The planters said they would be ruined if the slaves were made free, as the black people would not work unless they were forced to do so. Besides, they had paid a great deal of money for their slaves, and it seemed unfair that they should be made to lose it all.

But, at last, all difficulties were smoothed away. The British Parliament said they would give twenty millions of money to the planters to make up for what they would lose in freeing their slaves, and, in the year 1834 A.D., most of them were set free.

Many other things were done during the reign of William IV., which you will find more interesting when you grow older. He died on 20th June 1837 A.D., having reigned seven years.

CHAPTER CI

VICTORIA—THE GIRL QUEEN

MANY years ago, in a big airy schoolroom, a little girl of eleven sat with her governess. The little girl had many lessons to learn, far more it seemed to her than other little girls of the same age, and sometimes they were terribly dull and uninteresting. But to-day they were not so, for she had found in her history book a page which showed how kings were descended from each other. This was very interesting. The little girl read the page carefully, then, looking up into the face of her governess, she said gravely, "So I shall be Queen of Britain one day." Then slipping her hand into that of her governess, "I will be good," she added, "I will be good. I see now why I have to learn so many lessons."

This little girl was Princess Victoria, the daughter of the Duke of Kent, younger brother of William IV. William IV. had two children, but they died while they were babies. The Princess Victoria's father had died when she was a baby, so she was the heir to the throne.

When William lay still and quiet in the great palace at Windsor, the Archbishop of Canterbury and the Lord Chamberlain stepped into a carriage and drove fast to the palace of Kensington, where the Princess lived with her mother. It was five o'clock in the morning when they arrived there. They knocked and hammered for a long time before they could rouse the sleepy porter, but at last they did so and got into the palace. But it seemed as if they were not to see the Princess, and that was what they had come for.

At last, after they had waited for a long time, a lady came to them. "The Princess is sleeping so peacefully," she said, "I cannot wake her."

We have come to see *the Queen* on affairs of state," said the Archbishop. "Even her sleep must give way to that."

The Queen! That was a very different matter.

In a few minutes the new-made Queen came into the room. Her brown hair was hanging over her shoulders, a shawl covered her nightdress, and only slippers were on her little bare feet. She was hardly awake, and she wondered, perhaps, if she might not still be dreaming.

And there, in the early morning sunshine, these two grave gentlemen, the Archbishop and the Lord Chamberlain, knelt to kiss the hand of this girl of eighteen who was their Queen.

Since the time of George I., the kings of Britain had also been kings of Hanover. But in Hanover there was a law that no woman could ascend the throne. Victoria could not be Queen of Hanover, so the crown passed to the Duke of Cumberland, another of the brothers of William IV. The British people were not very sorry to be rid of Hanover, and they were quite glad to be rid of the Duke of Cumberland, for no one loved him.

Not long after Queen Victoria came to the throne she married her cousin, Prince Albert of Coburg Gotha. Very often kings and queens cannot choose whom they will marry as other people can. They have to do as they are advised, and marry for the good of their country and people. But it is pleasant to know that this Queen and Prince really loved each other, and that they were happy together with their children, just like ordinary people.

Britain had been long at peace, and I wish I had no more wars to tell about. But, unfortunately, during the reign of Victoria there were many wars, although wise men did all they could to avoid them, for we see now more and more clearly how cruel and terrible a thing war is.

I cannot tell you about all these wars and their reasons; indeed, I cannot tell you about nearly all the important events which have happened since Victoria began to reign. Things happen and changes come now much more quickly than they used to do, and to tell of all the wonderful events of the nineteenth century would fill a whole book, and much of it would not interest you.

CHAPTER CII

VICTORIA—WHEN BREAD WAS DEAR

SOME time after Victoria began to reign, the poor people were in great distress. Work was scarce and bread was dear, and many died of hunger.

Long ago, most of the people in Britain used to live by cultivating the land; that is, by ploughing, sowing, and reaping. In those days enough corn was grown in Britain to feed all the people. But as years went on, the great lords, who owned the land, found that they made more money by rearing sheep for their wool than by growing corn and wheat for food. So year by year less and less corn was grown in the island. Year by year, too, more babies were born and grew up into men and women, so that there were more people to feed. Then discoveries began to be made and factories were built, and the people who used to plough and sow went into the towns to work in the factories. And so, because it became more difficult to find people to do farm work, still less corn was grown. Gradually the supply of corn became very small and, in consequence, very dear. For it always happens that if there is only a little of something which a great many people want, that article becomes very dear and only those who are well off can afford to buy it. That is what happened to corn in Britain. There was not enough for all, and it became so dear that only the rich people could buy it, and the poor people starved. Bread was so dear that, however hard men worked, they could not earn enough to feed themselves and their children.

There was plenty of corn in other parts of the world. In fact people in other parts of the world had more than they wanted. They would gladly have sold it to Britain, and have bought instead, the beautiful cloths which were being made in the British factories. In that way the people in Britain would have had plenty to eat, and the people in other parts of the world would have had better clothes to wear, and every one would have been happier and better off.

But, unfortunately, some years before this, a law had been passed that no foreign corn might be brought into the country until British corn cost eighty shillings a quarter, which is very, very dear indeed. The people who made this law meant to be kind to the farmers and help them to get a good price for their corn, but they did not see how unkind they were to the poor.

At last a few people saw what a dreadful mistake these Corn Laws, as they were called, were, and they began with all their might and main to try to have them altered. The chief of these people were John Bright, Richard Cobden, and Charles Villiers, but they found it was very difficult to make others think as they did.

For a long time they fought in vain, while the people grew poorer and poorer, starving, struggling, dying. Even little children and old men had to work hard all day long, always hungry.

"Child, what has thou with sleep to do?
Awake and dry thine eyes:
Thy tiny hands must labour too;
Our bread is tax'd, arise!
Arise, and toil long hours twice seven,
For pennies two or three;
Thy woes make angels weep in heaven,
But England still is free.

"Up, weary man of eighty-five,
And toil in hopeless woe;
Our bread is tax'd, our rivals thrive,
Our gods will have it so.
Yet God is undethron'd on high,
And undethron'd will be:
Father of all! hear Thou our cry
And England shall be free!"

But there was worse still to come. In Ireland nearly all the poor people lived on potatoes only. And the potatoes all went bad. In a few weeks the food which ought to have lasted for a whole year became rotten.

This was such a terrible misfortune that some of the men who had been against the repeal of the Corn Laws went over to the other side and tried to do away with them as fast as they could. Among these men was Sir Robert Peel, who was now Prime Minister. They knew that unless corn could be brought cheaply into Ireland there would be a famine.

A famine did come, and the people died in hundreds. Little children cried in vain to their mothers for something to eat. The mothers had nothing to give. It was a dreadful time, worse than any war.

Rich people sent money and food to the poor, starving Irish, but in spite of everything that was done, the misery was terrible. Some of the food and money came from the United States of America—from the colonies which Britain had so lately lost. The owners of ships and railways did what they could too, and all parcels which were marked "For Ireland," were carried free on their trains and ships. When at last the famine was over, it was found that nearly a quarter of the people in Ireland had died.

But the Corn Laws had been done away with.

CHAPTER CIII

VICTORIA—PEACE

QUEEN VICTORIA'S husband was called the Prince Consort. He was a clever man, and, after he married Queen Victoria, he tried to do all he could for Britain. Although he was German, he learned to speak English almost perfectly, a thing which some of our German Kings had never troubled to do.

The Prince wanted to help trade and to keep peace. So he asked people to come from all parts of the world and bring with them the beautiful and useful things which were made in their countries, and also the things which grew there, such as plants and fruits. These were all to be gathered together in one great building so that the people of each country might see what the people in other countries were doing, and, having seen, might go home with new ideas. In this way the trade of the whole world would be helped. The Prince thought, too, that if people of different countries met together and came to know each other in this friendly manner, they would be less likely to want to fight with each other.

Although we have since had many great Exhibitions or World's Fairs, then, it was quite a new idea. It was so new that many people did not like it. They thought that it would be bad for Britain to bring a number of foreigners there. But in spite of difficulties, the Prince had his way.

One great difficulty was how to make a building quickly enough, and big enough to hold the beautiful things which were to be brought from all over the world. The Prince wanted to have a pretty building, and no one could think of anything except ugly brick sheds.

At last a gentleman, called Sir Joseph Paxton, said, "Why not use glass and iron?" And he sat down and drew a sketch of what he thought the building ought to be.

This idea of a glass house was quite as new as the idea of having an Exhibition at all, and the Prince was delighted with it. Very soon a palace of glass began to rise in Hyde Park and it seemed so beautiful that the people called it the Crystal Palace.

And very beautiful, indeed, it looked on the opening day. It gleamed and glittered like a fairy thing, it was decorated with the flags of all nations, with palms and flowers, with statues and fountains, and crowded with people from every country in the world.

Queen Victoria opened the Exhibition, and she was glad and happy, both because it all looked so beautiful, and because she knew it was the thought of her husband whom she loved so well. Bands played, a great choir sang, the world seemed full of sunshine and joy.

"And lo! the long laborious miles
Of palace; lo! the giant aisles,
Rich in model and design;
Harvest-tool and husbandry,
Loom and wheel and enginery,
Secrets of the sullen mine,
Steel and gold, and corn and wine,
Fabric rough, or fairy-fine,
Sunny tokens of the Line,
Polar marvels, and a feast
Of wonder, out of West and East,
And shapes and hues of Art divine!
All of beauty, all of use,
That one fair planet can produce,
rought from under every star,
Blown from over every main,
And mixt, as life is mixt with pain,
The works of peace with works of war.

"O ye, the wise who think, the wise who reign,
From growing commerce loose her latest chain,
And let the fair white-wing'd peacemaker fly
To happy havens under all the sky,
And mix the seasons and the golden hours;
Till each man find his own in all men's good,
And all men work in noble brotherhood,
Breaking their mailed fleets and armed towers,
And ruling by obeying Nature's powers,
And gathering all the fruits of earth and crown'd,
with all her flowers."

The Exhibition was a great success. Never before had there been so many people from strange countries gathered together in London. Never before had so many beautiful and curious things been seen all at once. When it was over, the Crystal Palace was not destroyed, but was taken down and built up again at another place. There it has remained ever since, and is still one of the sights of London.

But although people hoped great things from this friendly gathering, their hopes were not fulfilled. Three years later, after a peace of forty years, Britain was again at war.

CHAPTER CIV

VICTORIA—WAR

RUSSIA is a great country in the east of Europe. But if you look at the map you will see that, although it is very large, it has not much seashore. That is bad for a country, for, unless it has seaports, its ships cannot easily sail to other countries with goods and bring back their goods in exchange.

To the south of Russia lies the Black Sea, but then as now half of the shore of that sea belonged to Turkey, and Turkey had the right to keep the ships of other nations out of the Black Sea. Russia was very angry at this, and formed plans to conquer Turkey and take possession of the country. The Emperor of Russia had another reason for wishing to fight with the Turks. The Turks, you know, are Mahometans, but many of the people who lived in Turkey had become Christian. The Emperor thought that these Christians were badly treated by the Turks, and he wished to protect them. This made the Sultan very angry, for he said that the Emperor was not really anxious about the happiness of the Christians, but merely wished to interfere with his rule.

The Russian Emperor hoped that the British would help him to fight the Turks, and be offered to divide Turkey, when conquered, with Britain.

But the British were on good terms with the Turks, and they had several reasons for not wishing Russia to conquer Turkey. So when war at last broke out, they sided with the Turks against the Russians, as did the French, who also thought that it would be a bad thing if Russia conquered Turkey.

For the first time, France and Britain, instead of fighting against each other, fought side by side. Lord Raglan led the British army, Marshal St. Arnaud the French. The war was fought in the Crimea, a little peninsula in the Black Sea, and from that it was called the Crimean War.

Both the French and the British sent fleets into the Black Sea, but they did not do much, as the war was chiefly fought on land round the fortress of Sebastopol, which the allies, as the armies of Britain, France, and Turkey were called, besieged. Ally comes from the same word as alliance, and means, "the friends" or "those who had joined together."

Britain had been at peace for forty years, and, although the soldiers had not forgotten how to fight, it seemed as if those in command had forgotten how to plan a war.

The winter in Russia is terribly cold, and the people who had charge of sending out clothes to the soldiers sent the things to the wrong places. So when the soldiers were shivering with cold at one place, great stores of warm clothing would be lying at another, perhaps not many miles off, but quite out of reach. Once a whole shipload of boots arrived, and, when they were unpacked, they were found to be all for the left foot. Terrible storms arose, too, which wrecked the ships which were bringing stores of food. These storms not only wrecked the ships, but they tore down and blew away the soldiers' tents, so that they had to sleep in the open air in the snow and bitter frost. They had nothing upon which to sleep except wet straw, and often they had no bed-clothes at all. And this in cold so dreadful that, if a man took hold of a piece of iron, it would freeze to his hand, so that he could not leave go without tearing away the skin.

So great was the suffering that many of the soldiers became sick and ill. The hospitals were soon filled, and many more died of disease than were killed by the Russians. In those days there were very few proper nurses, and the poor sick soldiers were very badly cared for, until a lady called Florence Nightingale went out to the Crimea, taking with her other ladies as nurses.

When Florence Nightingale and her nurses arrived in the Crimea, the dirt and horror of the hospitals were dreadful. The great wards were crowded from end to end with sick and wounded, dead and dying. No one did anything for the poor soldiers, their wounds even were often not dressed; they were brought there to die. But Florence Nightingale worked so hard that soon the hospitals were sweet and clean, and the men grew well instead of dying. The soldiers loved and adored her, and she never seemed to tire of working for them. Long after every one else had gone, she would walk through the wards carrying a lamp in her hand, moving softly from bed to bed, doing what she could for the poor wounded men. "She would speak to one and another," said one poor fellow afterwards, "and nod and smile to many more; but she could not do it to all, there were so many of us; but we could kiss her shadow as it fell, and lay our heads on our pillows again, content."

"Lo! in that house of misery
A lady with a lamp I see
Pass through the glimmering gloom,
And flit from room to room.

"And slow, as in a dream of bliss,
The speechless sufferer turns to kiss
Her shadow, as it falls
Upon the darkening walls.

"As if a door in heaven should be
Opened and then closed suddenly,
The vision came and went,
The light shone and was spent.

"On England's annals, through the long
Hereafter of her speech and song,
That light its rays shall cast
From portals of the past.

"A lady with a lamp shall stand
In the great history of the land,
A noble type of good,
Heroic womanhood."

Once Florence Nightingale went out into the trenches among the soldiers to get a good view of Sebastopol. When it became known that she was there, they sent up such a shout that the Russians behind their strong battlements heard it and trembled, not knowing what it might mean. There was not a man there but honoured her as he would a queen. Florence Nightingale worked so hard that at last she, too, became ill of the terrible Crimean fever. Then there was sorrow indeed. Little could the men do for her who had done so much for them, but even in that wild place they found flowers to bring to her to cheer her loneliness. And she did not die, but still lived to bring joy to many.

Since Florence Nightingale worked among the soldiers in the Crimea, army nurses have worn red crosses upon their sleeves, as the crusaders did long ago. But those who wear the cross to-day do not go to battle to fight, but to help the wounded and the dying. Over the hospitals on the battlefield too flies the red cross flag, and no enemy ever fires at it or injures any one who wears the red cross badge.

The British soldiers were brave, and in spite of sickness and suffering they fought gallantly, but they were often badly led, and many mistakes were made. One dreadful mistake was made at a battle called Balaclava.

There was a brigade of cavalry called the Light Brigade. Lord Raglan sent a message to the officer in command, telling him to prevent the Russians carrying away some guns. The officer thought he was meant to charge right forward, and he did so. But it was a mistake. He and his men rode straight to death. For a mile and a half they rode with Russian guns in front of them, Russian guns on either side of them, thundering death. When their comrades saw what the Light Brigade was doing, they stood watching in horror and wonder, as six hundred men of the brigade rode down the lane of fire and smoke, and disappeared in the bank of smoke beyond.

It was horrible! What was happening to these gallant soldiers? They rode straight up to the Russian guns and drove the gunners away. But they could not stay there. The whole Russian army was arrayed against them, so they rode back again—back through that awful lane of shot and shell. Six hundred and seven men went, only one hundred and ninety-eight returned.

It was a splendid show of bravery, but utterly useless. What was the order given? What were the men meant to do? No one can answer the question. "It is magnificent," said a French officer who saw it, "but it is not war." Yet all the world saw what Britons could do in obedience to a command.

"Half a league, half a league,
Half a league onward,
All in the valley of Death
Rode the six hundred.
" 'Forward the Light Brigade.
Charge for the guns!' he said:
Into the valley of Death
Rode the six hundred.

'Forward the Light Brigade.'
Was there a man dismayed?
Not tho' the soldier knew
Some one had blundered:
Theirs not to make reply,
Theirs not to reason why,
Theirs but to do and die:
Into the valley of Death
Rode the six hundred.

"Cannon to right of them,
Cannon to left of them,
Cannon in front of them
Volley'd and thunder'd;
Storm'd at with shot and shell,
Boldly they rode and well,
Into the jaws of Death,
Into the mouth of Hell
Rode the six hundred.

"Flash'd all their sabres bare,
Flash'd as they turn'd in air,
Sabring the gunners there,
Charging an army, while
All the world wonder'd:
Plunged in the battery-smoke,
Right thro' the line they broke;
Cossack and Russian
Reel'd from the sabre-stroke
Shatter'd and sunder'd.
Then they rode back, but not
Not the six hundred.

"Cannon to right of them,
Cannon to left of them.
Cannon behind them
Volley'd and thunder'd;
Storm'd at with shot and shell.
While horse and hero fell,
They that had fought so well
Came thro' the jaws of Death,
Back from the mouth of Hell,
All that was left of them,
Left of six hundred.

"When can their glory fade?
Oh! the wild charge they made.
All the world wonder'd.
Honour the charge they made,
Honour the Light Brigade,
Noble six hundred."

The siege of Sebastopol lasted about a year, during which time the Sardinians joined the allies. Sardinia was a very small kingdom, but the people were brave; they wanted to take a place among the great powers of Europe, and the allies were very glad to have their help. During the winter, too, the Russian Emperor died. He was so sad and disappointed because his soldiers were being beaten, that he did not care to live. He died of a broken heart. When the Emperor died, people hoped that the war would come to an end, but it did not. His son, the new Emperor, still carried it on.

At last the French and British made a fierce attack on Sebastopol, and, although they did not succeed in doing all they meant to do, the Russians felt that they could hold out no longer. Next morning Sebastopol was empty and in flames. The Russians had set it on fire and fled.

After this, the war soon came to an end, and a few months later peace was signed. Russia had failed, and Turkey was neither conquered nor divided.

CHAPTER CV

VICTORIA—THE LAND OF SNOW

IN days long, long ago, men knew very little of the world, and all the countries it contained. But in the time of Henry VII., great sailors began to sail into far seas and discover new lands. From that time onward there have been many great and daring sailors who have sailed the seas and discovered more and more lands, until the blue of our maps has became marked with islands and continents.

The way to India and China is long, and, in the days when there were no steamers, it was dangerous too. In the time of King Henry VII. a man called Sebastian Cabot tried to find a short way to India, by going round the north of America through the Arctic Ocean. This began the quest of what was called the "North-West Passage."

For hundreds of years men struggled to find this North-West Passage, but all in vain, and many brave lives were lost in the bitter frost and snow of the far north. As new lands were discovered, the map of the Arctic region began to be filled in bit by bit, but the North-West Passage remained undiscovered.

At last the British Government decided in 1845 A.D. to send out an Arctic expedition, and Sir John Franklin, who had already been on two voyages of discovery to Arctic regions, was put in command.

Sir John was no longer a young man, but he loved the sea and the north, and he went out like an old sea-lion, eager to find the long-sought passage.

He sailed away with two ships, called the *Terror* and the *Erebus*, manned by a hundred men and more. The last good-bye was said, the last handshake given, and away sped the ships further and further north into the white and silent land, never again to return.

A year passed, then another. At home anxious hearts waited and waited for news, but no news came. Then, as nothing was heard of the ships and their gallant crews, both Sir John Franklin's wife and the British Government sent out expeditions to try to find the *Terror* and the *Erebus*.

These new ships sailed to the north, keeping as much as possible in the course Sir John had gone, but they could find no trace of him. Here and there sailors landed on the bare, white shores which they passed, and left supplies of food under great heaps of stones or cairns as they are called. They also left letters telling which way their ships had gone. This they did hoping that some of Franklin's men might pass that way and find the food and letters. The sailors also caught white foxes which run about wild in these cold countries. Round the necks of these foxes they put copper collars on which were engraved directions how to find the ships and the stores of food. The foxes were then let loose again, in the hope that some of them might find their way to the *Terror* and the *Erebus* and bring comfort and encouragement to Sir John and his men.

But nothing was of any use. No sign of Franklin and his brave men could be found, although expedition after expedition was sent out. At one time as many as fifteen ships were looking for Franklin, but each one failed.

At last, after about twelve years, the searchers were rewarded. They found a cairn in which was a tin can containing a paper which had been put there by one of Sir John's men. This paper told how at last the North-West Passage had been discovered; how Sir John had died a few days later, and how as the ships were stuck fast in the ice and could not get through to the sea beyond, the men had at last left them and started southward on sledges. That was all.

None of the men ever reached home again. They all died of cold and hunger, and here and there along the way they had gone their skeletons were found bleached and white.

The people who live in the cold, far north are called Eskimos. When they were questioned, some of them remembered having seen white men travelling southward with a sledge. "But they were very thin," said one old woman, "they fell down and died as they walked."

The Eskimos had among them silver spoons and forks which the searchers knew had belonged to Sir John. These were all collected and brought home, but of the ships themselves nothing was ever seen.

All through the long search it was Lady Franklin who urged the explorers on, and when at last she knew that her dear husband was indeed dead, she raised a tomb to his memory in Westminster Abbey. She herself wished to write the words which were to be carved on the stone, but she died before they were written. The great poet laureate, Tennyson, wrote them instead.

"Not here! The White North hath thy bones, and thou,
Heroic sailor soul,
Art passing on thy happier voyage now
Towards no earthly pole."

Although it is now known that there is a North-West Passage, it is also known that it can be of no use for trade. Even if the passage was not blocked with ice, the danger and suffering from the cold are too great to be endured.

There are still wonderful things to be learned in the cold, white north, and there have been many Arctic expeditions since the death of Sir John Franklin, but I have told you about him because he was one of the most famous Arctic explorers. He really discovered the North-West Passage, and his death in the far north caused many other expeditions to be sent out, and, although they did not find Sir John, they learned much that was new about the Arctic regions.

CHAPTER CVI

VICTORIA—THE SIEGE OF DELHI

A HUNDRED years had passed since the terrible night when the British had been murdered in the Black Hole of Calcutta; a hundred years had passed since Clive had gained the victory of Plassey. Since then the British power in India had steadily grown and grown until, instead of a few sepoys, there was a great Indian army; instead of a few factories, the whole of India was under the rule of Britain, and British rule in India seemed firm and certain. But suddenly, from out the calm, rebellion blazed.

New guns had been sent to India for the use of the sepoys. The powder and shot for a gun is made up with paper into what is called a cartridge. In those days the end of the cartridge had to be bitten off before it could be used. The paper of these cartridges was greased, and somehow the sepoys came to think that the grease was a mixture of cow's fat and pig's lard, and they refused to use the cartridges.

These Indian soldiers were not Christians, but Brahmins and Mahometans. The Brahmins worship the cow, and they thought that it was dreadfully wicked to put into their mouths, or even touch, what they held as sacred. The Mahometans, on the other hand, thought that pigs were unclean animals, and their religion forbade them to touch anything which was considered unclean. So they, too, felt that it would be wicked to use the cartridges.

The governor, Lord Canning, sent out a proclamation telling all the people that the cartridges were not greased either with cow's fat or with lard. But the sepoys did not believe him, and a terrible rebellion, known as the Indian Mutiny, broke out.

It was a most dreadful time. There were very few British soldiers in India, and Lord Canning knew that it would be many weeks before others could arrive from Britain. But the British had been fighting in Persia, and Lord Canning sent for the soldiers there, and also for some who were on their way to fight in China.

The Mutiny first broke out at a place called Meerut. There the native soldiers one day suddenly fired upon their officers, and killed some of them. Then they murdered many of the white people in the town, broke open the gaols and freed the prisoners, who joined in rioting and plundering. But at last the few British soldiers who were there succeeded in driving the sepoys from their barracks, and they fled to Delhi, another town near.

At Delhi there lived an Indian Emperor of about eighty years old. He was an emperor only in name, for his whole empire was under British rule. But now the sepoys, driven from Meerut, rushed to his palace and loudly clamoured for him to come and be their Emperor once more. They would no longer have British rulers, they said. They would sweep them from the land. Dreadful deeds were done in Delhi, but British troops besieged the town and took it again. When the Mutiny was over, the old Emperor was put in prison, where he died.

At a place called Cawnpore, some of the most cruel acts were done. There were only about three hundred British troops there, and more than three thousand sepoys. Sir Hugh Wheeler, who was in command, was a very old man. He knew that with his few soldiers he could not hold out against so many sepoys, and he sent to Lucknow, to Sir Henry Lawrence, for help. But alas! Sir Henry could not help him, for Lucknow, too, was in great danger, and he needed every one of his men.

So Sir Hugh sent to a native called the Nana Sahib, and asked him for help. The Nana Sahib had always pretended to be a friend, and Sir Hugh believed that he was. Really, he hated the British. Now he came with three hundred men, professing to be glad to help them. He got into Cawnpore with his soldiers and his guns, and then he turned against the British.

Sir Hugh and all the white people had gathered into an old hospital for safety. The magazine, the place where the gunpowder and fire-arms were kept, would have been a far better refuge for them. It is difficult to understand why Sir Hugh did not go there, but he did not, and it fell into the hands of the sepoys.

The hospital was surrounded by a low wall of mud, which was all the defense there was between the white people and the shrieking, yelling mob of sepoys. Within these walls there were nearly one thousand white people, and more than half of them were women and children. The sepoys thought that it would be easy to kill them all. But they found out their mistake. The white people fought fiercely, and the sepoys were driven back again and again.

The suffering within the old hospital was dreadful. The women and children died by hundreds. The fierce Indian sun blazed down upon the almost roofless house. There was little to eat, and less to drink. Water could only be had from a well which was within the range of the enemy's guns. To go for water seemed to the bravest to be going to certain death. During the whole siege not a cupful could be spared to wash with.

Thousands of yelling sepoys were without the low mud walls, yet so great was their dread of the white men that they dared not leap over. At last the Nana Sahib, out of the deep wickedness of his heart, proposed terms.

He promised that all who would lay down their arms should be allowed to leave the town; that he would give them boats to take them to another town where they would be safe; and that they should have food for the journey. All he asked was that they should go away.

What joy there was within the hospital when it was known that the terrible siege was at an end. The women and children were utterly worn and weary, the men were wounded, sick, and hopeless. The joy and relief were almost too great.

The day came. Everything was ready, and the long, slow procession passed down to where the boats were waiting on the river. Gently the sick and wounded were placed under the straw awnings, with which the boats were covered to protect the passengers from the blazing sun. Then the women and children stepped in, lastly the men. The Indian rowers took their places and pushed off, when suddenly a trumpet was heard. In a moment the straw-thatched roofs of the boats were in flames, and the rowers, throwing down their oars, made for the shore. A moment later both banks blazed and roared with gunshots, and a horrible rain of bullets fell upon the boats. To make the horror worse, the boats drifted upon the mud banks and stuck fast.

At last the firing ceased. The women and children who were still alive were taken ashore again and shut up this time in a place called the Savada House. The men were all killed. So the Nana Sahib kept faith!

But the British were coming. General Havelock and his brave soldiers were not far off, and the Nana made haste to finish his cruel work. He ordered his sepoys to fire at the women and children through the windows of the Savada House. Even the sepoys, however, turned from this awful work and aimed high, so that the shots fell upon the roof and did no harm.

But in the evening five men went into the house. Horrible shrieks were heard, then all was silence. The work was finished. All the women and children were dead.

The bodies of those poor women and children were thrown into a well, and when the British took Cawnpore, the horror of that well was one of the first sights they saw. Now it is covered over. A marble angel, holding a palm branch, guards the spot, and a garden blooms where that ghastly house stood.

The Nana Sahib was never punished. When his sepoys were defeated before Cawnpore, he galloped away and was seen no more. People said that he was not a man, but an evil spirit, and that when his work was done, he vanished as a spirit would.

CHAPTER CVII

VICTORIA—THE PIPES AT LUCKNOW

LUCKNOW, too, was besieged, and terrible things were happening there. The chief officer at Lucknow was Sir Henry Lawrence, who had so sadly to refuse to send help to Cawnpore. He was a brave and wise man. But he was killed almost at the very beginning of the siege.

One day while he was talking with some of his officers a shell burst into the room. When the smoke cleared away a little, some one said, "Are you hurt, Sir Henry?"

There was a moment's silence. Then Sir Henry said quietly, "I am killed." He died two days later. "Never yield," he said, "let every man die at his post rather than yield."

For nearly three months the siege went on. The white people were shut into a strong place called the Residency, and although they were better off than the poor people at Cawnpore, many died of wounds and sickness. It was three months of horror beneath a blazing sky, amid the shriek and roar of cannon. Men grew hard-eyed and gaunt, women drooped and faded. Would help never come?

At last General Havelock, having defeated the Nana Sahib, marched towards Lucknow, but he had lost so many of his men that he dared not attack. He was obliged to wait for more soldiers, and the waiting was hard for men with the memories of Cawnpore in their hearts.

But at last Sir James Outram joined Havelock, and together they marched to Lucknow.

As week after week passed, and no help came, the brave defenders of Lucknow grew sick with longing and despair. One evening a sergeant's wife called Jessie, who had been ill, was lying asleep while her mistress, who had been nursing her, sat by her side. Jessie stirred and muttered in her sleep, then, suddenly springing up and turning her startled eyes on her mistress, she cried, "Dinna ye hear them? Dinna ye hear them?"

The lady thought that Jessie had gone mad. "Jessie dear, lie down," she said, "you are not well."

"No, no," cried Jessie, "I'm well, I'm well, it's the Campbells I'm hearin'. Dinna ye hear them? Dinna ye hear them?"

It was indeed the sound of the pipes.

Soon not only Jessie, but all that weary band heard the glad sound. The terrible agony of waiting was over. General Havelock and his Highlanders were at the gates. Lucknow was relieved.

"Pipes of the misty moorlands, voice of the glens and hills;
The droning of the torrents, the treble of the rills—
Not the braes of broom and heather nor the mountains dark with rain,
Nor maiden bower, nor border tower, have heard your sweetest strain.

"Dear to the Lowland reaper, and plaided mountaineer,
To the cottage and the castle the Scottish pipers are dear—
Sweet sounds the ancient pibroch o'er mountain, loch, and glade;
But the sweetest of all music the pipes at Lucknow played.

"Day by day the Indian tiger louder yelled, and nearer crept;
Round and round the jungle serpent near and nearer circles swept.
'Pray for rescue, wives and mothers,—pray to-day,' the soldier said;
'To-morrow death's between us, and the wrong and shame we dread.'

"Oh, they listened, looked and waited, till their hope became despair;
And the sobs of low bewailing filled the pauses of their prayer.
Then upspake a Scottish maiden, with her ear unto the ground:
'Dinna ye hear it?—dinna ye hear it? the pipes of Havelock sound.'

"Hushed the wounded man his groaning; hushed the wife her little ones;
Alone they heard the drum-roll and the roar of sepoy guns.
But to sounds of home and childhood the Highland ear was true;—
As the mother's cradle crooning the mountain pipes she knew.

"Like the march of soundless music through the vision of the seer,
More of feeling than of hearing, of the heart than of the ear,
She knew the droning pibroch, she knew the Campbells' call:
'Hark, hear ye no MacGregors'?—the grandest o' them all.'

"Oh, they listened, dumb and breathless, and they caught the sound at last,
Faint and far beyond the Goomtee, rose and fell, the pipers' blast.
Then a burst of wild thanksgiving mingled woman's voice and man's.
'God be praised—the march of Havelock! the piping of the clans."

"Louder, nearer, fierce as vengeance, sharp and shrill as swords at strife
Came the wild MacGregors' clan call, stinging all the air to life.
But when the far-off dust-cloud to plaided legions grew,
Full tenderly and blithsomely the pipes of rescue blew.

"Round the silver domes of Lucknow, Moslem mosque and Pagan shrine,
Breathed the air to Britons dearest, the air of Auld Lang Syne.
O'er the cruel roll of war-drums rose that sweet and homelike strain;
And the tartan clove the turban as the Goomtee cleaves the plain."

But although the coming of Havelock and his men saved Lucknow for a time, they were not strong enough quite to defeat the sepoys, and take all the women and children to a safe place. So the siege began again and lasted for about two months more. But at last Sir Colin Campbell landed in India, and, a few days later, marched to Lucknow. This time it really was relieved.

Little more than a week later General Havelock, who had fought so bravely for his countrymen, who had endured so much to bring them help, died. India is very far from Britain, and in those days news travelled very slowly, so the Queen, not knowing that Havelock had died, made him a baronet, that is, she gave him the title of "Sir," in reward for his brave deeds. But three days before the Queen did this, the brave general was lying still and quiet, resting after his great labours.

General Havelock was a good as well as a great man. Like Cromwell he taught his soldiers to fight and to pray, and "Havelock's saints," as they were called, were well known in India. But Havelock's saints, like Cromwell's Ironsides, showed that they could fight as well as pray.

After the relief of Lucknow the Mutiny was nearly at an end. Lord Canning made a proclamation offering pardon to all except those who had actually murdered the British, and gradually the country became peaceful again.

The East India Company, which until now had practically ruled India, was done away with, and the Queen took the government into her own hands. As Victoria could not herself live in India, she appointed a viceroy. Viceroy means one in place or a king. Lord Canning, who, through all the terrible days of the Mutiny, had proved himself to be a good governor, was made the first Viceroy.

CHAPTER CVIII

VICTORIA—UNDER THE SOUTHERN CROSS

"Let no one think much of a trifling expense;
Who knows what may happen a hundred years hence?
The loss of America what can repay?
New colonies seek for in Botany Bay."

IN the days of King George III. there was a great sailor called Captain Cook. He made many voyages into unknown seas and discovered new lands. Among these lands were the islands of Australia and New Zealand.

It was in April 1770 A.D. that Captain Cook first landed in Australia, in a bay which he called Botany Bay, because there were so many plants of all kinds there. At that time the island was inhabited only by wild, black savages, and Captain Cook took possession of the whole eastern coast in the name of King George, calling it New South Wales.

While America was a British colony, wicked people, instead of being sent to prison for punishment, as they are now, were sent to work on the cotton plantations or farms there. After America was lost, convicts, as these wicked people are called, could no longer be sent there, and British statesmen began to look round for some other country to which they could be sent.

Then it was that Australia was thought of. It was decided to form a convict colony there. It was hoped that free people would go too, and that soon Australia would become as great a colony as America had been.

So there sailed out from England a little fleet of ships, carrying Captain Philip as the Governor of the new colony, and nearly a thousand people, of whom more than seven hundred were prisoners; the rest were officers and marines to guard the prisoners. They took with them food and clothes enough to last two years, also tools for building houses, and ploughs and everything needed for farm work.

As the ships passed the Cape of Good Hope, they stopped there to take in more food, and also animals with which to stock the farms which the British hoped to make in Australia. They took so many animals on board that the ships looked more like Noah's arks than anything else.

When the ships reached Australia, Captain Philip landed, a flagstaff was planted, and soon the Union Jack floated out to the sound of British cheers. The health of the King was drunk, and then Captain Philip made a speech to the convicts. He told them that now, in this new country, they had another chance to forget their wicked ways, and to become again good British subjects. It was the first speech which had ever been made in the

English language in that far land, and, when he had finished, the silence of the lonely shore was again broken by the sound of British cheers. So the town of Sydney was founded.

Governor Philip and his strange company of rough, bad men soon set to work. Everything had to be done. Trees had to be felled, and stones quarried and broken for the building of houses, and the making of roads and harbours. There was so much to do that little time was left for farm work, and the settlers in this new colony nearly starved. It seemed as if the people at home had forgotten them, for the food which they had promised to send never came.

Day by day eager eyes looked out vainly over the blue sea, straining for the sight of a white sail. But no ship came. Prisoners and warders alike grew gaunt and pale. Nearly all their food was gone. The Governor even gave up some sacks of flour which were his own. "I do not wish," he said, "to have anything which others cannot have. If any convict complains, he may come and see that at Government House we are no better off than he is."

Still no help came. Little work could be done by men who were starving, and the weary days dragged slowly past for the handful of white people who, utterly cut off from all others, were ignorant of what was happening in the great world, which lay beyond the blue waves.

But even in the darkest hour, they never forgot that they were Britons. "Our distress did not make us forget that this was the birthday of our beloved King," wrote one. "In the morning flags were displayed, and at noon three volleys of musketry were fired as an acknowledgment that we were Britons, who, however distant and distressed, revered their King, and loved their country."

At last, after three years, a sail was seen. Oh, what joy! Help at last, and news at last from home! But alas! the new ship brought little food, and many more convicts. It brought, however, the assurance that the little colony was not forgotten. Other ships had been sent with food, but they had been wrecked on the way.

A fortnight later another ship arrived, then another and another. The colony was saved for the time at least, although famine threatened them again more than once. At one time things were so bad that when any one was asked to dine at Government House, he was requested to bring his own bread with him.

In a few years, free settlers began to come to Australia. They were farmers, and soon corn was grown in such quantities that the colony was freed from all fear of famine. Later still, a gentleman brought wool-bearing sheep to Australia, that is, sheep which have fine fleeces, and now the rearing of sheep for their wool is one of the chief industries of Australia.

As the free settlers increased in number, they objected to having convicts sent among them, for, because of these wild, bad men, the colony began to have an evil name. When gold was discovered in Australia, many more people flocked there. Then Queen Victoria and her government decided at last that it was not a good thing to send convicts to the colonies, and so in 1867 A.D. the last convict ship set out for Australia. After that the British shut up those who did wrong in strong prisons at home.

Australia has grown quickly into a great and wealthy country. I cannot tell you the history of it here, but although it is now called the Commonwealth of Australia, and has a Parliament of its own, it is still part of the Empire of Greater Britain.

Australia lies quite at the other side of the world from Britain, and when it is day in the one it is night in the other. And when Australians look up to the sky at night they see the stars of the Southern Cross, instead of the Pole Star and the Plough which the British see. Yet the people in the two islands are friends and brothers, and ties of love draw them together across the ocean waves.

CHAPTER CIX

VICTORIA—FROM CANNIBAL TO CHRISTIAN

IN 1769 A.D., Captain Cook landed in North Island, New Zealand. He cut the name of his ship upon a tree, planted the British flag, and claimed the land in the name of King George III. Then he sailed all round the island, proving to himself and his officers that it was indeed an island. In January of the following year, he landed in South Island, again hoisted the Union Jack, and again claimed the land, and all the lands near in the name of King George.

For many years no white people settled in New Zealand, for it was peopled by a wild and warlike race of savages called Maoris. These Maoris were cannibals, that is, people who eat human beings. After a battle, those who were killed would be roasted and eaten by the victors. The Maoris fought among themselves, and they fought with the white traders who came from time to time to their shores. Yet although they were cannibals, the Maoris were not nearly such a low kind of savage as the Australian, and a missionary called Marsden, hearing about these islands and their people, made up his mind to teach them to be Christian.

Mr. Marsden was working among the convicts in Australia, and one day he set sail from there, and landed in New Zealand. For the price of twelve axes, he bought two hundred acres of land from one of the Maori chiefs, and there he founded a missionary settlement. Mr. Marsden himself could not stay, for his work was in Australia, but he left two men behind him who taught the natives, and he often came back to the islands and was greatly loved by the Maoris.

For many years Britain did not acknowledge New Zealand as a colony. Dreadful deeds were done there, but when the British Government was asked to put a stop to them, the answer was that the islands were not within His Majesty's dominions. Yet at other times the Government acted as if the islands were part of the Empire.

It was only very gradually that white people went to live in New Zealand. The first colonists who came did not stay long, for the dreadful customs of the savage Maoris frightened them away again. That was not to be wondered at, for, in spite of all the missionaries could do, many of the Maoris remained cannibals.

When Queen Victoria came to the throne there were only about two thousand white people in all the islands. But, as many of these were British, it was felt at last that it was the duty of the British to do something to protect their colonists against the Maoris, and also to protect the Maoris from being cheated and ill-treated by bad white people, who went there to steal the land from the native chiefs.

So a governor was sent out from Britain who was told to make a treaty with these native chiefs. This treaty was signed at a place called Waitangi, in North Island.

The Governor, with all the principal white people, sat upon a platform which had been set up in an open space near the town. Round them sat the Maori chiefs, and behind them stood all the rest of the white people. Beyond gleamed the white of the British tents, gay with flags, which showed brightly against the background of waving green trees.

When all were gathered, the Governor spoke to the people, and, as he could not speak the Maori language, one of the missionaries translated his words to them. He told them how the great White Queen in an island far away was anxious that they should be happy and at peace. And because so many of the great White Queen's own subjects had come to live in these islands of New Zealand, she felt that she must send a governor to rule them and to see justice done between them and the Maoris. The great White Queen asked the Maori chiefs to acknowledge her as over-lord, promising that if they did so she would protect them, their families, their people, and their goods, as she protected all her other subjects and their possessions.

Then the Maori chiefs spoke. Some of them did not want to sign the treaty. "Send the man away," said one, springing up and pointing to the Governor, "do not sign the paper. If you do you will become slaves, you will be made to break stones upon the roads. Your lands will be taken away from you, and you will no longer be chiefs."

Another chief then rose. He spoke so calmly and so well, that all the white people were quite astonished. "You will be our father," he said turning to the Governor, "you must not allow us to become slaves. You will keep all our old customs, you will not let our land be taken from us."

This chief was a very great man, very mighty in battle, so the others listened to him, and, after more talking, it was agreed that they should think about it for a day, before signing the treaty. Then with cheers from both the natives and the white people, the meeting was ended.

Next day, with firing of guns and great ceremony, the treaty was signed. The great chief who had spoken in favour of the treaty signed his name as the missionaries had taught him to do, but the others made marks like the marks called tattooing with which their bodies were covered.

A few months later the chiefs of South Island also signed the treaty, and the Union Jack was hoisted amid the thunder of guns and the cheers of the people. So New Zealand became an acknowledged British colony, nearly one hundred years after it was discovered and claimed by Cook.

Many years have passed since the signing of this treaty, and many things have happened of which I cannot tell you here. New Zealand has become an important part of the British Empire. Instead of two thousand white people there are now about seven hundred thousand in the islands. It is a self-governing colony and, like Australia, has a Parliament of its own, and in New Zealand the women help to choose the members for Parliament, just as the men do.

CHAPTER CX

VICTORIA—BOER AND BRITON

IN the days when Cromwell was ruling Britain with his iron hand, a few stern-faced, silent men sailed out from Holland and landed in South Africa. There they made their home, and there they grew rich and prospered.

In the reign of George III., while Napoleon was conquering all Europe, British soldiers landed in Africa and took possession of Cape Town. Later still, when Napoleon had fallen, the Cape of Good Hope became a British possession by treaty with Holland. Soon thousands of British settled there, and slowly but surely the colony grew.

So side by side these two races, Dutch and British, spread and prospered. But they could not live together in peace. It seemed as if in all the wide veldt there was not room for both.

I cannot tell you here of all the quarrels and dispeace; of how the different colonies called Orange Free State, Transvaal, Natal, and Cape Colony arose; of how the Transvaal at one time owned British rule and at another did not; of how Britain fought and suffered until at last the long years of unrest and trouble ended in the great Boer War;—I cannot tell you of all this, for it would take too long, and much of it would not seem interesting to you. I will not talk much either about the Boer War, for the tears it caused are hardly dry; the graves it made are hardly green.

All through this book I have tried to give you reasons for the wars of which I have told, and, although now that we have come to our own time it becomes more difficult, I will give you one reason for the Boer War, which you may understand.

From the very beginning of our story you have seen how Britons have fought for freedom, and how step by step they have won it, until at last Britons live under just laws and have themselves the power to make these laws. For it is now acknowledged that the Briton who pays taxes has the right to help to frame the laws under which he lives. You remember how America was lost because King George III. tried to force the Americans to pay taxes, although they had not the right to choose and send members to Parliament.

Now the Transvaal was a republic, and the government was in the hands of the Boers, as the South African Dutch had come to be called. Yet in some vague way the Boers owned the Queen of Britain as over-lord. Those who lived in the Transvaal were chiefly Boer farmers, but gold was discovered in the country and then many other people went there hoping to make a great deal of money. Many of these people were British, and although the Boers were not glad to see them, and wished they would keep away from the land which they considered their very own, these British helped to make the Boer country rich. They paid heavy taxes, but they were called Uitlanders, which means, "outlanders" or "strangers." They were harshly treated in many ways, they were not allowed to vote for members of Parliament, and so had no voice in making the laws under which they had to live.

You have heard how Britons for centuries had fought for this very freedom which was now denied them in South Africa, and you can imagine how hard it was for Britons to bear what seemed to them so great an injustice. This is only one reason why the Boers and Britons could not live in peace together, but it is one which you can understand. The Boers, too, had their troubles and their grievances, and, when war came, they fought as patriots fight for their country.

The British in South Africa appealed at last to the mother-country for help. The mother-country gave help, and in October 1899 A.D. war broke out.

It was a dreadful war, and lasted for two years and a half. We have not yet forgotten the days of sick suspense during the long months when Ladysmith and "brave little Mafeking" were besieged; nor the gloom which fell upon us as we read of disaster and defeat; nor the cheers and sobs which greeted the news of the relief of Ladysmith and then of Mafeking.

But in the darkest hour one thing became certain. The little island was not fighting alone. The Empire of Greater Britain was no mere name. From all sides, from New Zealand, Australia, Canada, from every province of Greater Britain, from every land over which the Union Jack floats, came offers of help. Britain was fighting, not for herself, but for her colony, and right or wrong, her colonies stood by her, side by side, and shoulder to shoulder.

At length the dark days passed, and the whisper of peace was heard. It was a whisper which grew louder until it was plainly heard.

The Boer leaders gathered at a place called Vereeniging to talk together over the terms of peace. Vereeniging means "union," so it seemed a good place at which to have the meeting. The Boers were treated as the guests of the British, who prepared a camp for them and did everything for their comfort, but as they were led to the camp, through the British lines, the Boers were blindfolded and guarded by soldiers of the Black Watch. This was done because the Boers might not have agreed to make peace, and then the knowledge they had gained of the British camp would have helped them greatly.

The meeting lasted about ten days, but at last, on Sunday, June 1, 1902 A.D., the good news reached London. Peace was proclaimed.

"Here, where my fresh-turned furrows run,
And the deep soil glistens red,

I will repair the wrong that was done
To the living and the dead.
Here where the senseless bullet fell,
And the barren shrapnel burst,
I will plant a tree, I will dig a well,
Against the heat and the thirst.

"Here, in a large and sunlit land,
Where no wrong bites to the bone,
I will lay my hand in my neighbour's hand,
And together we will atone
For the set folly and the red breach
And the black waste of it all,
Giving and taking counsel each
Over the cattle-kraal.

"Here, in the waves and the troughs of the plains
Where the healing stillness lies,
And the vast, benignant sky restrains
And the long days make wise—
Bless to our use the rain and the sun
And the blind seed in its bed,
That we may repair the wrong that was done
To the living and the dead!"

The south of Africa is now entirely a British colony, and we hope that soon it will be as loyal, as happy, and as prosperous as any other British colony.

Queen Victoria reigned for sixty-three years, which is longer than any other British sovereign has ever reigned. When she had been on the throne fifty years, great rejoicings were held.

On the 21st of June, the anniversary of the day upon which she ascended the throne, the streets and houses were everywhere decorated, and bonfires and fire-works blazed. This year was called the Jubilee Year.

Ten years later Victoria was still upon the throne, and again the people rejoiced. The whole air was filled with shouts and cheers as the white-haired lady, who was Queen of half the world, drove through the streets of London on her way to St. Paul's Cathedral, there to thank God for her great and glorious reign. This was called the Diamond Jubilee Year.

Three years later, while the dark war cloud still hung over the land, the news was flashed through all the great empire, "The Queen is dead." At the close of a dull winter's day, the sad toll of muffled bells rang out the message to every town and village; and from east to west, wherever the flag of red, white, and blue floats, hearts were sad.

"May children of our children say,
She wrought her people lasting good;

"Her court was pure; her life serene;
God gave her peace; her land reposed;
A thousand claims to reverence closed
In her as Mother, Wife, and Queen;

"And statesmen at her council met
Who knew the seasons when to take
Occasion by the hand, and make
The bounds of freedom wider yet

"By shaping some august decree,
Which kept her throne unshaken still,
Broad-based upon her people's will,
And compass'd by the inviolate sea."

"God of our fathers, known of old,
Lord of our far-flung battle-line,
Beneath whose awful Hand we hold
Dominion over palm and pine—
Lord God of Hosts, be with us yet,
Lest we forget—lest we forget!

"The tumult and the shouting dies;
The captains and the kings depart;
Still stands Thine ancient sacrifice,
An humble and a contrite heart.
Lord God of Hosts, be with us yet,
Lest we forget—lest we forget!"

LIST OF KINGS FROM EDWARD THE CONFESSOR

SAXON KINGS.

- Edward the Confessor reigned 24 years, from 1042 to 1066 A.D.
- Harold II. reigned a little more than nine months, from January 5th to October 14th, 1066 A.D.

NORMAN KINGS.

- William I. reigned 21 years, from 1066 to 1087 A.D.
- William II. reigned 13 years, from 1087 to 1100 A.D.
- Henry I. reigned 35 years, from 1100 to 1135 A.D.
- Stephen reigned 19 years, from 1135 to 1154 A.D.

PLANTAGENET KINGS.

- Henry II. reigned 35 years, from 1154 to 1189 A.D.
- Richard I. reigned 10 years, from 1189 to 1199 A.D.
- John reigned 17 years, from 1199 to 1216 A.D.
- Henry III. reigned 56 years, from 1216 to 1272 A.D.
- Edward I. reigned 35 years, from 1272 to 1307 A.D.
- Edward II. reigned 20 years, from 1307 to 1327 A.D.
- Edward III. reigned 50 years, from 1327 to 1377 A.D.
- Richard II. reigned 22 years, from 1377 to 1399 A.D.
- Henry IV. reigned 14 years, from 1399 to 1413 A.D.
- Henry V. reigned 9 years, from 1413 to 1422 A.D.
- Henry VI. reigned 39 years, from 1422 to 1461 A.D.
- Edward IV. reigned 22 years, from 1461 to 1483 A.D.
- Edward V. reigned a little more than two months, from April 6th to June 26th, 1483.
- Richard III. reigned 2 years, from 1483 to 1485 A.D.

TUDOR KINGS.

- Henry VII. reigned 24 years, from 1485 to 1509 A.D.
- Henry VIII. reigned 38 years, from 1509 to 1547 A.D.
- Edward VI. reigned 6 years, from 1547 to 1553 A.D.

- Mary I. reigned 5 years, from 1553 to 1558 A.D.
- Elizabeth reigned 45 years, from 1558 to 1603 A.D.

STUART KINGS.

- James I. of England and VI. of Scotland reigned 58 years, 36 as King of Scotland only, from 1567 to 1603, and 22 as King of Great Britain and Ireland, from 1603 to 1625 A.D.
- Charles I. reigned 24 years, from 1625 to 1649 A.D.
- The Commonwealth lasted 11 years, from 1649 to 1660 A.D.

STUART KINGS.

- Charles II. reigned 25 years, from 1660 to 1685 A.D.
- James II. of Engand, VII. of Scotland, reigned 3 years, from 1685 to 1688 A.D.
- Mary II. and William III. reigned together for 5 years, from 1689 to 1694 A.D.
- William III. reigned alone for 8 years, from 1694 to 1702 A.D.
- Anne reigned 12 years, from 1702 to 1714 A.D.

HANOVERIAN KINGS.

- George I. reigned 13 years, from 1714 to 1727 A.D.
- George II. reigned 33 years, from 1727 to 1760 A.D.
- George III. reigned 60 years from 1760 to 1820 A.D.
- George IV. reigned 10 years, from 1820 to 1830 A.D.
- William IV. reigned 7 years, from 1830 to 1837 A.D.
- Victoria reigned 68 years, from 1837 to 1901 A.D.

11623198R00199

Printed in Great Britain
by Amazon